ADVANCED PRAISE FOR

How to Love an American Man

"*How to Love an American Man* offers an important, new perspective on relationships from a bright young author. Kristine Gasbarre not only gives young women advice for understanding men but she also inspires women of all ages to share the beauty and the wisdom of the female experience. This book answers critical questions about the mystery of love."

—Marci Shimoff, *New York Times* bestselling author of
Love for No Reason, Happy for No Reason,
and *Chicken Soup for the Woman's Soul*

"Kristine Gasbarre is a modern-day Jane Austen. . . . With sparkling wit, this spunky heroine faces modern women's search for love with the complications and joys of freedom and independence. That's where her grandmother comes in, gently schooling her in the art of courtship and, ultimately, identity. A page-turner that leaves you guessing until the very end."

—Jean Twenge, Ph.D., author of *Generation Me*
and coauthor of *The Narcissism Epidemic*

"*How to Love an American Man* is a beautifully written, heartfelt gem. Disguised as a romance, it is actually a story of familial bonds, personal growth, and faith. With the help of her grandmother's wisdom and her own hard-earned insights, Kristine Gasbarre discovers what it means to live in a relationship with 'an American man.' And while she may or may not have found 'true love,' she has definitely found herself."

—Lisa Oz, *New York Times* bestselling author and radio host

"Tradition can be a refuge or a prison, family ties, likewise, both comfort and burden. Krissy Gasbarre maintains a perfect balance. But then there's love. And love ain't so easy. Krissy puts all bonds on hold and sets out on her search for fulfillment. In a world of mental palates dulled by the sugars of instant gratification, Krissy's voice is freshly squeezed orange juice. Krissy writes with style and grace and plenty of humor. Hers is no passing fancy. Hers is a genuine quest. In these times, when love is more precious than ever, Krissy Gasbarre opens wide all her windows and doors. In *How to Love an American Man* tradition meets today. Up close and personal, here is a bright light on the road to love."   —Alphie McCourt

How to Love
an American Man

How to Love
an American Man

—*A True Story*—

Kristine Gasbarre

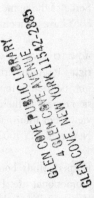
HARPER

NEW YORK · LONDON · TORONTO · SYDNEY

HARPER

HOW TO LOVE AN AMERICAN MAN. Copyright © 2011 by Kristine Gasbarre. All rights reserved. Printed in the United States of America. No part of this book may be used or reproduced in any manner whatsoever without written permission except in the case of brief quotations embodied in critical articles and reviews. For information address HarperCollins Publishers, 10 East 53rd Street, New York, NY 10022.

HarperCollins books may be purchased for educational, business, or sales promotional use. For information please write: Special Markets Department, HarperCollins Publishers, 10 East 53rd Street, New York, NY 10022.

FIRST EDITION

Designed by John Lewis

Library of Congress Cataloging-in-Publication Data is available upon request.

ISBN 978-0-06-199739-6

11 12 13 14 15   OV/BVG   10 9 8 7 6 5 4 3 2 1

For Mom and Dad.

Thank you for raising me with such deep love and intrigue of family, and encouraging me to prove Grandpa's words true: A girl can do anything she wants to do.

Bonds with family are priceless, and bonds between women are necessary. A thousand thanks to my grandma who shared so many stories and insights with me as I worked on this book. I believe the most powerful legacy a grandparent can give her family is a stronger sense of identity, and I will always appreciate the joy you found in teaching me more about where we come from and who I am. Love you, Glo.

CONTENTS

INTRODUCTION

I HAVE ALMOST NOTHING in common with my grandmother.

One Sunday when I was about twelve I burst through her front door to announce with great fanfare to all of my extended family that my cousin had just gotten her first period. While my three aunts rushed to said cousin's side to nurse her like Sleeping Beauty's fairy godmothers, Grandma groped her chest with both hands and ducked into the kitchen. I followed her and popped a shrimp cocktail in my mouth. "Grandma, what?" I said. "This is huge." In response, Grandma scrambled to the stove to stir Grandpa's spaghetti sauce, which she's ordinarily too daunted by his perfect recipe to touch. I think in that moment she'd have done anything not to have to show me how my frankness had flustered her.

Our views of womanhood have always been this different. I discuss with great candor topics that cause Grandma to blush red like a beet, and while she honors my youth and modern spirit by remaining silent, the discrepancies between us crash as loud as the sea. She never knew her father; mine is her affectionate and smiling third son. She never finished college; I graduated with my master's. She never traveled or lived alone; I spent all of my twenties questing and introspecting to understand where I fit in the world. She married my grandpa when she was nineteen; last year at twenty-eight I moved back in with my parents to decide whether it was time to wrap up my quarter-life adventures of living in New York and Europe.

On the spectrum between traditional and contemporary, Grandma Gloria occupies the demure, cross-ankled, ladylike end, while I dance loud and proud at the opposite extreme. Intellectually we understand our inherent responsibilities to love each other, and we do—but to say we *understand* each other would be, to employ Grandma's 1940s terminology, a fib.

However, there is one subject on which we see eye-to-eye: my grandfather. In the year and a half since he died, just two months before their sixtieth anniversary, I have grown to appreciate that my grandma and I share an equally intense affinity for the first-generation all-American alpha male that our family and community adored. She was his wife, I was his firstborn grandchild, and of course Grandma's relationship with Grandpa was very different than mine. But she and I had a similar goal: in everything we did, we both hoped to please him.

To me, Grandpa was the perfect man. He was a self-taught engineer and entrepreneur of our family's now-international business that makes industrial parts for cars and appliances. He'd helped to liberate the Jews from the concentration camps as a soldier in World War II. He went to Mass most Sundays, raised money for our schools, and threw parties so legendary that last year at our tenth annual bocce ball tournament we toasted with his signature martinis to celebrate his memory. And he took care of my grandma with such unshakable devotion that you could've sworn she was the only woman God had ever created.

For her every need and insecurity and reason for excitement or celebration, he was there. With all of his hard work and dynamism and steadfastness, he built a modern American life for the two of them—five smart kids, twelve happy grandkids, three houses, golf on the weekends, and a pontoon on our central Pennsylvania lake. Grandpa had a vision for his life and his family, and he *made it happen*. He was a great guy and an amazing man. About two years ago, just a few months before he was diagnosed with lung cancer and still smiling and well, I told him that if I ever found a man as enterprising as he was, I'd be the happiest girl in the world.

Since I was a kid my grandpa had always cheered on my achievements very vocally, but just before he got sick he confided in my parents something he'd kept silent about: he was beginning to worry I'd never find a husband and settle down. During a regular call to him after church one lonely Sunday as I strolled past couples brunching at bistros, I gently set the record straight. "I live in New York, Grandpa," I told him, trying to talk over the roar of traffic but not loudly enough for people on the street to hear me. "The men here are impossible, all they're after is sex and money and when I date them I feel invisible." Then I spotted the lean, tan boyfriend of a tiny blonde in a tube dress.

He was dropping a bite of French toast on the sidewalk and encouraging their puppy to snatch it up. *Well,* I thought, *almost all the men here are impossible.* I myself had a hard time locating the ones who were . . . let's say . . . *possible,* and I blamed our American pursuit of self-advancement for my romantic drought.

In an effort to replenish my hopes about men (and any sense I'd ever possessed of feeling alluring), I planned a vacation in Italy to visit the village outside Rome where Grandpa's parents were born and married before settling in rural Pennsylvania in what's now my hometown.

That trip to Italy was pivotal, to say the least. For two weeks tanned men in windy linen pants flocked to my friend Elena and me like we were sparkling, big-toothed movie stars straight from Hollywood. "American women?" they'd smile, shaking their hands in prayer position and looking up to the sky. *"Mamma mia!"* Elena and I flirtatiously accepted their admiration, giving each other high-fives and mouthing *Oh my God!* when they weren't looking.

The Italian men grandly bestowed after-dinner shots of limoncello and gelato upon us from a carnival vendor on a hill overlooking Florence. They popped us onto the backs of their motorcycles and rode us off to quaint, authentic dinners. They invited us on Tuscan bicycle rides and to parties full of stylish Europeans who hung on the words of us American women, and suddenly I perceived myself completely differently than I had back home. It was as though my exhausted, work-driven American existence had transformed into the flowery cadence of a Romance language; as though I'd dressed in the wardrobe of some irresistible theater character and took on the deliciousness of her traits. The more fun I had with this goddess I'd adopted, the more the European men seemed to respond with their attention. I relished this vivid version of myself so much more than the one who sneaks out of humiliating speed dating events for— exciting!—buttoned-up book publishing dinners for work. *I felt so much more beautiful there than I did at home!*

I spun into a panic attack when my grandpa's cousin Rocco drove Elena and me to the airport in his Fiat to catch our flight back to New York. I'd fallen in love with the European me— this carefree, glowing manifestation of my real spirit—and I didn't want to return home without her. This was the Krissy who didn't just want beauty and romance, but who *was* beauty and romance.

The last site Elena and I visited before we boarded the plane was the enchanting Boboli Gardens in Florence. Through the vines of fresh flowers and bushes heavy with lemons, we came upon a marble and seashell pedestal that made me stop dead in my tracks: a Renaissance statue of Adam and Eve.

I couldn't move.

The middle finger of Adam's hand was broken off, but he caressed his beloved's wild curls on his shoulder as they both stared back at me with vacant, woe-filled eyes. It was them against the world, committed for eternity; the first man planted here with his wife, still standing witness to their love as time marches on and the rest of the earth turns. *I* wanted a love like that. I took a snapshot so that at the very least, I could have it digitally.

When I landed at JFK, I felt radiant from all the holiday

fantasy and international male attention . . . and, honestly, quite certain that I'd never find it at home. The very next night I didn't much help my case, when I got embarrassingly drunk on a date with a young CEO named Chuck and then tried to blame it on jet lag. The following week the distinguished friend who had introduced me to Chuck sat me down for a talking-to about how I might want to behave on dates. While I was utterly nauseated at my behavior, the experience made me long even more to meet someone who would accept me just the way I was. Surely there had to be a man down-to-earth enough out there to *love everything about me.*

My grandpa's smart and handsome and successful and he loves me, you American creeps! I wanted to yell in the streets. *You knobs just don't know what you're missing!*

TWO WEEKS LATER I met Adam Hunt. It was during a bachelor-ette party that my college roommates from Cleveland had flown in for; an August night so sensuous and humid that as we mean-dered the twinkle-lighted bar patio on the Lower East Side, our perfume seemed to stick to the air behind us.

Adam and I spotted each other by complete accident, when I was pulling my heavy hair off my neck and resting my Miller Lite bottle against my skin. He smiled thoughtfully at me, and quickly I looked away. I could tell he was English by his sharp button-down shirt and blond faux-hawk and the way his sul-try blue eyes seemed to have seen a thousand wars. My heart pounded and I tried earnestly to engage myself in another con-versation as he and his friends approached us. He waited patiently for me to spin around to him, and when I finally gained the courage to turn slowly, he asked me my name.

"I'm Krissy."

"Krissy." He sized me up. "That's very American, isn't it."

"I guess it is." His accent and his eyes were melting me but I tried to stay cool. "And yours?"

"Adam."

I raised my eyebrows in fake ambivalence and took a sip from my bottle as my mind flashed back to the Creation statue in Florence. *Adam*. It was the name of the first man; a name that meant heart, loyalty, and strength. Finally.

I tried hard to remain aloof and barely interested as his friends and mine huddled off to the next club together. Up at the bar, Adam handed me a cold beer and then knocked the lip of my bottle with the bottom of his, sending a fountain of foam rushing to the top so that I had to chug it to keep it from spilling down the front of me. When I reciprocated by slamming the bottom of my bottle against the top of his, the lip of his bottle shattered. He shrugged and moved the bottle toward his mouth. "No," I pleaded, wrapping my grip around his. "Please don't, there could be glass inside." The bartender leaned in for me to yell my order over the music, and I smiled to pass Adam a fresh Corona. He marveled at me.

"That's the nicest thing a girl's ever done for me." His *girl* came out like *gihl*. I wanted to slather butter on his words and eat them with tea.

I leaned my back against the bar and looked out at the crowd. "It wasn't nice, it was necessary." His invitation to dance made me feel shy and on-the-spot, so then he set his hand soft on the small of my back.

"Can I kiss you?" He smelled like Hugo Boss and cigarettes and summer.

I lifted my chin to his face like some hard-hearted old-time film maven. *"Adam,"* I said, "I'm an American woman. If you want to kiss me, then you kiss me. You don't ask."

His lips landed soft on mine, and I opened my mouth to taste Marlboro and the lime from his Corona. The warmth of his breath against my lips instantly loosened my limbs and my good judgment, but I could sense his friends surrounding us like schoolboys. I pulled away.

"I'm only here another week but I'm calling you for dinner!" he called behind me.

I smiled back at him, disappearing through the crowd and into the lights outside.

My friends and I squealed over his English accent as our cab pulled into uptown traffic. The romance that ensued as a result of that chance meeting is now, as they say, history.

GRANDPA WAS THE ONLY one who believed in my decision to move to Italy. "If it's something you've always wanted to do, then you have to try it," he said. "You can't listen to what your parents want for your life and your career. What have I always told you: You can do anything you want to do."

I was visiting him and Grandma at their winter home in Florida for Valentine's Day, and lamenting over the difficulties of my long-distance relationship with Adam. "If I take the nanny job in Italy and he's in London, then we'll just be a short plane ride apart from each other. Grandma . . ." I paused cautiously. ". . . do you think it sounds like he's really serious about me?"

She set down a bowl of spaghetti on the table. "You want the truth?"

No, I didn't. "Yes, I do."

"To me it sounds like a fling."

Ouch. Where had she gathered that? Grandpa poured me more wine—first into Grandma's glass, then mine, then his own. As she sat down and slid her napkin onto her lap, she told me, "Don't move for this relationship, move because living in Italy and learning about our family is something you want to do for yourself."

"Oh, oh, of course I wouldn't move just for the relationship, of course this is to learn about our family." I pictured myself throwing the encyclopedic family tree that Grandpa created out the top of a convertible as Adam and I whipped with abandon through the hills of the English countryside. "I have my priorities straight," I lied, and then Grandpa raised his glass.

"To our first grandchild," he said. "You make us happy when you come to visit." I smiled; we clinked glasses. After dinner Grandma kissed us both good-night and excused herself to bed, and Grandpa shut off the hall light so she could sleep. Then he joined me back at the table, where he and I stayed up all night talking.

The next day he had a heart attack. He and Grandma and I were watching Oprah interview an author whose book I was doing marketing for in New York. If Grandpa's distraction from my connection to Oprah—"Grandpa, only one degree of separation between us!" I'd said, shaking his knee—didn't make it obvious that something was wrong, his expression did. He braced himself to lie down on the couch—he was never known to rest—and apparently when I was out of earshot, he told Grandma that his chest and stomach hurt. That night we rushed him to the hospital, and they admitted him for procedures.

Cheery and chatty as ever, Grandpa spent the next five nights in the hospital. I kept him company and helped Grandma process the doctors' decisions, delaying my flight back to New York by two nights until my parents could arrive from Pennsylvania to take over. Grandma and Grandpa were a notoriously independent couple, but immediately decided to sell the Florida house to be close to the family year-round. The doctors had discovered that Grandpa's red blood cell count was decreasing rapidly, although they couldn't determine what was causing it.

Three months later when June poked its head, I moved to Italy anyway. The urge to go was growing more desperate as my relationship with Adam continued to flounder on its back over the deep, cold Atlantic; plus, if I was to complete any real digging into my family's background, I wanted to do it while Grandpa was around to bounce the research off of. I wanted to make him proud that I was so invested in understanding his roots. His was the most inspired life of anyone I ever knew, and *I came from him*—I wanted to be able to wrap my head and heart around how truly significant that made my existence.

I found a job as a live-in English-speaking nanny for a family in Milan, which was the ideal location for my pursuits—on

Fridays after I finished nannying I could hop on a plane and be in London by dinner; on holidays, a train could rush me to Rome to visit my grandpa's relatives in three hours. From Milan, I could pursue the two men I wanted in my life more than anyone.

The events that took place during my year abroad changed my perception of relationships forever . . . but the biggest change happened right here at home, where I sit in my teenage bedroom as I type this story. When I lost the two men who made me feel beautiful and important, I gave up the world and returned to my family. For the first time, it would be a *woman* who would change the way I looked at myself and at relationships. When I moved back to small-town Pennsylvania, I started learning about love from my grandma.

Grandma's brand of love was different from the books I'd seen experts promoting on *Oprah*, and *way* different from the kind I'd read in *Cosmo*. Forget "Eighty-six ways to blow his mind tonight" or "If he's not calling you, then he's just not that into you." I sat down over a period of months with Grandma to discuss her sixty-year relationship with my grandpa and learn what I'd been doing wrong when it came to understanding men—and myself.

Grandma's insights transformed my thinking about relationships forever. She taught me to quit chasing romance (you mean like all the way to Europe, Grandma?); to stop hanging my hat on contemporary self-help one-liners (because it's possible he *is* just that into you but not in a good place in his life to enter a relationship—be grateful that he was forthcoming and had the strength of character to not drag you into something slow and painful); and to start practicing kindness toward him and re-spect toward yourself when you finally meet someone who may be worthwhile. Forget the games or brow-beating, Grandma said; what women and men need from each other are respect and understanding.

My grandma became the unexpected but ideal relationship guru who finally led me to see exactly what real love looks like. Her idea was that in a relationship, a woman has one main re-sponsibility: to love by radiating her unique, inherent beauty. That's it. But as simple as it sounds, and just when I thought I'd returned to my tiny hometown for safety and certainty, I took off on a huge adventure of the heart. Grandma's legacy to me would be a year-long journey together, in which she taught me about all the lessons in love and being a woman that I'd never, *never* been able to grasp before. It was from my grandma and her guided reflection on what it means to be female that I learned the lesson I'd been so recklessly seeking: in order to love any man, a woman has to know herself first.

1

Know When to Say I Love You

"Why do you fly today?"

I'm buckled into the left window seat of an Alitalia flight, spreading soft white cheese on a roll. I pause apologetically as if to tell the man, *I'm afraid my answer won't be pleasant.* "My grandfather," I tell him. "He's dying."

"Ah." The man smiles politely. I wait for him to extend his compassion for my sorrow, or at least offer me his coffee stirrer, since the Italian stewardesses have disappeared down the aisle. Instead he runs his tongue down the tiny plastic straw, adjusts his glasses, and goes back to reading today's *La Repubblica*.

Mister, did you even hear what I just said? If I weren't so accustomed to European insensitivity after five months living abroad, I might want to explode. In exactly what time zone did dismissiveness become acceptable? Decency must be hovering somewhere over the Atlantic before the UK, where I last saw Adam, because every time when I *tried* to bond to another individual (particularly a man) in Europe, I've been blown off as defenselessly as an eyelash from a fingertip. It's now the end of January, and there are more mushrooms on a slice of pizza than the number of times I've heard from Adam since I landed in Milan in June.

I spent my summer nannying on the Riviera and in the Alps at remote locations where most Italians have never even heard of the Internet, not to mention needing a digital IV hooked up to their arms like I'd grown so used to in my pursuit of connection (ha!) and career accolades. On the rare occasion I spotted a café with Wi-Fi, my heart sunk when the name "Adam Hunt " was perpetually absent from my in-box. If he replied to my texts at all, it was to brag that he was "quite drunk! xx" at expensive wine tastings and spending his summer evenings at exclusive clubs in downtown London. I would receive his texts, then scan the gray, collapsing, water-damaged Italian holiday cottage where I'd been trapped for a month, these toddlers killing each other at my feet. Then I'd craft a stabbing reply like, *Again?! Wow, your poor English liver. At Riviera now, so amazing, rode in a Porsche last night—so fast!* Then I'd add an *xo*, one meager attempt to pull us both back to center, back to the affection we'd once both found unmatched comfort in. But I could see it was no use. The more Adam appeared to be forgetting me, the more I strived to prove how effortlessly I too was climbing the European social ladder . . . and the only thing that turned me off more than the way he was acting was the way I was acting. I hated begging for his attention. The xx's and xo's may as well have been invisible, mere formalities evaporating to zero meaning. We'd traveled quickly to becoming lovers and kept the relationship flying for almost a year, and now suddenly we were complete foreigners again. Geographical proximity wasn't bringing us closer—instead, we mysteriously repelled each other.

When I hadn't heard from Adam in three weeks while I was still at the seaside, I finally called him on Skype from a café on my Friday off from the *bambini*. I caught him just as he was leaving work:

"Oh my God, hi. Are you okay, chicken? Are you safe?"

"Yes," I answered, with reserve. "Adam, I haven't heard from you in almost a month. I've been worried."

"Ah, baby. I'm sorry, I should've told you." He paused. "I've taken a job in Bahrain."

I take a punch in the stomach. I want to double over and vomit.

"Are you there?"

Ah yew theh? The sweet properness of his accent weakens me yet, and my voice comes out deflated. "I'm here."

"Are you there, darling?"

"I'm here!" I snap. "Where is Bahrain?"

"In the Middle East, near Saudi Arabia."

"You're moving to *Saudi Arabia*?"

"I'm moving *near* Saudi Arabia." He is losing his patience. "I go on the twenty-fifth."

"The twenty-fifth of September." Certainly he didn't mean two weeks from now.

"No, August twenty-fifth. Week after next."

"Good luck, Adam. I don't want to keep you."

"Wait, chicken, you're okay?"

"Yes, I'm fine. I'll let you go."

But I couldn't let him go. Everywhere I went, he was still there with me. I remember a hike one day in the Alps a few weeks after that conversation. I walked with the five children I was nannying for what felt like miles along a stream. I stayed behind and chuckled to myself at the grandma-style kerchiefs wrapped around their little toddler heads; how they skipped along in their knee-high woolen socks and hikers. When we decided as a group that we were good and hungry we found a flat spot to picnic, straight across the path from three thin grazing cows. "*Guardate le mucche!*" Alfonso cried, and with all their energy the kids took off to the wood fence to marvel at the cows. As I flew our picnic blanket open and spread it on the grass, it hit me: *Hey, would you look at that, I haven't thought of Adam since we started the hike two hours ago!* And then I wanted to kick myself because, of course, I'd just thought of him. That was the longest period that the concept of him agreed to leave me alone, but then he returned. For months after that he never left again.

WHEN WE LAND in Pittsburgh eight hours later, the fool in the seat next to me checks his watch. He leans far across my half of the armrest until I can taste the coffee on his breath. Have I heard what the captain said about the weather? "Snow," I tell him. He says he's relieved to be here for business and not holiday, then folds up his paper. I look out the window to study how gray the Pennsylvania sky turns this time of year; how night intrudes on the afternoon, so unwelcome to fall so early; and how, in town, traffic has probably already turned the bright snow into gray sludge peppered with gravel. *Grandma will have to mourn in this*, I think, and wonder if it's more helpful when the weather tries to perk up loneliness with its shine or when it chooses to sympathize drearily with a sad mood. It may not matter. In either case I don't believe that my grandma will ever recover after Grandpa is gone.

After sixty years of marriage, he's her life. He's all she has going on. They travel together. When he needs a hearing aid, she gets one too. Every day she knows it's four o'clock when he says, "Hey Glo, feel like making me a martini?" I'm as pained for Grandma to lose him as I am for myself.

A moan escapes me as I reach under my seat for my single carry-on packed with only black clothes for my week's stay, and a one-ounce bottle of expensive balsamic vinegar from my boss to my family. *I might consider appearing as though I actually live in the world's fashion capital when my family sees me.* I smooth on a coat of lip gloss, and the "Unfasten seat belts" bell dings. The man next to me rises and exits without saying goodbye.

In the last two weeks the phone calls from my parents had grown so frequent and frantic that it became very clear they weren't just panicking. It was officially time to book a flight home: Grandpa was about to die. When I enter my grandma's front door into the living room and drop my bag down, I feel naked like in a dream where no one knows how to react to you. Apparently my arrival from Italy is the official signal to my aunts, caught laughing and drinking wine around the dining room table; to my dad and uncles, resembling modern Greek centaurs in their dress shirts and pajama pants and their Wi-Fi and BlackBerries buzzing through the house; to my cousins, lounging with magazines on the couch and playing poker in the kitchen with their hats turned backward: the last of us has just arrived, and from far away. Their vigil is nearing its final hours.

Grandma emerges from the scatter of family and clinches tightly around me. I lean down so she doesn't strain and I pat her back gently, the way a new mother hopes to ease a restless baby to sleep. I can't fathom how to console a woman who is but days away from losing her husband of six decades—not hearing from Adam for a few months all but destroyed me—so I just hold her. Her skin smells floral like Oil of Olay, and her hearing aid hums in my ear. When we separate, she braces my shoulders and smiles through her tears. Then she clears her throat and smooths herself over. "I'm very happy you've made it," she says, as though she's addressing members of Parliament. "He was asking for you."

"I'll go to him. Grandma," I thumb my kiss off her cheek, "Are you doing okay?"

She nods hastily. "Yes," she says, and sniffles. *I'm trying.* She doesn't notice when I reach for her hand to walk back to the hall, so I just follow her to the guest room where they've set up Grandpa's hospital bed, along the way studying her immaculate brown curls and her tiny frame. She's not showing any signs of dementia yet, although I examine her for a change in appearance the way I did when my friend Lynne in New York told me she was six weeks pregnant.

Grandma and Grandpa announced to the family two weeks

ago, right before he took permanently to the bed, that two years ago Grandma had been diagnosed with early dementia. They decided last month, when the doctors determined that Grandpa's lung cancer was terminal, that it was a good time to loop us all in. They had been sick together and fulfilled a solemn pact to keep the information strictly between them for as long as possible. To my grandparents, suffering is not a noble condition. The capacity to fulfill a promise to another person, on the other hand, is. Will I ever trust someone so unshakably?

My parents and aunts and uncles crowd the doorway as Grandma pioneers her way straight to Grandpa's side and waves me in next to her. "George?" she calls. "Krissy's here."

Not a muscle moves.

"Huunn," she sings. This is the first I've ever heard her call him anything other than George; suddenly she's lighthearted and congenial in a way I've never seen her. "Sit down, Kris."

I sink carefully into the desk chair with wheels that sits at the rail of Grandpa's bed. They've propped an ottoman underneath the chair. It's upholstered with bright tapestry and regal bolts, like it was designed to sit at the foot of a queen's throne. I presume it's for Grandma, and I don't feel familiar enough with this situation yet to rest my feet there in comfort. I have to go through the initiation into this horrible setting that all the rest of the family knows as their new reality.

"Hun, there's a granddaughter standing here. She just arrived from Italy and wants to say hello." She urges me. "Go ahead."

I search for something normal to say. "Hi, Grandpa." I can't force out anything else. As I scan his body, I observe that everything from his ribs down is tucked in tight between the sheets. I focus on Grandpa's skinny hand and run a single finger down his tendons, defined as the prongs of a fork. *My God, where has he disappeared to?* He's lost twenty pounds and gained thirty years since three weeks ago when we hugged goodbye at New Year's. The muscles in my throat strain open, and a tear races down my cheek and lands fat on my hand. I want to collapse and wail.

"We'll leave you two alone." Grandma and the rest of the gang, watching from the doorway, disappear down the hall.

I scan Grandpa, his gaunt cheeks and olive skin washed out to a surrendering gray. I admire his stillness, his vulnerability. Here he is, yet again, even more tender than I'd ever perceived him before. Suddenly his eyes open, and widen, and he lets out a relieved sigh. *You're here!* he wants to say.

"Hi," I coo softly, as though he's a waking baby. I scoot to the edge of the chair, and he smiles. "I'm here." He sighs again, then smiles, then rests his head slowly back into the pillow. My throat, this pressure. I pull the St. Christopher medal that I always wear to travel from around my neck and loop it around the bar of his bed. Certainly this voyage he's on is much more demanding than mine just was.

Laughter explodes from the living room, punctuated by Grandma's girlish giggle. Our family has turned this bedside vigil into a cocktail-slumber party. I understand why. Grandpa wants us to take care of Grandma and help her carry on as uninterrupted as possible. The two of them have made all the arrangements; they've signed the wills and bought this house we're sitting in now, a one-story bungalow with a sun porch and emergency pull cords so that in case Grandma falls, she can call for help to the nursing home across the road, the one where I worked the nighttime switchboard all through high school.

With the business that my grandpa founded, his mark is impressed all around this small town. My grandmother will never be able to escape the thought of her husband after he's gone. He built a wing with a computer lab onto the Catholic high school from where the last of my cousins will graduate in a few months. Grandma will pass that building every day on her way downtown. Grandpa was usually her partner at Mass; I wonder how she'll bear the solemnity of church without him. Our factory sits proud in the middle of the industrial park, the GASBARRE PRODUCTS, INC. sign shining brightly at all hours, starring the masculine green logo that Grandpa designed. I can't even hear an English accent without pining for Adam—how will my grandma be able to continue without Grandpa after he's passed?

For four long days the family operates in shifts around the clock to sit with Grandpa. For his sake, I'm glad he wakes only every so often, because we'd be driving him mad with our hanging around by now—the man always valued his space. Early each morning, my mom and my aunts, my grandparents' three daughters-in-law, arrive after a good night's sleep fresh-faced and velour-suited, with huge breakfast casseroles and Perkins pancake takeout. They pour fizzy mimosas and brew hot coffee, and soon the aromas of bacon and syrup fill the air so strong that they travel back to the bedroom. "I'm hungry," Grandpa says.

I look up to my dad for guidance. "Yesterday the nurses said nothing solid from now on, right?"

"Yeah," he whispers. "Poor fella." My dad has the heart of a puppy. He puts his hand over Grandpa's. "They said his swallowing reflex is going. Oh God, he's hungry, and he can't eat." Dad wipes his own eyes with a handkerchief, and Grandpa's eyes now pour a constant steam of tears from the creases, which Grandma's "Stages of Death" booklet says is an indicator that the patient's passing is imminent within hours or two days at most. "Maybe just some fresh ginger ale."

"I'll go." I look at Grandpa. "Grandpa."

"Yeah?"

"How 'bout some ginger ale, does that sound good?"

"Mm-hmm," he mumbles. "Sounds good."

"Okay, you stay here with my dad and I'll be right back."

"You here, Billy?" Grandpa says. (The nurses have explained that he's losing his vision, but he's growing hypersensitive to light.)

"Yeah, Dad, I'm here," my father says, nearing Grandpa. "Krissy's gonna get you a drink, okay?"

"Yeah," Grandpa says, although the word is barely distinguishable. "Okay." As I walk down the hall I hear him say, "Billy?"

"Yeah, Dad?"

"Give me a hug."

Grandma is back to her old flustered self when she follows me into the bedroom. "George?" she says. "I'll be back shortly, I just have one more hand to play with the boys."

My gob-smacked gaze meets my father's. Shocked, we both start laughing. Her husband is hours away from his death and she's *playing poker*? Is this what sixty years of marriage do to a woman?

Later that night, after Grandma washes her face and combs her hair, she announces that she'd like a glass of warm milk before bed. "Who is she, the friggin' queen of Sheba?" my mom asks. "Her hands and legs don't work now?" But obedient as a saint, Mom knocks on her mother-in-law's door and passes her a full glass. When Grandma checks to make sure it's lactose-free and latches her door for the night, Mom says, "You know, sometimes I don't know if she needs a hug, noogies, or a smack upside the head." Then she goes in to hold her father-in-law's hand.

Through the nights after Grandma has gone to bed, the rest of us take our posts. Whoever's seated next to Grandpa at any given moment painfully observes that his breaths are growing more spread out and agitated. His gasps are hollow and cavernous, as though the River Styx is flooding his chest. During the hours when we most crave sleep, he is at his most listless. He shocks us with his new contempt for the nighttime, and frail as he his, it takes my dad, my uncle, and me to stop him from standing up and walking out of the room. When we finally get him settled down and tucked back in, we are too drained to cry . . . even though seeing this man, the hero of our family, in such a troubled state is enough to rip our weeping hearts open.

Three nights pass. With the arrival of first morning light there is a detectable shift in spirit, a raw dichotomy of hope and horror that today, he could go. The smallest crack of light between the blinds delivers Grandpa's cherubic troop of hospice nurses. As they scoot their snowy shoes off on the linoleum foyer floor and drift in a hushed pack to the guest room, there's a stir among us tired watchdogs. The coffeepot starts, the face-washing sink runs, and our vigil reconvenes. We relieve each other effortlessly, in a seamless cycle of sitting, feeding, eating, and waiting. Comforting this beloved dying man is less a chore than it is a pleasure and an honor.

Monday night I volunteer to sit up at Grandpa's side. In an armchair in the corner, I doze between sleeping and waking, the same way he floats between earth and the supernatural. "I have to die today," he says, plain as day, and I jolt awake. I stand to hover over him, stroking the smooth top of his head. He has to die today. For now, we are the only two who share this news. It makes me want to crawl in the bed with him and bawl. By the glow of the stained-glass night-light, I memorize his features—the mole on his eyelid, the pores across his nose, the precise Cupid's bow curving across his top lip. When he stirs, I whisper to him.

"Grandpa."

"Wha . . . ?" He is too exhausted to pronounce the *t* at the end of the word.

"I have to tell you something. Lay down first though, okay? Come on, there we go. Good job." I speak to him with steady encouragement. "There. Okay, listen."

"Okay."

I put my lips close to his ear. "I love you, Grandpa."

He opens his eyes. "I love you too."

My throat tightens. "I know."

"Boy, do I love you."

His eyes close again. I rest my head on the pillow next to him so his cheek hovers so soft against mine, and I can actually sense from him that it's hurting him to put me through this pain. I look up at the colored shadows on the ceiling as endless tears stream past my cheeks, over my jaw, around the back of my neck. Nothing in my life, no struggle or victory or heartbreak, could hold as much significance as this single perfect moment. The person I treasure most in the world loves me back. I'll never have to accept anything less from a man again.

When morning arrives, Father Ed, our parish priest, follows the nurses into Grandpa's room and they call us all in for a prayer. In our sweatsuits and our resolve to see this through to the finish, we gather around the bed smelling like breakfast burritos and dirty hair. The nurses have washed Grandpa down so he's fragrant as an angel, warm soap and aloe and clean linens on the bed. Grandma and Ruth, the head nurse who's also an old friend of our family, take seats at Grandpa's side and when we pray the Our Father in unison, Grandpa finds the strength to take both their hands and kiss their palms. After Father Ed's blessing the nurses exit the room, gripping each of our hands and looking us steady in the eyes. Everyone understands now that he'll pass today. We have only a few hours with Grandpa left.

There is no more poker. There is not much laughing or commotion, only the coming and going of my cousins as they make trips to the convenience store for a break. Grandma finally seems to understand the inevitability of these minutes, and she has committed not to leave Grandpa's side. She asks for music. I carry in the Bose stereo and pop in the only CD they own. It's a live performance of a jazz band they'd taken a bus to see last year, before they knew Grandpa was sick. "Find something he'll recognize, Kris," Grandma says, and we skip to a song that reminds me of Sinatra, with swooning violins and upbeat brass:

> *I'm sure that I could never hide*
> *The thrill I get when you're by my side!*
> *And when we're older, we'll proudly declare,*
> *Wasn't ours a lovely love affair?*

Grandma stands bracing herself over the bar of the bed and staring over Grandpa, and in a fresh alertness he stares back up at her. In the middle of the song when the orchestra swells to crescendo, Grandpa says, "Kiss me, Gloria." Grandma leans down and they kiss long and tender on the mouth. They are both crying. When Grandma finally pulls away, Grandpa pleads, "Do that again," and she does. It occurs to me that I have never seen my grandparents kiss before.

> *Our love affair was meant to be*
> *It's me for you, and you for me . . .*
> *And when we're older, we'll proudly declare,*
> *Wasn't ours a lovely love affair?*

When the song ends I play it again. Grandma sits at the edge of her seat stroking her thumb lightly over Grandpa's hand, and

I've never seen her so composed. "Peace, George," she says, and tears roll down the corners of Grandpa's eyes as he sleeps.

AFTER DINNER we all cheer when Ruth peeks her head back in the door. She smiles and goes to the bedroom to find Grandma at Grandpa's side. "It'll just be you and me with him for a little while, okay, Gloria? Whaddya say we give the troops a break?"

"Okay then."

Ruth winks and gently asks us to leave them for a little while. My mom had heard that the dying often won't pass in front of their loved ones, and she leans into me. "I bet you Ruth knows: it's time."

I nod slowly. Maybe it is.

After half an hour of silence from the back room, Ruth calls in my dad and his siblings. Their stampede is followed shortly by a loud gasp, and my mom and aunts and cousins and I all look around. Ruth enters the kitchen with her lips to her hands, which are folded in a steeple. Her eyes are fixed on the floor. "I think he's gone."

My cousins and brother and all of our moms exchange expressionless glances again, and slowly we rise out of our chairs. In the back room my dad and his siblings and my grandma are sobbing silently. When my dad's head finds my mom's shoulder, he breaks down. She holds him. "It's better this way, honey," she says, but her face is red and wet and she's trying to keep from hyperventilating. My aunts all embrace their husbands, and it occurs to me that not only have I never seen my uncles cry before, I have never seen them hug their wives. In this moment

I understand that relationships aren't just a blessing, they're a necessity. The trials of the individual are never enough reason not to love.

We each take turns kissing Grandpa's face. He still smells like soap, and he's warm. We move into places around the bed when Father Ed arrives again to pray over his body. Grandma remains at his side, in a trance. After we make the sign of the cross, she finally breaks down, saying, "I love you so, George."

Wasn't ours a lovely love affair.

I hope I'll be a good wife at someone's side one day, strong and loving and calm. I imagine sitting at Adam Hunt's side, smoothing the hair on his freckled arm, giving him sips of ginger ale through a straw, kissing his mouth one last time.

I can imagine all of it . . . except the kiss. It's been seven months since I've seen him, and no matter how hard I try, I can't quite remember his face.

2

Learn to Listen

"Well, I'm surprised you took this way."

Grandma and I are heading toward the doctor's office, and I've taken Brown Street instead of Arminta. When I was in high school I loved driving this street to work at the nursing home every day. It's curvy and requires attention to cars coming from the other direction, but I loved the challenge of maneuvering it patiently. And—full disclosure—it leads to the spot where my first love and I used to go parking: indeed, this road is full of thrills. I respond to Grandma treading lightly and with patience. "You have to remember, Grandma, I haven't lived around here for ten years. I don't know these streets like I used to. This will take us to the same place, right?"

"I suppose," she pauses, then adds this: "Grandpa used to take this way just to spite me." With her tone I'm beginning to think it's no wonder! Not every woman her age has a grown granddaughter who can drop her responsibilities for a whole afternoon to accompany her grandma to the doctor's, who cares what route she takes!

Grandma wants to go home before we head to lunch, although she can't really tell me why. I'm getting used to these stalling tactics—the more time she keeps you doing things for her, the less time she has to spend alone. Since Grandpa died four months ago, loneliness has become her worst enemy.

During my last four months in Italy it had become mine too. Grandpa's last days and his funeral composed a week-long family affair with a bond that I had completely forgotten since I left home a decade ago. When I was sitting around Grandma's dining room table for dinner, I felt *part of a group* again. For years my grandpa's colleagues have joked that it's hard to distinguish our "family" from our "family business," with wine and food and laughter and business talk characterizing both our company board meetings and the weekend family get-togethers that I knew constantly when I was growing up. Being away from these people for so long, then returning to witness our greatest tragedy together, allowed me to view the family I come from as an outsider looking in. How unique is this family, who at moments disagree about business but almost always agree on what's best for the family and how Grandpa would want us to handle things. I felt that for the last decade I'd been looking into a mirror with a big chunk taken out of the glass, and suddenly my family had moved in to help me put the missing piece back in place. With them behind me, I saw myself as whole.

It was the first week of February when I landed back in Italy after Grandpa's funeral. Every moment that I wasn't tutoring English for the family I was living with, I was in my room, quietly reading or writing in my journal. In the mornings the kids' mother, Isabella, would knock on my door and ask me whether I wanted to join her at the gym or take the train with her to Rome to meet a diplomat. (Isabella's husband manufactured parts for Italian sports cars and was known as one of the most prominent men in Italy. They had to be among the most generous families in the country too.) Usually I formulated some excuse related to the hope that I was *so close!* to finally seeing some success in my fledgling freelance writing career, convincing Isabella that there was some editor in America tapping her foot, waiting for me to hand in an assignment on the best girlfriend-getaway biking routes in Italy.

In tight Armani jeans and a blouse with poet sleeves, Isabella would smile, nod patiently, and say quietly, "Okay. I understand very well."

She did, but I wished she could explain my self-inflicted solitude to me, because the truth was, I didn't understand it at all. Through the week, I would sit with the blinds shut in my room and shower only at the very last minute before my shift to teach the kids. Finally, when the weekends arrived, I jumped on the metro across town to see Celeste, my best friend from college who, after her own painful breakup, had moved to Milan with me on a last-minute whim. With her fine blond hair and sparkling blue eyes, Celeste was faring swimmingly in the land of Latin love, dating a sexy opera conductor named Giuseppe and even signing her nanny contract for an extra six months. But I couldn't imagine spending another season away from home. I wanted my family.

One afternoon my mom and I were on the phone and she said she'd begun counting down the hours until I arrived back in the States. "Mom," I told her, "I've been giving a lot of thought to what I'm going to do when I come back."

"Well," she said patiently, "what have you come up with?" If you prefer clichés, my mom sort of grew up on the other side of the tracks from my dad, even though they lived just blocks apart in town on Pollock Hill. The Hill's where our three Catholic churches form a topographical triangle, and in those days a family's status and involvement in the community could be discreetly determined by which parish they belonged to. My dad and his four siblings were raised around the corner from St. Catherine's cathedral; Mom and her four siblings sang in the rear choir loft at St. Mike's. Mom says this was always a relief because it kept the people in church from noticing that she wore the same outfit week after week.

Mom started working from the time she was twelve to try to stay in style among her classmates at the public school, and she sometimes talks about the moment in junior high after she and her dad got in a brutal fight and she stared at her own face in the mirror and said, "You're better than this." Her own mother, whom my brother and I call Nana, insists Mom had a fabulous life growing up on the Hill, but Mom quietly retorts, saying that my dad rescued her from poverty and made it possible for her to make a career as the wife and mom she dreamed of being. Throughout my own upbringing my friends loved and counted on my mom—both to present elaborate finger Jell-O at class parties and to make us all feel loved and safe under her roof. Mom strikes an affirming balance between her unparalleled mother-bear sensitivity and her unmatched sense of humor—always speedy, usually raunchy—that's a sign of her being raised with brothers and her resilience to rise above a pinched childhood.

So there was no need for me to hold back when I tell Mom, "I need a few months back home."

"Home, home? Like, living with Dad and me?"

"Yes."

"I think that would be okay." She cleared her throat, which I translated to be the containment of a cheer.

"I just need time with everybody," I said, now breaking down and crying like a little kid. Tears had been creeping up on me out of nowhere like this for the last few months in the strangest moments—when I was driving past sunflower fields, in the village square while I sat watching a lump of sugar sink through the foam in a cappuccino, and especially anytime I sat down to write in my journal in the lone hollows of my nanny's quarters. Ever since January twenty-ninth when Grandpa died, there were pages smudged full of watery blue ink with paper that had turned hard and faded with my tears. "It's just weird to try to absorb that Grandpa's gone," I told my mom. "I feel like I have to see it for myself. You know?"

"Yeah, I do," she said. "We've had a chance to digest the reality of it, but I wonder sometimes with you being so far away if it's really sunk in for you yet."

"No, I don't think it's sunk in yet. And every time I call Grandma, she just sounds *so sad*—the grief gets worse instead of better."

"Tell me about it."

"The least I could do is try to pitch in and help you all get into a rhythm of taking care of her." There was a second of

silence, and then I realized what I was saying: "Mom, we promised Grandpa."

"Honey, she's my mother-in-law and I love her, you know that,"
my mom says, "but without him, she's becoming a handful."

I blew my nose in the phone. "Sorry, Mom," I sniffled. "You
mean with the dementia?"

"Not so much that as just needing a lot of attention."

I pause. "Should I think about . . . *moving in* with her?"

"Oh God! It's a nice idea but honestly, honey, nobody would
expect you to give up your life to do that."

"But I could."

"Krissy, it's generous. But your dad will have a heart attack if
you're not either writing for ten hours a day or looking for work.
I mean, okay, I'm exaggerating . . . a little. And anyway, no one
under the age of sixty-five is allowed to live in her development.
The most you could even stay over there would be four nights."
Mom scoffs, "And she ain't leaving the place, believe me. Grandpa
set her up there. They take the old ladies on shopping trips, on
buses to see plays in Pittsburgh, they have catered neighborhood
dinners every week, and I tell you, that community center is *ritzy*.
Except for missing Grandpa, your grandmother has it made. Just
come home and spend some time with her. I know everybody will
be happy to have you here. Especially Dad and I."

Two months later I'm up to my elbows helping with
Grandma—no, literally. I'm holding her arm from the doctor's
office to my dad's car, which I'm driving during what psycholo-
gists are calling us Boomerang kids' "temporary incubation period" at home.

"You said you wanted to run back to your house for an umbrella, Grandma?" The June sun shines blissfully through the windshield. "Then do you want to get takeout, or eat in the restaurant?"

"We'll eat it there." I can hear her thinking: *It'll keep me out for a bit.*

I don't mention that I'm on a story deadline or that I have a dentist's appointment in two hours. She needs help and company, and for now, I'm the only one in the family who's able to offer both on a nearly full-time schedule. I'm silently growing worried that my writing is falling behind, and I'm getting the same vibe from my dad, who used to send me inspirational quotes in Italy, à la my Grandpa: *You can do anything you want to do* and *Writing is your passion. Make it work.* If only I had time *to* work.

"Oh!" Grandma says as we come up on the pharmacy in the row of shops downtown. "Stop here! I have a question for the pharmacist."

As the bell jingles to announce our entrance, the gentlemen behind the counter look up, then disperse. Suddenly I'm certain that every medical professional within an hour radius wants to duck and cover when they see my grandma enter their doors.

"More acid reflux, Gloria?" the stocky pharmacist grumbles.

"The doctor said it's a side effect of the antidepressants, but it's *really* upsetting my digestion."

"You're out of refills on the antacid."

"Well, see, that's just what I was coming to ask you about . . ." Her voice trails off and the pharmacist glazes over, and when I try to translate her stutters and mumbles to him, she cuts me off. I leave to go browse the mouthwash aisle.

Twenty minutes later we are in the car, no antacid, no patience, no lunch. "You know what, Grandma? I think we're gonna be okay without that umbrella. What do you say we go straight to Ruby Tuesday's, I'm starving."

She pauses, pissed off. "That'll be fine."

Grandma's head spins when the hostess asks her where we'd like to be seated. She looks left, right, left, right, until finally I say, "We'd love a window seat, if you've got one."

"And somewhere close to the salad bar, just keep me away from that cheese."

"And close to the salad bar, please." I smile in peacekeeping fashion, trying to play down Grandma's high maintenance. My God, just how did my grandpa do it for sixty years, and *why*? She's a handful, she's ungrateful, she can't make a decision, and for the woman who used to be the waspiest, most rigid person I know, her new favorite topic of discussion is her gastrointestinal discomfort. I'm realizing that in all the years I've known her, in all the late nights over rigatoni and wine, it was my grandpa who did all the talking. It should have occurred to me before, as he was always the more gregarious and open of the two.

Grandma burps and slams her hand on the table in frustration before excusing herself and covering her mouth with her napkin. "This *belching*!" she says. It's the first time I've ever seen her practice less than perfect manners.

"You know, Grandma, have you considered that the problems you're having with your esophagus could be due to the simple fact that you're talking more now than you ever have before?"

"What do you mean?"

"I mean, Grandpa was the one really known for all the story-telling and gabbing. And around the house you two knew the other was there, but you didn't actually *talk* a whole lot, like a lot of longtime married people. So now, not only does it just so happen that you're talking more, but you're finding it *necessary* to talk to work through the sadness and longing you're feeling for him right now. When you think about it, you've never talked this much in your life!"

She looks up dumbstruck from her broccoli soup, which she decided to take a chance on. "You know, I've never thought of it that way before."

Grandma can't be left alone. When she tells me this, she doesn't mean it in a high-drama, I'm-not-sure-what-I'll-do-to-myself kind of way; it's just that every day the minutes crawl by and she's so lonely she cries. Eating by herself is the worst, she says, and I think of the first time I challenged myself to have dinner at a restaurant alone, in the summer during college. It was at the Olive Garden, and I waitressed there, so I knew my waiter but figured it still counted. There was no one actually seated across the table from me, and I conquered it. When I worked in New York it was a luxury to grab a salad or a coffee alone and read a book during lunch. As long as I had something to occupy me, being alone didn't make me feel uncomfortable or vulnerable. Usually I actually liked it. But for Grandma and people her age, meals are for sharing. Eating dinner without anyone to watch the news with feels like a cruel punishment.

"You think maybe that's why I'm still single, Grandma?"

She looks up from her salad. "What's that?"

"Could it be that people like me are more okay with being

alone than people in your generation, because we have more to distract us from actually feeling lonely?"

"I imagine that's some part of it. But how can you expect to meet anybody if you've got those things in your ears all the time. You wear that thing at the gym? Oh, what's it called—that little thing that plays music?"

"What, my iPod?"

"Mm-hm."

"Yes, that's why I got it."

"Well, there you go. If somebody wants to say hello to you, he's gotta pantomime. Feels silly talking and not knowing if the other person is listening or not."

I remember walking down the street in Cleveland, where I stayed the year after I graduated from college. My apartment was in Little Italy and a little old man tipped his hat to me in the street. I gasped and smiled to tell him thank-you. Then I stopped in front of him and said, "You know what, sir? I wish every girl my age knew what it felt like to have a man tip his hat to her."

He winked, placing his hat back over his silvery scalp. Then he thought for a second and said, "You know what, young lady? I wish that too."

When Grandma and Grandpa and the man in Little Italy were growing up, strangers made an effort to connect and be less of strangers; people expressed their appreciation for the mere existence of one another, and they communicated. It may be no wonder I haven't had a man tip his hat to me since that day—shortly after it happened, I moved to New York and instantly invested in an iPod to experience the city in my own world, the way just about everyone else did.

I tell Grandma the story, thinking it'll make her smile, but instead she turns almost preachy. "Well, of course he tipped his hat to you," she says. "That's how men back then were raised to treat woman."

"Okay, but . . ." I push my plate aside. "What did it *mean?*"

She squints her eyes, critical of my overanalytical approach to understanding a simple male gesture. "Well, what would you think? He was acknowledging you, paying respect."

"Okay, and what should I have done back?"

"Just what you did! You heard what he was trying to say, 'Hello, and I think you're lovely.' You stopped and thanked him, it was more than enough! It was just a normal, easy exchange."

But to me it wasn't normal; it was a really special moment in my young womanhood. Its simplicity and sincerity struck me in an instant . . . but maybe that's Grandma's point: I complicate things with all the noise I live inside and my journalistic interpretations of what men do. *He texted, what does it mean? He's not calling, what's he trying to say?* But Grandma's explanation is that it's all right there in the message. So from even *before* the start of a relationship, she says that people my age need to *learn to listen.*

What, Grandma?

Just kidding.

GRANDMA AND GRANDPA met at the ice cream soda shop downtown one early summer night just after she had graduated and he had been in Germany fighting in World War II for two years. When America won and he returned home for good, he spotted Grandma walking past the ice cream shop on her way to meet her mom after work. He stopped her in the street to say hello. "I remembered him from school," she says, and giggles. "He was very popular with the girls."

When she talks about him, she melts from cold as snow to warm and indulgent as hot fudge. A wistfulness enters her gaze, as though 1947 is playing back in a silver screen right over my head. "He called me the next day and asked me out on our first date. When he called, he asked for Florence! He confused my name with my street, Florence Street. My mother almost hung up on him, she thought he had the wrong number." Grandma says he never would have called her if they hadn't stopped to chat that night. I try to imagine where we'd all be if Grandma had been listening to her iPod.

She takes her time eating her salad like a little bird, and even though it's all I can do to resist looking at the time on my phone, I don't dare. I think of how many rushed lunches I've eaten by myself, then of how many silent dinners she has ahead of her. While sometimes the quiet is nice, too much of it is lonesome and unnatural. When we feed one another it's the nurturing instinct at work, the maternal message to the other person that you wish for them to thrive. I watch Grandma carefully slicing her cucumber, how it takes her so much more effort than it takes me, and the long strain her neck makes for her lips to find her fork. She wipes her mouth fragilely then grins at me, and my heart crashes open with compassion.

Grandma and I each get a cone at the Dairy Queen after lunch. My licks try to keep up with the melting ice cream, and when Grandma laughs at me, I remember the afternoon in Hyde Park in London when Adam and I sat and watched the swans, and then he bought me a vanilla cone at an ice cream truck. He had the vendor stick in a chocolate flake for me for fifty pence extra, and he took one lick and left the rest for me to enjoy.

I know he's the one who screwed things up by taking the job in Bahrain and not telling me, but I could've given more too. I hadn't shared enough. E-mails and texts—talk is cheap. Would dropping a card to him in the mail have been so hard to manage? Wouldn't an old-fashioned love note have been nice? And why did it take me ten months to go visit after we met—couldn't I have saved some cash over three? He didn't give enough, but maybe I didn't either. I'd been afraid to really connect, fearing that I was dealing with someone who wasn't as great as he appeared or that my beauty and its need to share itself could be rejected. In the end, isn't the result the same? Whether he was good or not, I held back, and now I don't have him. Some time-tested, in-the-flesh contact might have helped things along. If I'd just been wise enough to know that an eighty-nine-cent stamp can be golden, to show him just an ounce of extra caring, to compromise a little more.

On the way home Grandma suggests we take Long Avenue. Even though Brady Street is faster and I'm running late, this time I listen.

3

Get Your Own Life Settled

I MAY NOT REMEMBER the best ways around town, but everything else about my move back home requires little reacquainting. Mom and Dad's miniature collies greet me out front like old times, making me certain with their excitement and kisses that I have done the right thing by returning home for a while. We got Rocky on my high school senior prom night so that Mom would have extra company around the house after I left for college, and now with his gray hair, I'm usually the only one in the family he's nice to. Our puppy was a surprise last fall, when Mom and Dad called me in Italy to ask me what we should name him. "Something cute and Italian," Mom said.

"How about Alfonso?"

"Little Alfie, that's your name!" Dad said in the background. "Your big sister will have to wait till she flies home from Italy for Christmas to meet you!" Now that I've moved back home, little Alfonso is a sweet addition to my world. Affection feels good—feels *right*—to any human walking through the front door.

In my brother's teenage bedroom Dad has set up my writing desk so I can look out onto Treasure Lake, the sparkling gem my brother, cousins, and I grew up on. For almost two decades we spent every summer weekend at our Landing—the family's lake-front company house two miles away from my house—when our dads' customers weren't there to occupy it. A decade later the lake is as glistening as ever, and my brother Jeff and my cous-ins don't miss a beat welcoming me back into the fold. Jeff's the master at mixing Long Islands behind Grandpa's long bar (so we've outgrown Shirley Temples, I guess?), and my cousin Zach mans the boat instead of my Uncle Phil . . . but the overall spirit of *la dolce vita*—the sweet life—still swims, in exactly the way my grandpa wanted to raise us when he bought the house in 1982. I remember his silver-dollar pancake breakfasts after all-family trampoline campouts; how he beamed after building the bocce court and tiny beach out back. Around this lake, on this trampoline, under these grand pine trees, I hear Grandpa reminding me: *This is your safe Landing. This is who you are.*

This is who I am, and no matter how I keep bracing myself for it, the reverse culture shock my New York friends keep warn-ing me about isn't kicking in. I. Love. Home.

I've been back for two weeks when my dear mother is burst-ing to reintegrate me into her social circles. Mom reminds me (but perhaps more herself) that we're about to see everyone we know at all the summer weddings we have, so together we walk the seven miles around the lake or hit the gym every morning. Then, in what feels like a flurry of grown-up, fluffed-down debu-tantes, arm in arm with Mom I'm hitting book clubs, country clubs, and baby and bridal showers. I'd forgotten this culture existed; this comfortable world where friends are so loyal that decorating for the wedding of a friend's daughter is as much a bustling community effort as an episode of something Ty Pennington would host. These women's beauty radiates not after spa day, like it did for me in New York, not from the glamarazzi fashion sense I grew to worship in Italy, but in their down-to-earth sharing with each other—and now, with me.

Apparently the buzz phrase around town has become "Oh Krissy, we're gonna fix you up." I'm amazed at how a girl's hometown dating prospects start to look up after she's been away for a few years. At picnics my mom's pals crowd around me to put their single nephews up for bids, and Grandma's bridge group insist they know the perfect guy for me. The poker crew at my brother's house on Wednesdays have invited me to join them, and while I'm rubbish at cards, their quest to find me a date is encouraging. I went to high school with most of them, good guys with blue-collar jobs and wedding bands. Sometimes, even when I'm surrounded by their spittoons and dirty jokes, I wish I hadn't pursued a career that took me so far on adventure, away from the grown-up procedure these guys live and do so well. Couldn't I have stayed back home all along and set up a simple life with a husband and a baby and a mortgage like my friends did? The contentment in their lives makes me wonder if I got the last decade all wrong.

I've recently vowed to give a chance to whoever comes my way—some small-town romantic straightforwardness would be welcome, no matter what kind of package it comes in. (I am still so emotionally browbeaten after going splitsville in Europe that when truckers beep on the Pennsylvania interstate, I wave back, then shrug at my mom: "Hey, you know what they say, a compliment's a compliment.")

However, there is a particular bachelor who sounds extraordinarily . . . provocative. His superlative description always overshadows the other candidates, suddenly making them look limp and unexciting, like week-old imported vegetables. Anytime a woman in the community says, "Krissy, these guys sound fine but you really *have* to meet Dr. Christopher," the other ladies wilt and shrink away, suggesting to me that the royal flush of all local males has just been dealt. Apparently the most important trait this doctor possesses is his semblance to the hero in a European romance novel—dark hair that sweeps to his collar, eyes blue-crystal like the sea, a smile big and shining with the power to comfort the most unfortunate of trauma patients or de-pants even the most resolvedly celibate female.

Grandma's heard that this Dr. Christopher is well respected among the hospital auxiliary, and my mom met him at a charity fashion show when he first moved to town. "You should've seen how some of those grown women pounced to touch the fur coat he modeled. I was embarrassed just watching," Mom said. The thought of a man in fur weirds me out until Mom explains that the event was a fund-raiser benefiting the community's free medical clinic for people who can't afford health care. The doctor is known to volunteer there regularly.

This information begins to make me curious.

According to the women in town, Dr. Christopher's talent as

a surgeon runs a close second to his looks. At a hospital charity auction, Mrs. Chapman—notoriously one of the most polished women in town—tells me Dr. Christopher practices "facial-aesthetic medicine." With sparkles in her eyes (and the arms of her Prada bifocals, notably), Mrs. Chapman explains that Dr. Christopher's specialization is more glamorous than oral surgery but less phony than plastic. She says he's rumored to hold world-class credentials out the wazoo and a bedside manner that heals wounds but breaks hearts. Mrs. Chapman looks up over her specs and points a manicured finger at me from around a lipsticked glass of chardonnay. "What Dr. Oz does to fight aging and Dr. Drew does for relationships, Dr. Christopher can do for your face." She winks, then gusts on to another conversation, and it dawns on me that her lips look really damn good for sixty-five years old.

Mrs. Chapman's not the doctor's only pining patient. One night at dinner with Grandma my cousin Tricia tells me that when Dr. Christopher put her under for her wisdom teeth, she told him she wanted to marry his hair. From what she remembers, he simply chuckled quietly and asked his assistants to make sure she stayed comfortable. Tricia says he's like Grandpa the way he's so intelligent that he doesn't know how handsome he is. Grandma leans in intently, hoping we'll say more to keep the thought of Grandpa present.

But if I'm supposed to be sold on the Doc Hollywood of DuBois, Pennsylvania, all these ladies' claims just make me skeptical. Essentially this guy's a small-town cosmetic surgeon who makes females swoon: how much heart can he really have? Then just when I start to crinkle my nose in doubt, my mom throws down the spirituality card. Apparently the doctor attends church every week (although no one seems to know where, and there are mom fist-bumps all around when Mom's best friend asks where we think *a* god would go to find *the* God. Mom eloquently adds that she'd very much like to be a witness to his steeple). Plus, Dr. Christopher is a known yoga practitioner. ("Krissy, *you* do yoga!" my mom exclaims. "And you go to church, how perfect is this!") He reportedly balances his physical health with great care given to his emotional side, which finally begins to sway me. Could this really be the perfect man?

Still, I confess: with all the buzz I hear about this guy, how is he not married? Is he gay? Commitmentphobic? A total player? The mystery begins to follow me everywhere, and I find myself hoping to run into him in the organic aisle at the grocery store or the gym. I decide I can't judge until I meet him. So, by the time my mom's fourth friend mentions "Dr. Christopher," I agree to *think* about looking him up.

Enter my own spirituality. During a sweltering June Mass that requires the summer-is-a-week-away fanning of the hymnal, I reverently place my forehead in my hands and pray that if I look this man up, God will never make me suffer a pain as severe as getting dumped in a foreign country again. When church is dismissed I visit Grandpa's headstone, which, despite his status in my perception, blends in normally among the other stones. He wanted simple, and we wanted distinguished and elegant, so it's a polished charcoal color that stands about two feet high and three and a half feet long and reads GASBARRE on the back in strong-looking serif font and on the front:

GEORGE PHILIP GASBARRE, SR.
SEPTEMBER 9, 1925—JANUARY 28, 2008
WORLD WAR II

I hate reading his date of death, a date that's already passed—more proof that he's gone. Next to Grandpa's plot is Grandma's:

GLORIA DELORES GASBARRE
(ELLINGER)
DECEMBER 11, 1928

What would it be like to be alive and see your own name already etched on a grave? Grandma's never mentioned it.

After I make sure no one's around, I tell him, just above a whisper, "My heart got broken in Italy, Grandpa. The English guy, remember him?" This feels silly, but it could help. "And then I lost you." A blessed breeze flaps the American flag to his right. "But I believe that there are guys out there who are good, and exciting, right? Like you. Can you help me find one?" I crouch down on my knees and feel the grass tentatively with my hands, both amazed and nervous that his body lies right underneath where I'm touching. "There's one in particular, he lives *here* of all places, and, it's so funny"—I laugh down at the ground, the notion really is so ridiculous—"but everyone, including Grandma, seems to think our spirits are destined for each other or something." I look back at Grandpa's stone as though I'm staring him in the face. "And I've just decided I'm going to contact him." I hesitate. "There's nothing wrong with a new friend, right, Grandpa?" I kiss his stone and run my hand over its letters.

This is the second time I've made this request to my grandfather—when he was sleeping, the day before he died, I asked him to send me my husband. "We've talked about this before. I know you hear me." I stand to brush grass off the hem of my sundress. "Thanks, Grandpa. Love you."

Late that week, Mrs. Chapman had called our house to say she dropped off Dr. Christopher's card and tucked it discreetly in the standing fern on my mom's front porch. I'd intersected the message before Mom had a chance to get to it—there was no need for anyone to get carried away with excitement, which would've turned me off completely. But now, when I get home from church and the cemetery, I finally fish it out, making a pact with myself that if I never get a response, I will let the whole thing go. If the e-mail doesn't bring our paths to intersect, then I'm simply not meant to meet this person.

I title the subject "New friend in DuBois" and craft three friendly paragraphs, cleverly smudging over the awkwardness of my left-field self-introduction with a warm, easy-breezy tone. I tell the doctor that it seems he's built a really respected reputation for himself in the four years since he moved here. His work sounds fascinating, I type, and I only wish we'd cross paths. "Depending on your availability," I say, "it might be fun to get together for lunch or drinks one of these days." This is my eloquent way of saying, "Based on what I've heard about you, there's not an Eskimo pie's chance in hell you could possibly be single, but just in case everybody's right and you are, then it might be real swell to get together."

I read the note three times, noting the importance of sounding self-assured but not overly confident; ladylike but not desperate. (This is ultradelicate territory, and even offering my phone number at this early stage could be perceived as too forward.) In the end the message reads cordially, and I have left my intent wide open: I could be a business acquaintance, a charming new friend, or an eligible bachelorette with attractive dating potential. I hold my breath and look up at my bedroom ceiling. *Am I really doing this?* I release the e-mail like a dove in the wind, anticipating never to hear anything back.

The whole family meets that afternoon for a barbecue at the Landing. In the buffet line I put my lips close to Grandma's ear. "Remember when we were talking about the doctor the other night with Tricia?"

"Yes?" Her eyes turn to me, as wide as the deviled egg on her plate.

"I e-mailed him today."

"Doh!" She nearly drops her hamburger, and her eyes light up like I haven't seen them since the night she cooked spaghetti with Grandpa in the Florida kitchen, a year and a half ago, before he was sick. She whispers, "Please let me know what happens!" We join the others around the outdoor bar and Grandma shoots me clandestine winks between birdlike bites of her burger.

That night after I've washed my face and brushed my teeth, I log on to my laptop in bed. *Certainly he doesn't check e-mail on a Sunday night, he's probably having dinner with friends or sex with the girlfriend who has to exist.* My heart jumps when I open my in-box. He replied!

Dear Krissy, he writes, *your e-mail is warmly received and I would very much enjoy meeting you in person. If you'll kindly share your phone number, then I shall call you to make the arrangements.* He sounds intelligent and kind, although his politeness teeters on the edge of prudence. He finally wins me over when he refers to our little town as a "hamlet" and says that New York and Italy, the two places where I'd mentioned spending the last half decade of my life, are two of his favorite spots as well. After another exchange we determine that it could be a while before we'll meet: this week I'm off to writing workshops in New York, and the day I'm scheduled to return, he'll fly to San Francisco to perform a rare eyelid surgery.

Rare eyelid surgery? I write back. *So cool!*

TWO WEEKS LATER on a balmy Friday evening, I step onto my front porch with my hair down and wavy. Instantly I'm relieved I took my mom's fashion advice. "Don't do jeans," she'd said from my bed as I held up wardrobe options from my closet.

"Why?"

"It's a *date,* he's a *doctor.* Don't you want to feel beautiful?"

I'd made my way to the mirror holding up a little black dress, looking at Rocky and Alfonso in the reflection. "You know, boys, Mama gives a lot of opinions," I tell them. Alfie cocks his head. "But she's usually right."

This is the first time in a very long time that a guy ("a fellow," as Grandma called him) will come to pick me up at my parents' house, and something about it feels really old-time and comforting. Just as I start to enjoy it, though, I find myself jittery—actually shaking—more than I'd ever felt before a date when I was in high school. As the doctor's Mercedes coupe flies past the lamppost and into my gravel driveway, I stop desperately fanning the humidity from my face.

In loose linen pants and a light blue button-down, Dr. Christopher steps out of his car and pushes his sunglasses on top of his head. A guy in flip-flops usually looks self-absorbed or, let's face it, not straight. But on him they remind me of a sexy artist in Florence who once closed his studio to give me a private tour on a Saturday afternoon. Yes, clearly I have graduated: this person presenting himself at my doorstep is indeed a full-grown man.

"I'm Chris," he says, speaking deeply from the ball in his throat. "It's nice to meet you." He holds out his hand warmly and looks intensely in my eyes.

All at once I'm flustered, but I feign calm to extend my hand. "I'm Krissy." He takes my grip by sliding his palm under mine and giving me the upper hand—his etiquette is keen, which is both winning and intimidating. I realize that in the ambiguous nature of my communication with him, I've gone and confused *myself* about my intentions. His eyes shine as he tucks a wisp of windy hair behind his ear. "Lovely to meet you too." Now I smile modestly, suddenly burning to tell him that I don't usually pursue men first.

"Hey, look, there are bricks in that tree," he says, wandering into the grass like an engineer surveying the base of the Brooklyn Bridge. I explain that the bricks keep the dead oak tree from toppling on our house. "It's our Keebler tree," I chuckle, half trying to recapture his attention. I remind myself to stay upbeat despite the possibility that he may be more interested in my landscaping than in me. No matter what, I tell myself, this is better than dating the self-centered guys in New York, and *definitely* an improvement over the mama's boys in Italy. I lock the front door, duck behind the garage and dial my parents, who are out to dinner. "Mom," I hiss, "you were right, he's gorgeous and has really nice teeth. Goodbye."

"Oh yay!" she squeals. I hang up.

Chris opens the car door for me and holds my hand as I climb inside. I try not to gawk around, but his car's a two-seater, and it's clean. It may be safe to judge that there are no children in the picture. "Oh nice," I observe, "is this a stick?"

"It is a stick," he answers gently, climbing in on his side and wrapping the seat belt around himself. There's no denying he's cute, tanned with damp hair, fresh from a swim in the lake, which he'd said he planned to squeeze in after work. His scent is something preciously male, like powder and water and pine. I have never encountered anything like it in my life; everything about this man is entirely new to me. "Before we head where I'm planning to take you tonight, I should ask: do you have any dietary restrictions?"

I laugh. "Uh, no. I wish I could be interesting and tell you I'm vegetarian or something, but I eat pretty much anything." I pause and look at him. "Nice of you to ask, though." I'm thankful his air-conditioning and his coolness have blasted away any evidence of my nerves.

"Good. We're having dinner at the farm of some friends of mine. It's all organic, and we'll eat in their garden. They said they're making burritos, does that sound okay?"

"That sounds . . . amazing, actually. Wait, it's around here?"

"Yes, half an hour away in Brookville."

"Wait, there's an organic farm in Brookville?"

There's a jolt of electricity when he looks at me and smiles. "You sound surprised."

"It's just, I don't know, I guess I don't think of this area as being so progressive. Wow . . . an organic farm."

"Yes," he says, eyeing either my Ballet Slippers manicure or the silver stack of bangle bracelets on my wrist. I got them in Paris. "I know what you mean."

The car ride is such effortless conversation that I wish we could just keep cruising. Fortunately he can't remember where the farm is and loses his bearings for a minute on the back roads, giving us more of a chance to chat. He's six years older than I am and originally from Michigan. He says he started out in dental school, then decided to go on for his M.D. to do oral and facial surgery. He moved to the area after he completed a successful rotation with an oral surgeon in town who vowed to make him a partner in the practice if he returned after med school graduation.

"Believe it or not," he said about his partner, "he's one of the pioneer oral surgeons in the country."

"Wow, and that's why you decided to join him?"

"Yes."

"Very impressive," I tell him.

He glances at me and smiles, as though I've just validated why anyone as worldly as he seems to be would move to such a small town. "Thanks."

"Would you like a piece of Swiss gum?" I ask him.

"Uh, *yeah*," he says, breaking out surfer attitude. "I've never had Swiss gum. Thanks."

"You're welcome. It's sugar-free. You know, better for the teeth."

"That's important," he says.

I shrug nonchalantly, being half cute. "Yes."

These extra minutes in the car afford another moment to inhale his perfect smell, which I'm now praying will linger in the halls of my brain forever. For the first time in my life the first date is spectacular. I'm used to the exhausting verbal volleyball of one-on-one conversation that either bores me to sleep or makes me want sex, either way leaving me craving my bed and not just relishing the moment.

Unlike any date I've ever been on, the focus is not entirely on us—the family on the farm plays as much a role as we do. Chris unintentionally charms me when he climbs a tree to talk with his friends' six-year-old son about how to get over the nightmares the little guy had been having. The couple shows me around their garden, which is bursting with lavender and rosemary and sage. For dinner just Chris and I sit under an arbor, eating grass-fed beef burritos and drinking sangria. *Uh-oh.* A faint buzz sets in, alarming me to make the conscious switch to water, until he says, "Isn't it amazing they don't consume any alcohol on these grounds?" No alcohol! I go back to the sangria.

On his phone he plays Sting and Eric Clapton—two of our mutual favorites, as we've determined that we're both what he calls "music people"—and it pleases me to learn that he's close with his grandparents. He reveals that since he's been in practice, he's been able to help them a bit financially, and in return his grandpa has begun to open up about his past. "It's so important for us to connect with our grandparents and learn as much as we can about them while we're still fortunate enough to have them around," he says.

Again I could swear I'm a little drunk and I choose my words carefully. "I completely agree with you."

Chris tells me that when he finished med school, his grandpa asked him if "that little blue pill" really works.

I stop cutting into my dinner. "No," I heave. "What'd you tell him?"

"I told him he might want to talk to his physician about that."

That gives me a charge. I could wrap a blanket around my shoulders and stay here sharing all night.

After dinner we linger around the family's gift shop, surveying their fresh herbs and materials to make organic soap at home. I'm genuinely stunned that a place like this exists in my, well, *rustic* hometown. Before we exit the shop, Chris buys me heavy wheat bread and citrus honey, juggling them carefully as he opens my car door. He extends his baseball cap to keep my hair tame after he puts the top down—from the outside you can't tell it's a convertible!—and blasts a blues song called "Bittersweet Surrender," which seems pretty apt. I rest my elbow on the windowpane. "Mind if we play that again?" I ask him.

A smile spreads wide across his face when he looks at me. "Please do." I hit the rewind button, then feel the engine accelerate underneath us. We are experiencing this rare, emotion-charged energy together. The car speeds and the bass booms and despite the ball cap my hair flies all around me, but I feel like the world has stopped moving and we are the only things in motion.

Maybe there's a reason all the other guys haven't panned out; maybe all the turmoil and disappointment and embarrassment other relationships have resulted in will be worth my struggle for this ideal mate. How encouraging that this genuine, successful man enjoys my company and appreciates my style. Isn't that every woman's most inherent need? With a couple miles left before my driveway, I'm delighted to determine: Chris is someone I could like.

It's only ten o'clock when he drops me off, walking me to my front door in true traditional fashion. His hands are in his pockets; mine are clutching my little purse. The anticipation, wondering *What will he do?*, takes me straight back to high school, where you're either dying for your crush to kiss you or dreading the impending unwelcome advance. Chris and I play as casual as we can, and I hope he means it when he says, "We should do this again soon." In perfect punctuation to end this incredibly pleasant night, his hands brace my shoulders as he leans down to gently kiss my cheek. We remain there a second, and he's surprised when I return his message by touching my lips to his smooth, warm face. "Thank you," he says.

I smile. "You're welcome."

He turns back toward his car and says over his shoulder, "I'll give you a ring."

I watch him pull down the driveway before I switch off the front lights.

Wait: Did he just say "I'll give you a ring"?

The dogs announce my entrance as I creak through the kitchen. My parents, tucked in bed watching the news before Leno, want to hear all about my night. "So, is he *normal?*" Mom says, propping herself up on her elbow.

I climb into bed between them, an old childhood habit that's quickly returning. "Not exactly normal," I tell her. "Which is awesome." Dad asks if he was a gentleman and I answer yes, in a way I've never really experienced before. "There's bread and citrus honey in the kitchen for breakfast—can you believe he did that?" Mom claps her hands together fast—not over the bread, but Chris's gesture—and I kiss them and the dogs good-night.

In my teenage bedroom I shut the door and climb on the bed with my journal. *I don't want to go to sleep,* I write. *I just know that in the morning I'll have forgotten his face.*

THE SECOND DATE is a disaster.

Chris invites me to yoga class, then winds up with patients three hours later than he'd expected. I research a story and paint my nails, thinking, *Seriously, I could've been to Philadelphia by now.* Are the wives of successful men perpetually frustrated? (And just *how* do they keep their makeup looking fresh?) I'd told him I didn't want to be out late because I had an annual Third of July sleepover with all my cousins that night. It's eight o'clock when the doorbell finally rings, and at this rate I'll be lucky to meet up with everybody by midnight.

Rocky and Alfie ambush Chris at the door, and I am so full of annoyance and nerves—and, okay, excitement—to see him that I can barely paste a smile on my face. He hugs me anyway, and we head out.

"I made you some music," I say, trying to ease in and pulling a plastic CD case from my purse.

He's looking up something on his phone. "You did?"

"Yes. Just a little Euro jazz I picked up when I was away. Would you like to listen?"

"Honestly, not really."

Oh.

"I'll save it for my trip to see my folks tomorrow."

I'm suddenly humiliated for burning the disc.

He looks up at me from his phone. "I was thinking we could go to dinner at that quaint little Italian place in Clearfield," he says.

"Clearfield? That's like a half hour away." It comes out snippy, then to make matters worse, I shock myself with my next question. "Are you afraid of the local grapevine or something?"

He's startled. "No. Why, are you?"

I want to crawl in the trunk and stay there till Christmas. *Why did I just insult him like that?* He was trying to think of a nice restaurant to take me and I accused him of not wanting to be seen out with me. My New York Girl insecurity is creeping in, oh no, where is this ugliness coming from . . .

I try to bounce back. "Well, I don't want to overwhelm you with the legend that is my family, but every year on the third of July they all gather at our lake house for a pig roast and sleepover.

You said earlier that you wanted to maybe do something outside, so, no pressure, but it's an option."

He swiftly maneuvers a U-turn in the highway. I call my mom to tell her we're on our way. Chris is wearing a button-down and pants again, and I'm in a ruffled blouse and heels . . . okay, maybe we're a *little* overdone for a pig roast. Shortly I will learn my lesson when it becomes fiercely evident that we should have just gone to Clearfield. What follows instead sends me running into the arms of another guy—and directly to my grandma's sun porch to explain who he is.

"I'm just surprised, I thought the doctor was lovely."

Well, you're *single now, Grandma,* you *date him,* I want to snap, but then my wits filter out the rudeness. "He was lovely, Grandma, but that doesn't mean he's right for me." It's a Monday afternoon in mid-August and the sun is so hot that even with the ceiling fan swirling and the blinds shut, the screened-in porch is a brick oven. Grandma and I had talked about going to four o'clock Mass—between her loneliness and my man confusion these days, Sunday morning solace barely lasts a day. But the way our conversation's starting to pick up, I can tell we're not moving anytime soon. Grandma has scooped me a bowl of Neapolitan ice cream in classic Gloria-portion size, which is approximately just enough to satisfy a sparrow.

"What went wrong?"

"Grandma, what *didn't* go wrong? You saw what happened at the party."

When I'd called my mom to tell her Chris and I were headed

to the Landing to join the pig roast, apparently she announced to our dozens of family members that Krissy and The Doctor were about to make a grand entrance. They all hovered at the front door of the house, like a surprise party that's dreadful at finding hiding places. Cautiously he and I took seats at the outdoor bar, and Grandma strategically placed herself across from Chris in a spot where she could absorb the details of this enigmatic doctor.

"Krissy, what are you waiting for," my mom directed under her breath. "Go get him a plate." Instantly my aunt, clearly already tipsy from the selection of red, white, and blue margaritas, started lining up cocktails in front of Chris, who had politely informed everyone that he wasn't much of a drinker.

"Then what's he doing with *this* family?" my brother mumbled. I shot him a look. Chris leaned in and whispered, gesturing to the patriotic cocktail under his nose, "Will I look like I kissed Smurfette if I drink this?" I smiled halfheartedly, grateful for his attempt at humor in this nightmare. I wished I could shrink to Smurfette proportions and hide. Stat.

My mom's friends drooled from their bar stools and asked Chris to educate them on the latest in skin care. Their husbands told loud, perverted jokes in the background while Chris explained to his growing female audience why every woman should be exfoliating—if not for the youthful benefits, then to slough off precancerous skin cells. Behind him my cousin laughed so hard at a testosterone-fueled punch line that he snorted, sending an insufferable echo across the lake.

My dad, wearing an outfit sloppier than I'd ever even seen him wear running, stumbled over to us with red eyes and a cigar. "You know what you are?' he slurred to Chris. I held my breath. "You're *refreshing*."

"Grandma," I told her afterward, "in no way am I surprised things went downhill from there."

"I thought he had a good time, he conversed a lot. Sure draws a crowd, reminds me of your grandpa. And those eyes! My heavens, I couldn't stop looking at him. What's his name again, I can never remember . . . oh right," pleasure diffuses across her face and her focus drifts off into the air, "*Dr. Christopher.*"

This is not going how I'd hoped. I've come to get Grandma's blessing because I'm officially dating someone new, someone who's actually proven himself to want a relationship with me. I'd envisioned Grandma would be thrilled that I'm finally spoken for, and instead here she is sipping Sprite from a highball glass and telling me I'm missing the picture.

"I thought you and Grandpa wanted to see me in a relationship."

"We've always wanted what's *best* for you."

"Grandma, what if this is what's best for me? I'm back home now, I've tried dating someone really handsome and successful, and it didn't work. So I went for the sure thing."

Grandma takes a deep breath and stares into her glass.

The party at the Landing kicked off a series of confusing dates with Chris. He got along with my family despite their frathouse partying, but then e-mailed to ask why the CD, which he played for his parents on the Fourth of July, had the F word on it. (*OHHHH NO, I BURNED THE WRONG SONG!* I wrote back, subsequently losing my appetite for three days.) He would call me to enthusiastically make arrangements together, and then show up hours late and with completely compromised plans from what we'd set out with.

One Saturday, for example, about a week after the pig roast, when for some reason he decided to see me again despite my burning him a song about getting drunk, smoking cigarettes, and fucking—classy!—he rode his bike to work and got a flat tire. So instead of going to an arts festival together that night, I picked up him and his eighteen-speed on the highway with barely enough time for us to squeeze in a swim before dark. We stopped at my house and, crazed, I dug up one of the considerably modest bikinis I still kept in my drawer from high school. Why did my year in Italy foster such an excess of bravery for me to purchase stringy, sequined bikinis that I spent a summer's nanny wages collecting? *I'll never even wear these things!* Then, while Chris took a work call in my garage, I raided the fridge to fill up a jumbo brown Bloomingdale's bag with groceries my mom and I had just stocked up on: grapes, sea-salted almonds, a wheel of brie and crackers, and blue tortilla chips with fresh-made guacamole. I grabbed two plastic cocktail cups and a bottle of prosecco, and Chris ended his call to help me transport our goods into my mom's SUV.

I set up our dinner on the Landing's outdoor bar, telling Chris to go ahead. "How's the water?" I called as his silhouette emerged from his plunge.

"It's perfect," he said, pressing his wet hair back away from his face. "Wait till you feel."

I pulled my hair into a neat bun and undressed on the sand of our tiny beach, careful not to pull things off with suggestiveness or tantalization. In the past I've always been brazen with men, but something about Chris feels different. My inclination is to operate respectably, not to force romance or make waves—so to speak. I wanted to moan in pleasure as I sank into the lake; the water was like a spa. Instead, I remained silent until I finally said, "You want to know something?"

"What?" He floated on his back in the water, a boat length away from me.

"You have a really beautiful natural scent."

The water made sensual sounds as he maneuvered to stand on his feet. Quietly, he said, "Do you believe in that?"

"What, pheromones? Oh yes."

"Me too." We stayed silent another minute, and I pretended not to be self-conscious as I slowly swam alone. "Look at that sky," he said. The moon was three-quarters full, surrounded by stars rising up to fill every centimeter of space over the mountains and trees. They shined in mirrored perfection off the water, making the night twice as bright as it actually was.

"I know," I sighed, ducking into the water in awe so the dangle of my Florentine coin earrings was halted.

"Is it deep where you are?"

"Um." I struggled for my feet to touch bottom. "I can stand, but I don't want to. It's all mud."

"Come here, then," he said gently, holding out his hand. "It's all rocks."

I waited a moment, and then slowly began to swim toward him. Suddenly I caught us both by surprise when I stopped paddling and said, "That's close enough." In the moonlight

I watched him drop his hand, slump down in the water and drift away.

I wished I could erase his confusion and reveal that my tentativeness was only because if I grew too near to him, then he might have done something to make me want to get even closer. Then, eventually I'd want to give him everything, craving things in return that he's not ready to give. It's a cycle more certain than the moon's.

"I'm getting hungry," I told him. "You too?" I was relieved that he wasn't cold toward me when he took my hand to help me climb the ladder onto the dock. Under the string of white lights over the bar, we snacked on munchies and sipped prosecco. "I love meals like this," he said, as though he was realizing it for the first time. "Light. Whole foods."

I wrapped my towel tighter around my wet suit. "Me too." I couldn't get enough of the intelligent conversations we have, and our stories and easy laughter made me certain I wanted to see him again . . . I just wished I could decide which one of us was causing my hesitation.

When I dropped him off at his house and helped take his bike off the back of my mom's SUV, he stared at me for a minute, then hooked his elbow around my neck and kissed me hard on the mouth. After he'd gotten safely into his house, I stood there in the dark for a few seconds pressing my lips together, bewildered over what he'd meant to communicate with that. Was it a *Thanks a million for your help with my bike today!* or a boyish way to say, *I'm starting to have feelings for you?*

The following Tuesday I was riding around town in a sloppy

ponytail and cutoffs, searching for saffron to test a mulled wine recipe that I'd just sold to a food magazine.

My phone rang. "What are you doing right now?" Chris asked.

"I'm out looking for saffron."

He laughed. "Saffron?"

"Yes, and do you know how hard it is to find saffron in small-town Pennsylvania? I'd have better luck digging for the treasure in Treasure Lake. What's up?"

"Are you busy right now?"

Uh, yes, horribly. "Um, not really."

"Come over to my house."

"Is everything okay?"

"Oh, everything's great. You'll see. Hey."

"Yes?"

"Make sure you bring your swimming suit."

"Uh," oh *God*, I needed to run home and shave my legs! "Okay then, see you shortly."

Shoot, I thought, I was on a deadline, but what could I say? I swung my mom's car around in the grocery store parking lot and raced home to find a bikini that might camouflage as many of my corporal misgivings as possible. Since when had swimming on third dates become protocol? Doesn't he realize I'd like to know him a little better before he sees my body? It was different in the dark, but today the sun is blazing.

When I arrived, he walked me down to his dock, where he'd lined up turkey subs on whole wheat and fresh cubes of pine-apple.

"Sit down," he said. "You have to eat lunch before your first sailboat ride." Had I told him that not sailboating while I was in Italy was my only regret? Had he remembered? And had he really done this all by himself? Amazing. Across the gingham tablecloth his eyes shined bluer than the lake, and when I observed this, I determined that I was officially taken with him. "What's that ring you're wearing?" I mused. I normally avoid guys with rings—too macho and self-indulgent—but the wide silver band around his pinky finger was . . . sexy.

"I haven't told you this," he said, pouring water from a crystal pitcher into wineglasses (*wineglasses*!), "but when you moved to Italy last summer, it's very possible we could've crossed paths. I took a holiday to Florence myself."

I tried to act subtle as my stomach flipped over the word *holiday*. "Last summer, you mean?"

"Yes. And during one of our free days, I took an excursion out to this tiny village where all these artisans were displaying their wares in the street to the half-dozen tourists wandering the place. I forget the name, it was really remote. So I find this ring, and the crafter and I try our darnedest to communicate about it—what type of metal, why he chose this layered design—but we wound up shaking hands and parting ways before I could really understand what the ring meant to him. But to me, I knew what it meant. It's my reminder every day that before I'm a surgeon, before I'm a doctor, I'm an artist."

I want to chime in so badly, to point out how in our work we share an eye for the beauty and significance in everyday situations. I keep my exclamation inside; but man, am I feeling for this guy.

During lunch I remembered the discovery that I first made in high school: when I'm with someone I like, I can't help but eat *really slowly* (and this is pretty much the only time I eat really slowly—just ask my grandma, who recently noted that eating is the only thing she's ever seen me do quickly).

When Chris saw that I had finished my sub halfway through, he wrapped it back into its white deli paper and packed it securely for me to take home. Then he placed his hand on my knee. "You've gotta see this boat." He dragged the boat from the bank of his yard into the water and invited me over. As I climbed on board, he cupped water in his palm and gently rinsed the tiny stones off my feet with the meticulousness of, well, a surgeon. It reminded me of the feet-washing scene in the Bible, and how feet washing is said to be the most profound act of service one person can offer another. I'd never been out with a man so caring before.

"Okay," he said, "so, the sail essentially steers the boat, but the wind is in charge of the sail. You'll hear me say, 'Keel,' and when I do, that means you need to duck your head down because I'm going to swing the sail over your head. You got it?"

I nodded. "I'll catch on."

"Here, take these." He slid his sunglasses down his Gabriel Aubry nose and turned them around, placing them softly on my face.

"How nice are you," I told him. "Thanks."

Off we sailed into the center of the lake, which he explained was a bit of a nautical vortex because it's man-made and surrounded by woodland. He knew more about this lake in four years of experiencing it than I do after eighteen years growing up here, and with him manning the boat's helm, I saw the lake more exotically and completely differently. He transported me someplace else, the way the memory of my grandpa does when I stare up into a muscular, protective pine tree in the woods.

"It's sort of hot, right?" he said. I looked at him, surprised. "You want to go for a dip?"

Oh, he meant the weather. "Sure—do you?"

"Yeah." He took off his soft gray T-shirt and handed it to me. I sort of hoped from under his sunglasses that he'd note my review of his body, as I stared at his chest for just a second too long. He didn't seem to catch on. "But we can only go in one at a time, so the other person can balance the boat when we have to get back in."

"Oh," I told him, trying not to scrunch my nose. What's the point, if we couldn't swim together? "Okay." I stretched my neck over the side of the boat as he did so perfect a swan dive that the water made just one soft ripple that quickly diffused to nothing. He treaded quietly for a couple of minutes, panning his gaze reflectively along the coast of the beach as though he planned to paint it later. When he pushed his upper body back on board, the boat didn't even rock. He rubbed water out of his eyes and told me, "Your turn."

"Okay." I handed him his sunglasses and peeled off the flowered halter cover-up that I'd bought as my final purchase in Milan. I stood to dive gracefully as he did, but as my foot hit the deck, it slipped so that I fell flailing into the lake. When I came up, gasping for air, spewing water from every orifice and wiping the mess of hair and mascara from my face, I prayed he was laughing his head off. Instead he stared intently into the distance, pretending he hadn't seen a thing.

Why God?

I hurled my arms across the deck of the boat, estimating that a Styrofoam beer cooler would be steadier than this jalopy. As I hoisted myself up, I sensed a draft in a most unmentionable location of my body: the top of my bum has peeked out to greet Chris hello. How polite! How opportune! I could think only one thing: my grandmother would *die* if she saw this.

Meanwhile Chris continued to act obliviously, but the bulging veins in his arms revealed how hard he was attempting to balance the boat and keep it from capsizing. I yanked at the uncooperative patches of material on my body, trying at the same time to swing one leg onto the deck. By the time I finally managed to get back on board, Chris said he was going to be late for a meeting. He lay on his stomach at the boat's bow, doing the butterfly stroke with his arms to lead us back to land. In a rush, he accompanied me back to my mom's car in his driveway, opening the door and waving to me as he closed it. I got it: we were no longer hugging goodbye, not to mention that we had completely demoted from the kiss he'd pressed on me just three nights ago.

Every time we progressed in connecting with each other, the palpable milestone inevitably would be followed by a humiliating setback . . . and I was getting tired of feeling so *silly* all the time. While I was growing accustomed to being flexible for this doctor, it was getting tougher to know him as a man. Why is he so attentive in some moments, and so distant in others?

What was stranger yet was my reaction to him. For the first time ever in Krissy Crush History, I didn't feel compelled to spill, "The problem is, I *like* you!" I did like him, but I needed to keep it to myself . . . at least until he opened up more, which didn't seem any more likely after that day, our fourth date, than it did on our disastrous second date. My friend Joy is a med student who swears that in matters of health, if an ailment grows more severe instead of better over time, it's usually a good sign to get help. I agree completely, also applying Joy's theory to matters of the heart.

"GRANDMA, I FELT like I was finally turning a corner in my dating life, like at last I was opening a grown-up chapter with men. But the door just keeps getting shut in my face."

At Grandma's feet there's a metal platform with two little pedals, like the bottom half of a stationary bike. She slips her feet into the Velcro stirrups to exercise while we chat. "Men aren't always easy to understand." She begins spinning the wheels, same as I felt I was doing with Chris. Now she's contesting the Mars and Venus thing—our cultural belief that men are content with dinner on the table, a hot wife on their arm, and sex. "The world demands a lot of them, and even though they don't let it show, they have some real needs."

"Grandma, *I* have needs. I need a guy to laugh when I fall off his sailboat. I need someone to demonstrate his interest in me by kissing me. I don't want to look across the dinner table at someone and wonder if his nose was *really* always that perfect. I'd like somebody who's content with a basket of chicken fingers and a Heineken. You know?"

"Well, sure I know." She slows her feet to catch her breath. "But if you're really concerned with finding somebody to love, then I'm telling you that you have to stop focusing on yourself."

"Grandma!" I catch the increasing volume in my voice, in case any of her neighbors are in their yards. "A woman should put her *own needs aside* for a man she cares about?" I'm waiting on her answer. *What year is this?*

She raises her eyebrows like it's a no-brainer. "If you love someone, that's what you do. It comes naturally."

And that's it: after a month of awkward dating—can you even call that *dating*?—it's clear there's almost no way I could ever love Chris. "Okay. Grandma, I'm sorry for getting so fired up about this, but it *stuns* me! So what are some things men need that I should be bouncing off the walls to be?"

"A friend, Krissy. A man needs someone who supports his work. Someone who hugs him and means it when he walks in the door at night." She stops pedaling and leans toward me. "You want to be with a really good man?"

I stare at her, thinking, *Girl, you're trippin'*.

"You have to have courage. And *patience*. Lots of patience."

Courage and patience. I'll give her that. Any girl who wants to date that doctor better be very cool with herself, and incredibly calm with him.

Grandma continues. "You have to get to a place in your own life where you're convinced you're strong enough to manage the challenge. Because you want to know a secret they'll never tell you?"

"Yes."

"The successful ones are usually the last to wear their hearts on their sleeves." She shakes her finger at me. "They're used to winning."

"And," it starts to dawn on me, "extra sensitive to taking a hit." I'm starting to get it. The night we'd gone swimming as I packed our makeshift dinner, Chris had been on a stressful phone call in my garage. He punched the tennis ball that my dad hangs from a string so my mom knows where to park her car so hard that he sent the fuzzy yellow sphere flying across the room, knocking half of my dad's tool chest onto the ground. When he couldn't rehang it, he rushed me into the driveway. "We have to go, we're late." He wanted to do anything he could to take my attention away from his mistake.

"You see? It's why I usually apologized first after every fight with your grandpa."

"Even when you weren't wrong?"

"Sometimes."

I moan and drop my head in my hands.

She gets it. "Krissy, you have to understand: strong men have a lot of pride. They won't let you see everything for a long time, until they really need to lean on you, and even then they need you to tell them that it's okay to be vulnerable." She points at me again, a warning expression on her face. "But *you* have to be strong first."

Maybe she would know. She spent six decades with my grandpa, who, I have to admit despite the perfection I always perceive he possessed, sounds like he had his moments of being a real handful. Grandma told me recently that he spent most of his twenties and thirties laying the groundwork for his business, traveling all over the country for weeks at a time—*before the age of cell phones,* or even pay phones—wining and dining with his cronies while she stayed home with their five kids. One story has Grandpa at a local bar during a brief visit home when one of his buddies asked him if he wanted to fly to Michigan to see an old colleague.

"Sure," my grandpa said. "Call me tomorrow, let's get it in the calendar."

"No," his buddy said. "I mean tonight."

"Tonight, pal? Nah, I don't think so." Get ready for the reason he said he couldn't go: "I don't have any money on me." (Nice Grandpa, forget the wife and five little faces around the dinner table waiting for you!)

"No problem, George," his friend said. "My plane's sitting up at the airport. Come on, we'll be back by dawn." And sure enough, off they flew to party for the night with a friend in Michigan. My grandma was sitting up in the living room when Grandpa arrived home the next morning, and even today she brags that she lasted all day giving him the silent treatment until bedtime that night. "All day I stayed fuming, and he knew it!" she laughs. "But we never went to bed angry."

"Grandma, look at me. I've invested so much in my accomplishments and, geez, especially my own self-respect." I try to imagine always going with Chris's flow. "Do you *honestly* think I could grow to be so caring?"

"*What?*" she squawks. "Sure you can! Come on, Krissy, you're braver than that. Just because there's something unfamiliar beneath a man's surface isn't good enough reason to run away from him. You have to believe that it's okay to trust another person."

I set down my ice cream dish on the glass end table and sit quietly for a minute. "Grandma." The word comes out defeated, almost in a whisper. "It's too late. Someone new came along, told me he's crazy about me," my eyes go wide, "*kissed me . . .* and he didn't leave room for any doubt." What I'm trying to tell her is that I've been on my own in the world for so long . . . I just can't take another thing that's uncertain.

I MET TUCKER through my mom (go fig). She and her coworkers at a law office in town organized a "Bring Your Kid to Happy Hour" day the week after the Fourth of July. Because all their kids are finally twenty-one and a lot of the office was meeting me for the first time, it turned into a big old shindig at an über-posh establishment known as, what else, Dingers Duck Dock. "I'm so excited for you to meet Tucker," Mom said. "Not to date him, good God, he's still in college. Just for a buddy. He's so fun. A real cutie too . . . but you're not dating him."

I was fixing my lipstick in the sun-visor mirror. "Please, Mom, like I'd date a guy who's twenty-two."

Tucker's mom had told him the same thing: "You have to meet Krissy, but don't even think about hitting on her." But he sat across the table from me, so adorable, with his sweet eyes and broad shoulders and perpetual smile. We joked across the table all night and he bought me a beer at the bar, but when he asked me to go to karaoke, I had to draw the line.

"You should go!" my mom said, thrilled I was such a hit among her work crowd.

"Mom, he's twenty-two and just a smidge too confident. It's time to call it a night."

The next week he called me. "My buddies and I are headed to the Ski Lodge near the lake by your house. Want to meet up?"

By this time I hadn't heard from the doc in a couple weeks and was up for letting loose. I hiked up my cleavage and let my curls go wild like I hadn't done since my Adam Hunt days. When I walked into the pub, Tucker approached me nervously and gave me a hug. "Everybody, this is Krissy," he said, wiping his palms on his jeans and ushering me into a group of cute guys.

"Oh, *you're* the one he can't stop talking about!" one yelled. "Says your mom's hot too." I put my hands on my hips and let mock shock take over my face, loving the frankness of it all.

That night over Jagerbombs, Tucker said, "When I met you last week, I told my mom you were the most gorgeous woman I'd ever seen."

He was laying it on thick but I was so hungry for affection I didn't care. That night I took him home, where I set him up in the guest room but spent most of the night with him. He embraced like a man and kissed like a man, and I warmed instantly to his touch. For our first date he borrowed his cousin's shiny pickup truck to take me to another one of our moms' work picnics. We created a buzz among the moms' work crowd, who pinned us as an unexpected but charming item. He was so familiar and easy to know that we spent four days together in a row. I appreciated that underneath his boyish shell lay an open, caring young man whose willingness to voice his needs—one of which seemed to be me—made me feel strong and adored again.

"So you think there's some serious possibility with this new guy." Grandma hasn't even asked his name.

"Well, I think so. I mean it's only been a few weeks, but once he finishes school—"

"You mean he's still in school?"

"Uh," that was the other thing I was meaning to tell her, "yes. Last year of college."

"And he wants to make serious plans."

I pause a second, not knowing the right answer. "Yes."

"I have one piece of advice for you, my dear. Get your single life settled first."

The Debbie Downer jingle goes off in my head. *Wonh, wonhhhhh.*

Grandma once told me that right out of high school, she and her best friend enrolled in nursing school together. Sometime during their first year the best friend died tragically, and Grandma was too upset to continue studying. She took a part-time job as a department store clerk downtown and basically hung around socializing, as it sounded to me, until something better came along.

It came along quickly, in the form of a suitor. My grandpa had been to the war and back and learned enough in the field about engineering to get involved in some entrepreneurial manufacturing endeavors. He wanted his life all in place, and he married my grandma.

"I've never resented not having a career," she says, "because that's just not what most women did back then. After you graduated from high school—*if* you graduated from high school—you typically took the first thing that asked you out. That was that."

Lately, though, ever since my grandpa died, Grandma's been saying how her friend who's also recently widowed has such an easy time staying busy. This woman was an artist for years and is having a grand time redecorating her house and getting back to her painting now that her husband has passed. The two of them go out to breakfast, and Grandma has said she grows a little envious that she doesn't have anything for herself.

"You know what, Kris? Now that your grandpa's gone, it would be good to have something to keep me occupied. There's only so much Silver Sneakers and bridge I can take."

I'm happily shocked—very shocked—when she says one of the smartest things women my age are doing is creating lives for ourselves before we commit ourselves to someone else. "You don't know," she says, "he might not be around forever."

"So Grandma, you actually think living as a single woman is a *good* thing."

"I really do. I'd go so far as to say it will make you a better wife."

I edge forward in my seat. "Really?"

"Well, sure. Take you, for example. You've lived in another country, you know how to get around a city, when a problem comes up you have a quick solution or you call someone who will. You'll be a good partner for somebody else's life because you have a lot of common sense."

Grandma reminds me of my education, the years I put into publishing. She says I don't get to just give those up because I'm uncertain about where my life is headed. "What are you planning to do for work now that you're home?"

"I'm writing."

"Is that enough to pay the bills?"

"Well, not exact—"

"Where are you thinking of living? Are you waiting to see where this boyfriend goes?"

It had crossed my mind.

"You're going to put your life decision on him? What about your career? For all you know, you might end up with a job elsewhere." She can see in my face that she's beating me down. "And are you ready to deal with the image out there that it's still a man's world? If he makes a decision for his career and you two are serious, it'll be on you to follow him."

Certainly she must be finished. I didn't get involved with someone to have my new love-guru grandma tell me it's not going to work . . . but while it's almost impossible to admit it to myself, what she's saying is reality. "And one more thing," she says. *Oh no.* "I think you should stay single until you find your next job."

My face goes hot. "But Grandma, what if a new job takes me someplace where I'll never meet a guy?" I want to cry. "Like in New York, it was impossible."

"Krissy, you can't settle down until you get where you're going. Get your own life settled first."

But that's just it, I don't know where I'm going. Since when did she take such a liberal stance, this woman who used to wait weeks for her husband to call from the road? I keep hoping that a relationship will give me some direction about where to go next. Funny how this woman went from peddling the doctor to talking me into flying solo a while; such a peculiar change of tune.

I'm not ready to just accept that the relationship I'm in is not the answer, nor do I want to believe that it's not likely to last . . . but Grandma is proving to know more about relationships— and women like me—than I ever imagined. I know following around some guy who shines a little attention on me isn't what she meant by "strong and patient." She meant being strong and patient for the partner who's right for me, and in the spirit of her new crush, Dr. Christopher, she's diagnosing that just by looking at the different places we are in our lives, Tucker and I are not a match.

Not an easy conversation to have, that. But I can't criticize my grandma: she had what I want—a devoted marriage and a bustling brood and a life full of love and purpose. When I let her words sink in, I know she's getting somewhere with me. She's making me face the demons that are actually standing in the way of my happiness. Am I trying to cop out of planning my future by waiting passively for a guy to do it for me? How did I decide that banking on life with the first thing that came along was a good move?

I mean, Tucker's mature for his age and incredibly caring— and quite frankly, the intimacy *rocks*—but maybe it's impossible that he's thinking ahead at twenty-two the way I am at twenty-eight. He asked me to marry him on our third date. I laughed, then startled. "Oh my God, you're not joking."

"I'm not joking. I want to spend my whole life with you." I

almost reminded him that he didn't have a job and that if we wanted to have sex we had to do it on the air mattress when his pothead roommate was out, but the point was hardly worth arguing. Deep down I knew that eventually this whole thing would fizzle. I've lived long enough to know that I'll never be a pickup truck kind of girl, or one who's thrilled with a proposal at the county fair on the third date.

I give Grandma a kiss on my way to the kitchen, the soft crinkles in her skin yielding to my lips. When I reach the sink, I stare past her windowsill's statue of Mary, holiest woman, to the hummingbird drinking nectar from Grandma's feeder in the sun. No noise, just its agreeable floating and enjoying life's juices—sort of how Grandma was in her marriage. The hummingbird bolts away when my bowl accidentally crashes into the basin, ceramic against steel, milky water from my bowl spouting around the kitchen.

"I'm okay!" I yell. "Don't worry Grandma, it's okay! Nothing's broken!" She giggles quietly and says something to herself, and when I finally get the spigot shut off, I hear the patient turn of her newspaper page.

How did I descend from this woman, this example of tranquility and virtue who spent decades feeling gratified to make sacrifices for someone she loved? I'm a bull in the delicate china shop of interpersonal communication; an aimless force bouncing in and out of commitments both when I care whether they'll last and when I don't. Is my hapless pursuit of relationships a cover for the fact that I'm not in any place to share my life with someone, because my self-actualization is still in the works?

And is that why I gravitate to guys in the same boat—in it till it's not fun anymore?

Grandma's cheeks glow warm as I slip on my flip-flops to go. More than the mini-exercise bike, our reminiscing about dear, sweet—and challenging—Grandpa seems to have brought some of her rosiness back . . . and our chat about men has brought us to eye level.

The following Sunday is our family's annual bocce tournament. This ten-year anniversary is huge not only because for the first time we have hundreds of participants to raise money for the Catholic schools in town, but also because it's our first year without my grandpa as its patriarch and master of ceremonies.

My mom's glare says *You're late* as Tucker and I scoot into the early morning crowd around Bocce Court Number One (over the last twelve years, Grandpa built three courts across the Landing's lakeside). As the eldest son, master speechmaker, and CEO of the family business (I joke that he's also CEO of the family), Uncle Phil is Grandpa's obvious successor as head of the tournament. He asks the crowd to give Grandma a round of applause as she rolls the day's first ball in honor of Grandpa. She looks tinier than ever in petite cotton capris and a ball cap with MORNING GLORIES, her team name, which honors her as captain and namesake, embroidered with two blue flowers.

Tucker makes his way to the bar with my brother, and it's obvious they're talking bocce strategy. I like how easily he gets along with my family. My mom brings me a mimosa and invites me to sit with her and her friend Nancy on the edge of Court

One. Today Nancy is characteristically put-together in a cute
I ♥ BOCCE! tank and kitten-heel flip-flops and purple toenails.
Nancy's cute sexiness is always a surprise, considering her very
discreet manner. She gestures for me to sit on the folding lawn
chair next to her. "Here, honey," she says, "let me add some
champagne to your drink."

"Thanks, Nance." My mom sits in the empty seat to my
left, and instantly a swarm of her friends follows. I think Mom's
height, no-nonsense style, and incomparable sense of humor
make her the queen bee among her friends—to say Mom is "the
funny friend" would be as apt a description as saying that the
President of the United States wields some influence over world
policy. Doesn't even begin to do her role justice.

Nancy apologizes that she wasn't here the night I had Dr.
Christopher over for everybody to meet. "We were on our way
home from the Outer Banks."

"Ugh, Nancy . . ." I drop my forehead in my hands. "Don't
apologize. It was like a volcano: entertaining to watch, disastrous
to experience."

"Your mom said it didn't go exactly as you'd hoped."

"Ha! No," I say.

"Ha! No," Mom echoes. "But I told her, a woman needs a
man who loves her unconditionally." Mom's in slim black shorts
and a T-shirt with the Italian map in red, white, and green
rhinestones. Mom is actually German, but with her high cheekbones, olive complexion, and almond-shaped eyes, apparently
she used to be mistaken for Sophia Loren when she and my dad
would travel to Asia in the nineties for Dad's work ("Seriously, I
did!" she says). Mom also made herself the master apprentice of

Grandpa's spaghetti sauce recipe, and so around the kitchen and the family it's easy to forget my mom's not Italian. "A girl needs somebody easygoing. Just look at our guys," she instructs us.

On the bocce court my dad is wearing his signature outfit (St. Louis Cardinals ball cap, khaki shorts, and Croc flip-flops) and biting a cigar as he performs his signature victory dance (gently wiggling his hips and fists in hand-mixer motion, commonly seen when he sells a machine, finishes a marathon, or, in this case, wins a bocce game).

"Right, Nance?" my mother says.

"That's right." Nancy leans in carefully and whispers, "But you liked Dr. Christopher, didn't you, honey?"

Mom leans in too, and their whole group of girlfriends follows, pulling their heads in closer. I'm growing aware that even though Mom treats the topic of Chris with a brush-off, she was more enamored by the thought of him and me together than even I was. I nod, and look at Nancy. "I did. But you know, it's funny, with other guys I've dated, I get so hung up on 'Why isn't he calling? What did I do wrong?' But this time, I don't know . . . maybe I'm just outgrowing the insecurities. Or maybe I'm just too jaded by men to bother dissecting it. But my point is, thank God, I'm not analyzing it to death." I brush my hands together, as though there's bocce court sand on them. "It's done. Moving on."

Mom lowers her chin clandestinely and says, "Although weeks ago, she did invite him to come today. It wouldn't surprise me if he just shows up."

"Oh Lord, Mother, he's not going to just show up—"

Right then Grandma catches my eye from across the court

and gestures with her chin to warn me, *Pay attention, someone's here to see you.*

It's Tucker. "Babe," he says, coming at me holding a beer. "Your cousins are taking the boat out. Wanna go? I'm gonna try to get up on the skis."

Truthfully, hashing things out with Mom's friends about Chris is just turning fun. But I hand Tucker my mimosa and take his hand to stand up. "Sure."

I widen my eyes at Grandma to give her an inconspicuous thank-you. It must've been growing obvious to observers that I was dishing about my old flame when the new one approached. *Be careful,* she mouths across the court. I know: she's not just referring to the boat ride, but to the situation I've gotten myself into.

4

Does He Know What He Wants for His Life?

ALREADY EIGHT MONTHS have passed since we lost Grandpa in January. Grandma has approached his birthday with reserve, the way one braces for a massive sneeze whose threatened attack brings dread but no catharsis. Grandma doesn't know how the day might shake her. She didn't want cake—no way, too emotional— but she did want spaghetti and family. That, we all agreed, we could manage. Grandma and I attend afternoon Mass in the chapel at the nursing home across the road from her house. Because Grandpa had worked closely in community organizations with some of the administrators there, they informed us that they'd be dedicating the service to him to commemorate his birthday.

When I pick Grandma up in the afternoon, I see that she's gone to have her hair done. Her lipstick is a deep shade of Victorian rose, and the aquamarine sweater set she wears lights up her eyes. She appears luminescent and perfectly prepared, as though she's seeing Grandpa for their first date in a long time. In a way I feel the same, and I've even slipped on a dress and patent leather heels. I get the sensation that the three of us—Grandpa, Grandma, and I—are all headed to the same place for the same purpose, like when we'd go to Mass at their church in Florida. For just a moment I allow myself to pretend that when Grandma and I arrive in the vestibule, Grandpa will be there waiting for us with a seat already picked out. She and I take the spot where we sit together every Sunday, on the left-hand side in the middle. The chapel was added onto the building at the same time Grandma and Grandpa's house was built three years ago, but somehow, despite its newness, the smell of incense and the stained-glass reflections give it an ancient feel. As Grandma and I settle into our pew and release the kneeler to pray, a tender, familiar solace creeps upon me and I'm reminded how I always feel at home in a church. I am protected, my worries lifted . . . and so it's true, Grandpa is here. As I rest my head on my knuckles, Grandma releases a loud sigh. This isn't going to be easy for her. The priest takes the altar, and right away I grow so immersed following the liturgy that I forget why we're here.

Two-thirds of the way through the Mass the priest leads, "And now for our petitions and the intentions in our hearts. Our response is, 'Lord hear our prayer.'" He runs through the usual suspects: world peace, wisdom for our leaders, the upcoming national election, the fulfillment of needs for the poor. Obediently I respond to all of these with such concentration that my eyebrows have furrowed. Then he says, "For the beloved George Gasbarre, to whom this Mass is dedicated." Grandma and I both respond—*Lord, hear our prayer*—but the reminder that Grandpa's left us takes the wind out of me. When we turn around for the sign of peace, a friend from Grandma's bridge group takes our hands and grips us tightly, as though she feels our pain as well. The way she attempts to comfort us with her eyes reminds me of the never-ending line of people at Grandpa's funeral viewing—how many of them shared stories about him that most of us never knew: he'd hired them when no one in town had work to spare; he bought a share of a colleague's ailing business and months later their orders were on fire; in the early seventies he borrowed a Ford truck for a business trip from a friend who was a car dealer and afterward the friend let him keep it and make payments when he could afford to. Grandpa stayed loyal by driving Fords for decades.

Just glancing around this tiny chapel, I can count half a dozen people whom my grandpa impacted with his kindness, his persistence, and his integrity. As the priest steps down from the podium, Grandma and I dab silently at our eyes, trying to maintain our composure. But a few minutes later when I allow her into the aisle before me for communion, I feel both of us raise our chests and walk tall toward the altar. The moment of mourning has passed. Now it's time to be proud for having been his happiness. Grandma lifts up her glasses and blots under her eye. When we're seated again I rub her shoulder gently, and she half looks at me with a closed-mouth smile. *I'm trying*, her expression tells me. We both are.

WHEN WE ARRIVE back at her house I remove my heels at the door to avoid tracking dirt across white carpets. The smell of garlic and onions and sauce bubbling on the stove invites us inside. I have to give Grandma credit—she's faced the day with as much courage as she could harvest, going so far as to take a stab at Grandpa's impossible spaghetti sauce—with meatballs. "Grandma," I swoon as the aroma from the kitchen pulls me with greater force, "this place smells *incredible.*"

She's pulling wineglasses down from the kitchen cabinet, making two rows of six goblets. "I'm a little worried it won't be ready when everybody gets here in a couple hours. This was always Grandpa's job."

"Let me taste it," I tell her, taking a teaspoon from the drawer to dip it delicately inside the pot like Grandpa used to do. "Oh, good *heavens,* Grandma." (At some moments I now find myself employing her sayings in all their grandmotherly glory.) I drop my spoon in the sink and take out a clean one from the drawer. "I think it's ready now." She's giggling silently when I turn to her. It's the first time I've seen her smile today. We travel together into the garage, Grandma holding tightly to the railing Grandpa installed for her. The room is in perfect order, with his workshop occupying the left back corner. Since he died I've only been out here to fetch drinks from the utility fridge, but I realize it was on purpose that I hadn't stopped to observe how Grandpa had left his favorite area of the house. Grandma turns around and points back at the screen door we just opened. "Close that," she says. "I want to show you something."

I slide shut the screen door that separates the garage from Grandpa's office. A piece of string the length of a shoelace drops down, holding a palm-sized silver cutout of Grandpa's company logo. Grandma's staring at me with amusement when I turn to her, puzzled. "He did that so we'd know that when the logo's at eye level, the screen door is closed."

"Ahhh!" I go to the door and open it, watching the pulley disappear into the door frame above it. "Look at that!"

"Isn't it something? I almost fell through it one day because I thought it was open—you see, it's hard to see!" She goes to the garage fridge and pulls out a chilled bottle of white wine. "He was always thinking," she says, more to herself than to me. "There's no doubt about it, that man was born to be an engineer."

I agree with her, surveying the perfectly organized contents of his garage. On the side wall he kept a collection of old-fashioned skeleton keys that he would examine and then duplicate on his machines just to keep his mind occupied when there were no other projects. Hanging here, they take on the feel of an exhibit at a history museum. "Grandma, come here," I say. "Look at this key—how beautiful."

"That one's from Italy," she whispers. "You know what to?"

I look at her.

"Your great-grandpa's house."

"Hey, I visited that house when I was in Rome!"

She beams. "I know."

I continue wandering the garage, peering curiously into Grandpa's shiny tool cabinet, the stacks of company-stamped ashtrays that he kept for posterity and pride, the shelves of non-perishable groceries lined up single-file like soldiers—a fixture for any household that had survived World War II and the Depression. "Hey, Grandma?" She's following me now, taking in the strength that Grandpa has left on every wall, above every shelf, in every corner. "Can we open up his pipe cabinet?"

"Oh, why not," she says, as though I've just asked her if I could have a popsicle before dinner. She unlatches the wood cupboard doors, and a couple dozen pipes of all different styles line the shelves. I take out one whose bowl is a yellow corncob. I giggle, bewildered. "He liked these corncob pipes, didn't he?"

"He did. He picked up on those when we lived in Missouri. Local farmers harvested the corn and Grandpa wanted to support the locals. But," she reaches, "this one was his favorite." She hands me a regal, shiny wood pipe with a perfectly round bowl.

"This *was* his favorite, huh?" I say. He left dozens of teeth marks on the pipe's lip. "Oh, Grandma." I put my hand on my hip as though we've just busted Grandpa doing something he shouldn't. "There's still tobacco in here!" We both laugh, but then the ashy tobacco inside the bowl makes it seem like he might have been smoking it just yesterday. I hold the pipe under my nose, and the scent paints an image of Grandpa standing right before me. He lights his pipe, shakes out the match, and winks. I put back the pipe and shut the cabinet. "Grandma, look!" On top of the cabinet sit a row of six candles designed to look like green martini olives lined up in a wax aperitivo dish. "We have to light these today!"

We travel back into the kitchen, each double-fisting bottles of wine. I light the candles while Grandma makes an attempt with the corkscrew. "Oh, your grandpa always took care of this," she says though her teeth. She gets on her tiptoes to give the cork one last fight.

I meet her at the counter. "Here, Grandma," I say gently. "Would you like me to try?"

"He took care of everything," she says, surrendering the corkscrew into my hand. "That was his mission in life. He was always in charge. *Always*." She laughs, but the whites of her eyes go pink and well up.

The cork finally exits with a quiet pop. I pour her glass, then mine, wishing I could be better at letting someone else take care of me. Grandma's scratching at exactly the idea that's been confounding me. Grandpa used careful placement of the building blocks of their life together; yet, he wasn't a control freak. It was as though he was on this mission in life to be a success, and when he met Grandma, she had a quick chance to jump on board and be part of it all . . . or not. And it's not that he would have been pleased forging ahead without her, but he was so self-assured and focused on his achievements that if he'd had to carry on alone, he still could have—and he still would have. It was like he was sitting outside that old ice cream soda shop on a steed, and Grandma looked up at him, took his hand, and climbed on for the ride.

It's such a compelling trait for a woman to find in a man, that cavalier manner; that passion to leave his mark; that battle against being ordinary. When I look at Grandma, I get a sense she couldn't quite *feel* Grandpa's drive or relate to it, but she loved it. She was all in. I don't even know whether she actually understood the things my grandpa cared about—the mechanism of the key, for heaven's sake, the physics behind a pulley, the economic role of the corncob pipe in twentieth-century America—but she found the man endlessly interesting. She was sort of like Dorothy in *Jerry Maguire*: I'll stand back and support you, even when I can't read your heart. And when you come home at the end of the day, I'll happily be your soft place to fall.

The way most men navigate the universe with such a determined path and such fierce passions absolutely mystifies me.

And we women, how we yield so pliably, how we take interest in *their* interests with such heartfelt sincerity. I used to research this when I studied psychobiology in college, the male hunter-gatherer capacity that is complemented by the woman's nurturing, by her devotion to home and hearth. This gender-psychic phenomenon has more to do with the human spirit than it does with science. A male is born into the universe with such an unstoppable approach to his goals and identity—for him there's always a victory to prove. And the female, she encourages him, or at least permits him, to pursue his battle . . . but does he notice that? Somehow the women around me have balanced their own desires in exchange for comfort and protection of a man. This clear interpretation of the male and female hearts . . . did I somehow miss the memo?

And when I think of it from this angle, it seems a little embarrassing that *I* am always trying to prove some feat of my own. What if I entertained the thought of sharing all my challenges with someone? "Grandma, you liked that Grandpa was usually in charge, didn't you?"

"Oh goodness, I wouldn't have had it any other way, really. He always knew what he was after. I trusted him." If I found a man with such ambition, would it inspire me to sit back and be cherished? Would it help me to stop worrying about opening the pickle jar—or, ha, the wine bottle—myself? And would one hundred percent of me *want* that? I'm proud of the self-reliance that I've fostered in my young adulthood, and it doesn't come in handy only when I'm alone. Just look at the work I've been doing for Chris: these days some men actually benefit from having a woman in their lives who can manage things on her own. But . . . what if that's not the same kind of woman who they perceive as making a good wife?

Grandma and I clink cheers. She sips at her pinot grigio and smooths herself over. "Let's sit down." She places a dainty napkin under my wineglass and sets out a tiny bowl for our shrimp tails. We nibble at shrimp cocktail and cashews, shifting our conversation away from memories to catch up on the last week.

Neutrally, Grandma asks me how things are going with Tucker. I tell her fine, nothing eventful, that we're just hanging out. "He's fun." I shrug. "He's nice company. But he's back at school now, so he's two hours away." Tucker and I have made plans for me to go out next week and help him get settled. Meanwhile I've been trying to gauge how the long-distance thing is going to affect us on top of our already hazardous age difference . . . and frankly, I should probably feel more concerned. Fewer than two months into my relationship with Tucker—innocent, harmless Tucker—I weeble constantly between feelings of affection, ambivalence, and annoyance. While fortunately the affection is the most frequent of the three, the intensity of the other two sometimes eats me alive. He called me last week to tell me he'd gotten caught cheating on a paper:

"Sweetie, it's the beginning of the semester," I told him. "Why are you already using someone else's work?"

"I couldn't figure it out!" he said. "I think chemistry was the wrong major. Hey, when I come home this weekend, do you think you could help me with my homework?" I looked at the phone and recoiled, then told him sorry, but he'd be on his own. It was growing apparent that

Tucker's lack of maturity was his tragic flaw in both text-book chemistry and the grown-up kind. I really couldn't tell how much longer this whole affair would last.

"And your doctor friend?" Grandma asks, raising her eyebrows cautiously. "Any word from him?"

I promptly occupy my mouth by munching on a shrimp. I smile with my eyes, gesturing charmingly—*Just one sec, Grandma, it's not polite to speak with my mouth full*—acting as though one baby shrimp had transformed into the size they serve on luxury cruises. I'm debating how to answer my dear grandmother. I'd been hoping the divisive topic of world-class surgeon wanna-been romances wouldn't play any part in Grandpa's birthday. Cans of tomato sauce, absolutely; even cans of pipe tobacco—sure. But this can of worms . . . do we *really* need to open it?

Looks like we do, as Grandma's gaze has turned from inquisitive to hopeful. *Ugh . . . can opener, please?*

I fill her in on the latest: two or three weeks ago, just before Tucker left for school, Chris's calls had grown strangely common. While I was usually legitimately too far from my phone to hear it ringing, one day it got me in trouble while Tucker and I were taking a break from packing moving boxes into his car to relax at the beach. Our swimsuits dripped wet while we snacked on subs and put a dent in a six-pack. When my phone rang I picked it up and jumped, then sent the call straight to voice mail.

"Who was that?" Tucker asked through a bite of ham and cheese.

"My mom."

"You suck at lying." He wiped his mouth with his arm. "Was it that doctor?"

"Tucker."

"He's still calling!"

"Only sometimes. He asked me to have lunch next week."

"*What!*" he squawks, alarming two toddlers who are dancing on the ruins of a nearby sand castle.

"Tucker, stop," I hiss under my breath. "It won't happen. I honestly never even catch his calls."

"But if you did, would you go out with him?"

"Tucker, of course not! I'm in a relationship."

"Well, I would hope not. Geez, before I met you I didn't think I had a prayer. That's all I heard about from those ladies at our moms' office, that 'handsome, rich surgeon' you were dating." He speaks the words with giant burden. "When's the last time you talked to him?"

"In the middle of July, right before his birthday—"

Tucker opens his mouth to object.

"Tucker, you and I weren't even hanging out yet. Anyway, he'd sent me an e-mail saying that for a birthday present he'd gotten himself eight stitches in his finger trying to fix the fan of some laser machine at his office. Then two days after he sent the e-mail he called, and I picked up. What, Tucker? I felt bad! His injury sounded graphic." I weakly throw a piece of my bun at the water for the fish to eat, remembering how Chris said that he could actually see the bone in his index finger. "The poor guy doesn't have any family around here." The thought saddens me so much that I can't take another bite of my sandwich. "He's all alone."

"Well," Tucker brushes sand off my knee, "the next time he calls or e-mails, you'll tell him you're seeing someone else?"

"Sure. I'll tell him."

"And that it's serious?"

"Yes, Tucker."

"Okay. Promise?"

"*Yes*, Tucker."

When I listened to Chris's voice mail later that day, he said he was riding around the lake and wanted to stop by my house to say hello; that he'd finally felt up to trying his bicycle using only nine fingers . . . such moxie. Explaining to my boyfriend why this handsome doctor with a three-thousand-dollar eighteen-speed wanted to just "drop by" would have been both unnecessary *and* futile, so I was relieved that I hadn't been home with Tucker—but surprisingly, sort of disappointed that I hadn't been home at all. For half a second I wondered how Chris's scent mixed with a clean sweat would have affected me.

The following Monday, I was preparing some questions about marital faithfulness for dinner with Grandma and realized I'd been procrastinating in my promise to Tucker. But seriously, I think, is this really necessary? Will Chris take me for presumptuous to think that just *perhaps* he'd wanted to be more than just friends? I pace around my brother's room and then sit down to craft the following e-mail—carefully:

Hi Chris,

I hope your Thursday is going well. I look forward to our lunch next week; I only wanted to drop a quick line to bring you up to speed on my current events, which have been a whirlwind lately!

In addition to the projects and family affairs that have been keeping me super-busy, I feel it's right to inform you that in the last few weeks I've become involved in a serious relationship. It's been a quick, surprising turn of events and he knows via the infamous local grapevine and my own reviews what a great guy I'd hung out with earlier this summer and that I think you're an amazing person and friend.

Life throws us things when we least expect it, doesn't it? (I know, I'm preaching to the choir.) In any case I'd love to continue fostering our friendship and am certainly all for our getting together to catch up. I'm excited to talk about developments in our respective work and personal projects. I just felt it best to fill you in on the latest so as not to surprise you when we finally do connect again!

Again, let me know of any changes to lunch plans. Otherwise I'll look forward to next Monday and can't wait to hear your updates (and share some of my own)!

Warmest,

Krissy

p.s. how is your finger healing, my friend?

Grandma is sorting out the logistics of the story now that she's up to speed on the whole ordeal. "So you *had* made lunch plans with him, but hadn't told Tucker."

"Well, yes. Knowing Chris's schedule, I figured that the lunch had as good a chance of not happening as it had of happening, so I figured I'd let sleeping dogs lie until it was really time to tell Tucker."

"And how did the lunch go?"

"Actually it was . . . dinner."

Grandma's eyes light up. She sits back and folds her arms, waiting for me to continue.

"He'd put in a really long day, patients and meetings and no lunch. So he told me he was totally understanding of my relationship situation—I think he actually used the words 'ten-four'—but said it was urgent that he sees me."

Grandma leans back in and purrs in an uncharacteristic manner that's reminiscent of Blanche Deveraux on *The Golden Girls*: "*Do go on.*"

Chris asked me to meet him at Peking on the boulevard, and I found his correct *pay-king* pronunciation of the Chinese restaurant's name even stranger than our town's hillbilly pronunciation, which makes it sound like a place one would go to worship the ruler of all urine. Anyway, I'd honored his request for me to bring something to write with, wondering what in the world all this could be about. Was he fleeing town and needed help devising a getaway? Did he feel an autobiography coming on and was in need of a convincing ghostwriter?

He climbed out of his Mercedes when I pulled into the spot next to him. He waited for me to walk over to him, and I noted that his greeting felt a little like embracing a cold fish—had he taken my e-mail personally? But when I pulled away from the hug and looked into his face, his eyes were the same vivid hue as his scrubs. Both his face and his outfit made my knees go woozy, reminding me that I was under the influence of someone powerful. Maybe I shouldn't have found it so thrilling, but I did.

When we sat down at the private corner table he requested, he greeted the only other occupied table—clearly a patient and his wife, who looked me over shamelessly. Chris ordered a fish and vegetable dish with brown rice and no sauce; I too decided to go light with the spicy vegetable soup. "So I need to tell you why I've brought you here," he said as he folded the cloth napkin onto his lap.

"Okay."

"I've actually had a project in the works for some months. There's a hospital in Southeast Asia that has commissioned me to start a cosmetic surgery division there . . ."

I took this as my cue to begin transcribing. My hand raced hastily across my notebook page, catching his key phrases and musings verbatim. But in my head I was trying to push down the sadness I was feeling: Chris was telling me that he's leaving.

"AMBITIOUS THING, ISN'T HE," Grandma cuts me off.

Ambitious? *How about selfish?* I bite my tongue against it. But who drops a bomb the way he did?

"Let me guess," she continues. "He wants you to help him prepare."

My eyes go blank, my mouth mute. How did she know that?

"You're a smart girl," she says, rising from her chair to put on water for the pasta. "Any man in his right mind would want you in his corner."

Was I really in Chris's corner? I couldn't decide. In the last week the two of us had begun working consecutive late nights together in the quiet of his office. We were compiling an extensive presentation for him to drum up business overseas, and it required a lot of research on my part about the cosmetic tourism industry. I was also managing the development of some marketing materials, and he loved the design I chose for his business cards and Web site so much that he told me he just wanted me to take liberty over all the aesthetic decisions.

When his staff stepped in to check out with him in the evenings, they scanned me up and down, questioning the nature of my presence there. Of course he couldn't tout to them his plans to move his practice overseas, possibly making their jobs obsolete . . . and his silence made me all the bigger mystery. "Ann," was all he might say as he filled out one last patient script, "you met Krissy earlier this week, right?" I'd smile innocuously, telling Ann it was nice to see her again.

"I don't remember you," she would reply. "Unless you were the one wearing wacky glasses on Monday."

"Yes, yes, that was me!" I'd respond, overlooking her insult at my reading glasses to prove with my friendliness that I posed absolutely no threat to her boss-crush. *I tried dating him already— go ahead, you take a stab!*

After Chris wished a good-night to all of his staff, he'd close the door to his office and lie down on the carpet. In free association he'd spill his exhaustion, his frustration, the fact that he'd just cried with a patient who said she needed Botox because she feels she's aged three decades in the six months since her daughter was diagnosed with cancer. He'd always turn off the harsh fluorescent lights over our heads, and working by the lamplight would give his office a hushed, trusting ambience. At such moments I'd find myself bubbling to tell him things about my day too, but I would always reconsider, thinking it best to maintain the professional boundaries. Mostly, though, I didn't want to interrupt him from opening up to me.

I don't tell Grandma all this. I don't tell her that when we're not working by jazz music we're working by classical; that I like the rawness of his scent after he's been busy all day; that one afternoon I took a break from loading presentation files into my car to walk down to the pond in front of his office to peer at the ducks, letting the breeze whip through my hair and my dress . . . and at that very second Chris knocked on the window from the inside, placed his fingers on the glass and slowly smiled at me. He'd caught me in this one feminine, beautiful moment, and he saw it. He saw *me*.

I end my details for Grandma after I list the projects we're working on, finding an excuse to step away from the stickier details by adding salt to the boiling water on the stove. I can't have the involvement of anyone else's emotions—especially fragile Grandma's—fueling my own confusion about Chris.

My mom and aunts arrive and take my attention from the matter completely, lining the kitchen counter with salad and Italian bread and pie. "Oooh, it's coconut cream!" I peer into the box. "Grandpa's favorite . . . mine too, actually." I open the cardboard and we all hover over the perfect mound of fluffy meringue.

"Gloria, no tears," my aunt says. "We agreed no cake, but nobody said anything about pie."

The guys each arrive separately, one by one from the office. Grandma lights up more and more as each attendant enters her feast. With all our commotion, we have successfully distracted her from the reason we're all here. I think of Tom Hanks in *A League of Their Own*:

"There's no crying on birthdays!"

It takes both my mom and me to transfer four pounds of spaghetti from the strainer to Grandma's colossal pasta bowl, when my dad finally makes his entrance. "Looks like a party in here, Mom!" he says.

"Well, it is a party, Billy!" Grandma calls from the kitchen. "You drinking red or white?"

The twelve of us take places around Grandma's dining room table, the guys loosening their ties to relax. We pass bowls and bread baskets and wine bottles until Grandma—is she tipsy?—calls for grace. We bow our heads, and after the amen, we raise our glasses. "To the birthday boy," Uncle Phil says, and we murmur our hear-hears.

Dinner is further cheered by the news that our company got a nice order today, putting an end to a near year-long business drought. Inconspicuously, I look up at the ceiling, past Grandma's chandelier: *You're still taking care of everything, aren't you.*

Even though our hero is missing from his own birthday dinner, this night feels like old times—including Grandma's laughter.

Together we celebrate the man who always knew what he wanted: autonomy in his work, and a partner who honored it.

5

Support His Work

THERE'S A TINY WINDOW every year when the landscape of central Pennsylvania deserves a description this big: it's magnificent.

It's the middle of October. Out the window there is an orchestra of color splashed around the woods, dancing from the trees, mirroring off the marina. Entering the lake, there's a great hill half a mile long, flanked on both sides by majestic, element-kissed trees that welcome you to the community like the arch of swords at Buckingham Palace marking the bride and groom's entrance into the Queen's dominion.

When I was away, I'd forgotten how these surroundings feel, this exclusive initiation into something grand and unlike anything you'd find anywhere else. Deep down, even though I admit it only to my mother, Chris's project is similar—more late working evenings to meet epic deadlines, lunches with his famed colleagues who fly in from around the country to invest their money or their interest in his practice overseas, and now, a road trip to New York. I'm leaning against the tailgate of his SUV as he sizes up his luggage in the garage of the house he rents on the lake. "Do you think five suits are enough for six weeks?"

"I'll answer if you scratch your chest like a gorilla again."

He stops and looks at me, puzzled and amused. "Like what?"

"Like you were just doing."

"This?" He does it again, taking both hands to his chest the way a freckle-faced little boy might scratch his head over a math problem. I double over. "Was I doing this?"

When I compose myself I peek one more time inside his garment bag at the Italian suits he had custom-tailored for this trip and tell him yes, I'm certain that he has enough clothes but he'll need to get his shirts pressed when he arrives. This is our working relationship now, caring and familiar the way the lead costars in a movie might hang out in each other's trailer between scenes. Chris and I are together so often that I know his teeth-brushing schedule, his bank account password, his mother's middle name, and that he keeps a picture of her in his car. The dynamic between us is so natural and agreeable that sometimes I wonder: is this how Robert Pattinson and Kristen Stewart started out in *Twilight*?

But even as we inch closer, there's a boundary that keeps us just out of reach from one another. All this contact over the last month hasn't been just for our enjoyment—it's for a purpose; for an end. And that contact is *about* to end for more than a month, because tomorrow Chris takes off for his first publicity tour in Asia to promote his practice over there. I know that if I weren't part of this business initiative, then I wouldn't be the one standing here right now, getting ready to climb into the driver's seat so he can call patients and plug away on his laptop for the next three hundred miles to Manhattan.

Tucker, poor Tucker, hates this trip. I think he's imagined every possible sabotage against it, and the worst part is, per Chris's request to keep costs down, I've booked only one hotel room. Fortunately it's a suite in the middle of Times Square so Chris and I each will have our own private space, but the thought of anything less than two hotel reservations was more than Tucker could stand—but I couldn't lie to him. I called Grandma early in the morning to tell her not to save me a seat at church today.

"Whatever you want to do!" she exclaimed. "I won't pressure you. And God doesn't mind—*He's* there for *us*; He doesn't depend on *us* to go and see *Him*." I exhaled, grateful that at least there was someone who was trying to take some pressure off me today. I stayed in Tucker's bed and pleaded for him to accept that this trip was for work, but he rolled toward the wall, not even wanting to look at me. When I left him I was still in tears and my pajamas, speeding home to shower and pack so I wouldn't be late for Chris.

But after we get Chris's gear loaded up and the car on the road, it occurs to me that my mood has lifted significantly. In the sun, the mountains on I-80 are on fire with leaves, and I decide there couldn't be a better week in the whole year to have to drive my boss across Pennsylvania. Chris rolls down the windows and cranks up jazz music, and we snack on buttery biscuits that my mom stuffed with mushrooms and Gruyere cheese.

I do not want him to leave the country.

He calls a patient for follow-up, and when I turn down the radio he thinks I'm being polite. I actually just love the soothing, accommodating tone his voice takes when he's talking to patients. He pops open the glove box in search of a pen, and just then a black plastic bag tumbles out onto his feet. He picks it up, looking at the logo from the jeweler downtown, and mouths to me, *What is this?*

"Just wait," I whisper, locating a pen in the middle console. When he ends the call he tips open the black velvet box, finding a silver medallion inside. Perplexed, he turns to me.

"It's St. Christopher," I tell him.

Gently, he pulls the chain from the box.

"He's the patron saint of travelers. Turn it over."

Chris flips the pendant carefully to the other side, where his initials are engraved. "Kris, what made you do this?"

"This trip is a big deal, and you're going to be doing a ton of traveling over there. I—" I hesitate. "I wanted you to be protected."

"You know what? My grandpa had one like this after World War Two. He gave it to me."

"There's no such thing as too much St. Christopher."

"Look, he's carrying a baby." Chris is studying the medallion carefully. To buy it cost me six hours' worth of work for him, but the look on his face makes it worth a hundred.

"He carries travelers on their journeys. And know what else?"

"What?"

"You're Christopher, I'm Kristine: he's the patron saint of us both."

We hit weekend traffic coming from the Poconos and don't get to the city until nine o'clock. Chris asks whether I mind if he goes to meet his former mentor for dinner without me, considering the time.

"No, go," I say. "I'll get us into a room that's not right next to the elevator, so you can sleep tonight."

I wander a block off from the bright lights of Times Square and stumble on a Greek restaurant on Ninth Avenue. There I sit, on the cushy wall side of a candlelit table that's meant for two, eating a spinach crepe and drinking chardonnay all by myself. I think of calling home or just playing with my phone to occupy myself, but instead I take in the city breeze blowing in through the open door, the passersby, and the waiter who has just delivered another glass of wine. He tells me it's from the owner, and I stretch my neck to offer a smile and thanks. I can't tell if they're admiring me or feeling sorry for me. I can't tell which I'm feeling either.

I remember how Grandma and I agree that for a woman on her own, Sunday nights are the loneliest time of the week. My cell phone clock reads 10:30 as I start back toward the hotel . . . but I'll try her. If she doesn't answer by the third ring, I'll hang up.

She startles me, picking up on the second ring. "Hello?"

"Grandma! Sorry to call you so late, you're still awake?"

"Yes, I can't sleep. Is everything okay?"

"Yes, I'm in New York, we made it fine. I was just calling to check on you."

"My dear," she says, "you won't believe this, but I think you're the answer to my prayer."

"What? Why?"

"I was just having a very blue moment, in fact I've been crying since I hung up with your dad an hour ago. Just to hear your voice makes me feel so much better."

I return to a dark hotel room and slip into my long-sleeve silk peejays to work—I brought my nicest pajamas, knowing he's going to see what I wear to bed . . . although the bra shall remain. Then I pull out the couch in the living area of the suite.

I'm sleeping in the living room, I text to Tucker. *He's still at dinner. See? No worries.*

He replies with this: *I'm out. Have a good night.*

Chris keys into the room around midnight, and it strikes me how metropolitan he looks in distressed jeans and a black V-neck. "Hi, how was your night, where'd you eat?" he says. "Why are you out here, I told you to take the bed."

"You take the bed."

He says it's not right, but I insist. "I'm not the one with a nineteen-hour flight tomorrow. You are."

He thanks me, moving into the bedroom. "Saul wants brunch with us tomorrow. He wants to meet you." I hear his words come out as he's pulling his shirt off over his head.

"Good, I was hoping I'd get to meet him while we were here."

He peeks his head out from the door frame, and I can see his bare, broad shoulders. He tilts his head thoughtfully. "What are you working on?"

"Writing for your site." I look at him only for a second, careful not to gaze at his bare upper body. Over the lid of my laptop I see him continuing to hover in the doorway. Is there something more he wants to say? I clear my throat and adjust my glasses, then look up and smile in a way that could be taken as either friendly or impatient. I point at the desk lamp. "Will this bother you?"

"No," he says, turning self-aware again. "Not at all. Sleep well, Kris."

"Thanks. You too."

"Good night." He closes the door and enters the bathroom through his side door, which is separate from my entry. I hear the trickle of water running, the sound of his toothbrush, then the flick of the light switch, then . . . silence.

I exhale. This facade of indifference for him is a challenge. I pull the chain on the lamp and hunker down to work in the dark.

In the morning I'm in heels and a leather jacket, juggling luggage, a cup of Starbucks, and some files when he bursts out of his bedroom. "Saul called, we're late," he says, and this pretty much sets our pace for the day.

We check out, lock our luggage in storage, and race through Times Square. It crosses my mind that every man who has ever succeeded at anything should thank the woman at his side who has dodged crowds in high heels to see him to the finish. I chase Chris at his heels, calling, "You know the marathon's not till next month." He speeds up.

"You know what we forgot to do?" he says. "We forgot to return that expensive camera case. It's too bulky to travel."

"I'm shipping it back this week, remember? We talked about this."

Suddenly I cannot wait for him to leave the country.

Facing Chris and Saul from my side of the plush booth and between quiet bites of tomato quiche, I take notes while the two of them brainstorm. Saul is one of the world's best known sleep experts and has met Oprah. Their voices grow louder as they think of all the reasons they should add a sleep lab to Chris's center—sleep makes your body younger. Sleep fights disease. Sleep makes you smarter.

I don't tell Saul that I slept for four hours last night.

Before we return to the hotel for our luggage and the truck, we stop for a Jamba Juice. Standing in line and pondering the menu, at once the mover-shaker-surgeon-entrepreneur is himself again. "What flavor you gonna get, cheetah?"

Cheetah, ha. That's funny. I order a small berry smoothie. He gets a jumbo immunity boost. "For the flight," he says and winks, dancing the straw in my face.

"Ah, right."

Everything about him is exhausting me. When the valet delivers the truck, I eye the backseat and fantasize about climbing in to snooze to prep for my five-hour drive home, but before his flight Chris has a meeting in New Jersey with another investor, and by the looks of it . . . yep, he's getting cozy with his laptop in the passenger seat. I'm driving. I tell him I'm going to need his eyes to help get us out of this traffic.

"Yeah, sure," he says. His nose is in his phone.

"Can you get out the navigation system?" I ask.

"Why?"

"So I can put in the address."

"I don't have the address."

I turn to him blankly. "You don't."

He shakes his head. He tells me he recalls that our destination is located at a very specific point in New Jersey where some junction meets some route. I smile, nearing wit's end. "Why don't we call their office?"

"Right."

Forty minutes later by the grace of the GPS gods we stand in the parking lot of a suburban office complex, the contemporary type that always seems to exist in the same neighborhood as a Cadillac dealership and a P.F. Chang's.

"Hey Kris?" He's standing outside the passenger door. "I've been wearing this sweater for two days. Can you take it home with you?" He tosses it to me.

"Okay." I count on my fingers with his black sweater stuffed under my arm. "You have your suits, your sneakers, lots of underwear, your computer . . . wait, your camera, do you have your camera?"

He points to the fancy new travel backpack we had overnighted last week. "Got the camera."

"Okay, good." He stands bracing his backpack with both hands and I try to fight my estimation that he looks like a little kid going off to his first day of kindergarten. *Would you can it already? This is your boss.* "So, are you excited?"

"Really excited." I love when his eyes say the same as his words. He opens his arms for a hug. "What will I do without the cheetah?" His T-shirt is soft against my cheek, the contour of his chest so strong, and, oh heaven, his scent. He is the only man in the universe who can conquer midtown Manhattan on foot, then spend two hours in a restaurant that reeks of French onion soup and still smell like something you'd want to rip out of a magazine and rub all over yourself.

Please don't go.

Then, as though he could hear my plea, he separates from me. "See you in six weeks."

He's not mine to worry about, and still I do. The investor hosting him at this afternoon's meeting has arranged for a car to take him to the airport tonight, but not having the precise itinerary in my grip is a pesky loose end. Chris gets carried away talking at meetings if someone's not watching the clock . . . or, heaven forbid, they start toying with some groundbreaking procedure. For any chance to learn something new, he'd gladly take his jacket off and stay a while, miss his flight, and land in Asia somewhere around the Fourth of July.

Can I feel *certain* he even remembers which airport he's going to?

But his logistics aren't all I'm concerned about . . . because there's also Chris's wellness. I want to know he'll be comfortable on the plane, that he'll have a few days' rest before he has to start operating, that the people there will be kind and helpful. I get that this is only a paycheck for me, that to him I'm probably just someone whose skills he needs right now . . . but if I don't care about how he fares out in the world, who will?

The next day back in Pennsylvania, I smoosh the button on the alarm and sleep in, snuggling in bliss for the first day in weeks that's not full of bustling phone calls and appointments. I pull Chris's sweater in closer from the pillow next to me and hold the soft cashmere to my face. I don't know why I thought sleeping with it like a teddy bear was any less weird than just *wearing* it . . . but I'm disappointed that already his scent is fading.

Mom and Dad are working, the dogs snooze without care, and the sun peers in and casts light across the room. With a lazy cup of coffee, I sit down to tackle some follow-up notes, paying Chris's cell phone bill and finalizing the ad we're running in the local paper so his patients know he won't be back until just before Thanksgiving. Then I call Grandma. "You up for some company?"

She says that sounds nice.

I clean myself up and head into town. It's been since just after Grandpa's birthday that we last sat down together, which guarantees she'll be full of a month's worth of stories. I stop to grab chicken and french-fry salads—a hometown legend—at my favorite restaurant. The smell of the hot food in plastic containers pushes out the last of the smell of Chris, his sweater sitting in the backseat to go to the cleaners. I crack the window.

When I pull into Grandma's driveway her garage door is open with the car running inside. She stands next to it fumbling with a piece of paper and an envelope. The focus it takes her to complete this one small task alarms me somewhat, but more, I can't help but want to help. She jumps when I say, "Grandma, are you okay? Why is your car running?"

"Oh! Goodness, Kris. I didn't even hear you arrive." I wonder if her hearing aid's off, but when I embrace her, it sings high in my ear. It's impossible that she didn't hear my arrival . . . the real problem appears to be that her ability to multitask is fading. "Hey, what you got there?"

"I brought us chicken salads from Luigi's. Grandma, your car. Did you mean to leave it running?"

She turns slowly. "No," she says, dazed, "I don't think so."

"I'll jump in and turn it off." I set down the bag of salads. When I reach the driver's side door, it's locked. For her sake I stay calm, but this is very odd. "Grandma, it's locked. It's locked, and it's running with the keys in the ignition."

"Oh dear," she says, still puzzled. Instantly, I worry about what would've happened if I hadn't shown up and she'd have gone in the house and closed the garage door. "Grandma," I say, conscious about holding my voice steady, "do you have a spare set of keys?"

"Well, oh goodness, when I think about it, I want to say your dad has them. Or maybe your Uncle Phil . . ."

I take off into the house, opening Grandpa's desk drawers in the office that separates the garage from the kitchen. In the middle drawer there's a remote key. I run to the garage doorway and point it at Grandma's car. It clicks. Grandma spins as I run past her to the driver's side of the car and turn off the ignition. *Jesus, I want to say to her. Do you do this all the time?* "Grandma, has this happened before?"

"Maybe a couple times," she says. "You didn't get me ranch, did you? I'm still having a terrible time with dairy."

Are you kidding me? I try to keep my patience with her, wondering why she's thinking about salad dressing when she's just put her life in serious danger. I almost want to blame her, to shout at her, but I have to consider that it's her dementia at work. "No," I tell her, "I got you sweet and sour. Isn't that what you always order?" We travel into the house together, Grandpa's pulley on the screen door falling with our entrance. "Grandma, did you want to close the garage door?"

"Oh yes, thanks. It's the left button—or is it the right one? No, I could swear it's the left . . ." until finally she decides that she won't know unless she can see the garage door controls herself. "It was the left, I can never keep that straight. Have a seat at the table, you want a drink?"

My water order turns into a complicated task. No, it's fine without ice; yes, a small glass is fine. I'm happy to get it myself, I insist, but no, no, she says she's got it, I should sit and relax.

"So, how was New York?"

I need to go along with her casualness and have my dad and uncles deal with this memory thing later. I'm learning that I can try to help with Grandma's emotional issues, but her physical health—her memory—is a challenge that's totally beyond me. "It was busy, Grandma. He drives me crazy."

She shrugs and asks, "Did you get to see any friends?"

"No, there wasn't time."

"Well, you were there for work, I suppose." She picks at the fries on her salad with her fingers, which seems out of character. I pass her a napkin. "You glad you can focus on your work again?"

"Yes, very glad. I had to ask three different editors for deadline extensions. I never do that." I stop slicing my chicken to look square at Grandma. "You know what I want to tell him, Grandma?"

"Hm?" She's fiddling with the melting shredded cheese.

"'Get a wife.'"

Nothing I say seems to cheer her up today; she is clearly and completely distracted. "Grandma," I continue at my salad, "what's new with you?"

"Well . . ." She sets down her fork and sighs. "I might as well come out with it: I got rid of Grandpa's shirts."

Suddenly my salad is too much; I'm completely nauseated. "Wow." Grandpa's shirts, his old work shirts? Why would she do that so soon? My nana has buried three husbands, and for years afterward she would wear their shirts around the house just to keep the thought of them alive . . . and, if she's lucky, their smell. Nana has always said that smelling a man's clothes as soon as he's gone is the most heartbreaking feeling in the world, but that after some time has passed it's often the only thing that brings any comfort. It's the only sign of them that's really left. She said that you can leave a man's closet door closed for a decade and when you finally open it back up, it's like nuzzling your nose in his neck. "What made you do that?" I ask Grandma. *And so soon.* It's all I can do to hold down my anger.

She's angry too. For the first time in the half hour that I've been with her, she's making sense and her thoughts flow fluidly. She's mad at him, she says. She's mad at him for leaving her with so much to take care of on her own. For sixty years she tended to his every need while he worked, even though he was the much better cook and even though at moments she felt she was running their whole lives by herself. She says one time she was running my dad to electric drum practice (to which I can only interject, "Wait, my dad played the *electric drums?*"), and the other four kids were carrying on in the living room, and for some reason they always had parakeets for pets, which Grandma thinks was something they picked up from the Italians, but anyway the bird, his name was Johnny, somehow he got loose from his cage just as she was heading out the door with Dad and his electric drum kit, and one of my uncles decided to get smart and slam the sliding glass door behind Dad to scare him and *wham!*, Johnny the bird got squashed in the door and fell dead to the ground, leaving five little kids in hysterics and one of them late for drum practice to boot.

(The story is horrifying, but I am trying so hard not to laugh.)

Grandpa was never home, Grandma says, and yet he was always needing her. She'd spend entire days picking up after the kids and then he'd get home from work and take off his dirty shirt to put a clean one on for dinner. She says she'd track behind him picking up the first one—"He'd actually drop it on the floor!"—that smelled like a day's work and was often smudged with grease from the machines he built or stuffed in the pockets with napkins covered in mechanical sketches. How did he think things always just landed back in his closet clean? "That reminds me," she said. "The tax receipt for my donation today is in my purse."

Oh, and then the dinners, she continues, don't even get her started. (I'm not.) How many nights did she host colleagues and customers or get dressed up at conferences and carry on small talk with executives and their wives, all for Grandpa and his business? "And when I'd want to have friends over, he'd cringe, and I'd tell him, 'George, all the meetings and dinners I go to for you, you can put up with one night with my friends.'"

Grandma says she spent her whole life looking up to him, looking out for him, looking after him . . . and what does he do? He leaves her by herself. "Today I looked up at the ceiling and I told him," she points up, "'This is all your fault, you know! If you're looking down on me, then you can see what you did when you left me!'"

I take a deep breath and think about my response carefully. "Grandma," I start, "when Grandpa was dying, do you remember how unhappy he was? How much pain he was in?"

She sits quiet.

"It made you sad too, remember? And you told him to go. You told him you wanted him to go, because you knew that was the best thing for him. You have to remember that. You loved him that much that for him to have peace, you'd have given up anything. Even him." She's crying now. "He wasn't happy anymore, you knew that. Remember how pissed off and frustrated he was after he got sick? He was too tired to work. He'd sleep in all morning and then he'd finally wake up before noon, and just getting dressed made him tired again. He spent the whole day wanting to be able to do something constructive. His mind just wouldn't shut off, do you remember him saying that? He kept doing this," I imitate the motion Grandpa made of a wheel turning fast in his head, "and saying, 'I can't make it stop!' It was driving him crazy."

She nods slowly, concentrating on her hands, which are folded in her lap.

"Grandma," I lean in, "it's *normal* for you to feel angry. You did so much for him. And you supported him *absolutely unconditionally*, like I have never seen any other woman do for any man, ever." She continues to sit silently. "You can be proud of that."

"I think I was in denial in those final days."

"You probably were."

"I just couldn't imagine that after sixty years, he was about to disappear."

"It was impossible to comprehend, Grandma. I felt the same way." I talk to Grandma the same way I coach a friend through a breakup: *These feelings are real because all that love happened. You have to honor your grief process after losing that relationship.* When I wrote the eulogy for Grandpa's funeral, I remember referring to my grandma's devotion to him as "pure" and saying that she was a holy woman. She is. She heard a calling to spend her life serving, and nobly, she responded. It shouldn't surprise anyone that she feels lost and lonely without him. "Grandma, tell me something."

She pulls a tissue out of the cuff of her sweater and looks at me with puffy eyes. "Yes?"

"Grandpa's business didn't actually take off until he was forty-seven, right?"

"Yes."

"Am I remembering correctly that before that, the business in St. Louis went under?"

"Yes, it did. Marie and Phil were in college, and your dad and Uncle Paul were about fifteen and seventeen, and Junior was nearing ten, and we put them in the U-Haul with all of our belongings—well, actually, not all of our belongings, we had to throw a lot out because there just wasn't enough room."

"Dad lost all his baseball cards, right?"

"Yes, years worth of baseball cards he'd collected, they were all gone. He was devastated, but," she shrugs, opening up her hands, "that's the way it was. We all had to give something up."

"And how was Grandpa? How did he act in that period?" Grandpa was notoriously proud—how did he deal with his failure?

"He was very quiet in that time. I remember after we packed up the boys in the U-Haul, I climbed in the front seat next to him and said, 'Well, where we going?' And he looked at me, then looked down and said, 'I don't know.'"

"Oh, *Grandma*." I put my head in my hands. That defeat would've *destroyed* my grandpa.

"We lost everything, we had nowhere to go. The day I got married I'd told my mother that I would never come back to her. I had no siblings, and we felt we definitely couldn't go to Grandpa's family." She reflects out loud. "Most of them had been waiting for years for him to fail."

Did she try to comfort him? Did she stay out of his way? "So when all that was happening, how did you relate to Grandpa?"

"I did what I had to do. That's all there was to it. The only thing we could do was start the car and pull out."

"No looking back."

She shakes her head. "Nope."

When they got on the road, they decided to drive to Grandpa's siblings in Rochester, New York, after all. They had no other options. They stayed there a few months, enough for Grandpa to reestablish his contacts in Pennsylvania and return here.

"Then when your dad and uncles finished school and got involved, well, you know the story. Everything turned around for the better." Reminiscing has turned Grandma's mood around for the better too, and now she's laughing. "Then their only worry was that I didn't get involved in the business! But," she adds, "sometimes they did need me to come in and answer the phones." When Grandpa first launched the company with his sons, they worked out of the garage of a gas station because it was the only floor space they could afford. Dad and his brothers were all hands on deck, taking turns as the receptionist, concepting for machines, and sometimes going outside and pumping gas for customers. Everybody had to pitch in.

"Grandma, did it bother you that Grandpa only wanted you helping him with the business when it was convenient for him, on his terms?"

"Noooo," she says. "I knew he was doing all that for the family, for our future. Besides, good grief, when you love somebody you just jump in. You give what they need you to. It's easy to put yourself aside."

She's sighing less and talking a lot more than when I first arrived. I'm realizing that these chats aren't only helpful for me to understand the recipe behind a happy relationship—they're also helpful for her. In this forum, at her table or on her sunny back porch, I suppose I give her an excuse to talk about the person whose absence so desperately pains her. Here, she gets to remember the happy parts of their marriage and to reaffirm in her own mind that when it came to loving the man in her life, she did a pretty solid job.

Then there's the man in my life . . . not my boyfriend, but my boss. He's become much more than someone I'm happy to part from at the end of every workday. I want to see him well, I want his surgical center to take off, I want to keep doing everything I can to help make that happen. This endeavor is one of the most important things I've ever been part of. Every cell in my body feels invested.

Dusk closes in around Grandma's house, and just as I go to leave, my phone rings with a number I don't recognize. "You know what, Grandma, let me grab this in case it's something for Chris. It might be his life insurance company."

"Oh yes, get it."

"Hello?"

"Kris?"

I gasp—it's him. "*Hi!* You made it?"

"I made it, I'm here. I just had to call and tell you something."

I move in toward Grandma's kitchen in search of something to take notes with. "Go ahead."

"So you know how I was riding first class on the plane?"

How could I forget, he'd only mentioned it forty-six times. "Yes?"

"Well, there was this woman sitting next to me, and she saw

me pull out my cards, and she looked over my shoulder and said they were the classiest business cards she'd ever seen. I just wanted to call and tell you thanks."

"Oh wow, what a compliment! They did turn out beautifully, if I do say so. I figured it was worth trying them with your picture on there."

"Yeah. Really, thanks."

"You're welcome."

We hang up and I turn to Grandma, laughing. "He likes his business cards, he's getting compliments from strangers."

She smiles. "You see, you do good work. Oh, before you go, follow me. There was one shirt I saved, I wanted to give it to your dad." We walk into her bedroom and she opens Grandpa's closet. It's completely empty except for one golf shirt dangling. "This." She takes it out and hands it to me; it's the shirt from John Carroll University that I gave to Grandpa for Father's Day my freshman year. The navy blue has faded and the shoulders hang down and it's worn from being on the hanger. "Your grandpa loved that shirt."

"I know, he wore it all the time."

"I didn't want to give it away to strangers."

We kiss goodbye, and when I climb in the car I breathe in what's left of Grandpa's scent—a combination of pipe, machines, and aloe—till it draws tears. Then I hang the hanger in the backseat, and the polo sways over Chris's sweater. *Oh, the hearts that occupied these shirts . . .*

I start up the engine, collecting myself and noting the energy that dances in my rearview. He's gone, and now there are places I need to be.

6

Don't Lose Yourself

IN LATE OCTOBER, for Tucker's fall semester break, we plan a long weekend at the Pennsylvania Grand Canyon. Until now I had never even heard of it, but according to outdoorsy Tucker, it's a spot in the middle of the state with a wooded terrain that runs two miles deep and is sliced down the middle by a giant waterfall. The purpose for this miniholiday, in my mind, is to show Tucker that I'm committed to our growing together. Dr. Chris has been out of the country for two weeks, and apart from the occasional e-mail with a marketing question or to update me on how incredible Southeast Asia is ("You would melt into this place," he wrote in the most recent one), he's nearly out of my consciousness. Away from work and school and our parents, Tucker and I will finally have our own space this weekend to spread out together and just . . . *relax*.

However, the purpose of the trip in Tucker's mind is to go fishing and watch football at bars and do all the things guys do that I admit I sort of . . . don't get. But I've convinced myself that it's worth a try. I was away from Pennsylvania for a long time, and it's possible that with open-mindedness I could really hit it off with the huntin'-fishin' crowd. I may begin to envision myself setting up house in a secluded log cabin, or heck, I don't know, start understanding what a wide receiver does. Grandma, however, is not as optimistic as I am that the weekend is going to be so transformative. When I tell her I've gotten my fishing license, I hear her guffaw through the phone. "Fishing license! Why, when was the last time you went fishing?"

"With Grandpa," I figure. "I must've been eight, max. But I caught a little rainbow trout, and Grandpa got a real kick out of it." See, I'd forgotten about that: maybe I have an inherent knack for the outdoors after all. I ask Grandma if she ever used to go fishing alongside Grandpa, and she says heavens, no, fishing was never her cup of tea and in fact Grandpa only ever did it socially. She explains he wanted to make memories on their annual camping trips in Missouri when their kids were little, and then did it just enough to teach us grandkids how to cast a line off the pontoon.

When I was probably about four, Grandpa bought this blue baseball cap with a big stuffed frog sitting on top of it because I got into this huge frogging kick for a while. When dusk fell on the lake, the crickets and toads would all rise to start their all-night a cappella of croaks and creaks that echoed off the quiet lap of the water. My brother and my two cousins had all just turned a year old, and after they were tucked in bed, Grandpa and I would head out to the bank of rocks at the shore with a bucket and a flashlight for hunting pet frogs.

"Grandma, did I actually ever catch any?" I ask her.

"Oh sure, sometimes. But by the next morning they would always escape," she starts giggling, "and you would be so confused about why they would want to leave the perfect little life you'd set up for them."

"What, a bucket and some grass?"

"That and a drink of water."

When I was seventeen and going to the prom, Grandma slipped me a tiny box with a stone frog inside. I hugged her, and she told me, "I don't know why, but you always loved these things." I think I must have loved them because it's my first memory of my grandpa and me sharing an interest together. Experiencing the things Grandpa liked gave me a better understanding of who he was . . . and, of course, it fused us together. When I turned twelve I stood elbow-to-elbow with him behind the bar, and he gave me my first taste of a martini. When I graduated from college, he bought me my first stocks and taught me about the market, and in the couple of years before he died he answered my questions about our family tree with off-the-cuff expertise. It didn't matter if nobody else besides us opened the spiral-bound genealogy book together—I felt it was mine and Grandpa's to share. I adored him with such abandon that anything I saw him take an interest in intrigued me too.

As we load up Tucker's uncle's truck with our gear, I tell him, "Wait till you see how I've pulled out all the stops for our first big camping weekend together." I bought a fancy plastic holder to display my fishing license on my person at all times ("on my person"—I'm even picking up the lingo of the Pennsylvania Fishing and Game Commission!), booked a rustic-looking, charming little bed and breakfast, and even ordered my very first pair of hiking boots. (As a demonstration of my enthusiasm to try life his way, I excitedly e-mailed the photo of my new hikers to him, saying, *They're cute, right?* He replied saying how cute they would look after they're caked in mud, and the reality of our adventure sank in for me: *Oh yeah,* I wrote back. *They're gonna get dirty, aren't they?*)

Our polar different attitudes toward preserving the glamour of new hiking boots foreshadows the weekend completely. A beast of a thunderstorm stampedes us just as we pull into the bed and breakfast. I insist on how fun it will be to spend the weekend in the woods during a storm . . . but Tucker says this is going to ruin our fishing. The woman in her mid-sixties who owns the wooded property has decorated the inside of our private cabin with a gaudiness and frill that may have been attractive decor for a séance leader in the 1950s, decked out with shelves of blinking china dolls and an eerily realistic two-foot statue of a little boy peering around a tree.

"This is . . . interesting?" I say.

"We're not doing it with him watching," Tucker replies.

I promptly carry the miniature peeping Tom into the bathroom and set him next to the toilet.

Did he just say "doing it"?

In our raincoats we pile back in the truck to explore the area's antique downtown. It's a singular strip of cars moving at a worm's pace, with a grassy divider separating the two-way lanes. On the right side I spot an art gallery that actually appears to be very modern and cool; on the left Tucker sees a tavern that's known for its burgers and looks like it'll have a game on television. *Try it his way,* I remind myself, watching a man in the gallery draw the shade in the front window.

Tucker's stuffed up, starting with a head cold. I suggest we head straight to eat, thinking maybe getting something in his stomach will do him good. The place is in a happy-hour buzz and my beer is going down easy, but he moans about the noisy crowd and says his sinuses are about to explode. When the waitress comes with our dinner, we immediately ask her for boxes, and Tucker holds his head and his hands as I drive us fast to find a pharmacy. "There, honey, wash it down with water. You'll sleep well tonight."

"I hope," he answers.

I steer us back to the B&B, flicking my high beams to ward off the giant horned elk that are known to wander these roads like pedestrians. Even if he's woozy from the cold medicine, at least we can snuggle, I reason in my head, balancing him up the cabin's stairs and latching the heavy wood door behind us. Tucker goes headfirst for the bed and asks me to scratch his back because it relaxes him. When he's passed out with a NyQuil mustache and snoring on my arm, I pull on flannel pajamas (sexy, I know, but it's grown pretty obvious there's no point in chilly lingerie) and take my time washing my face and brushing my teeth, warming up a cup of tea before I climb in bed.

I wish I'd packed a book.

I move in next to Tucker's ear and whisper, "Honey, I'm making some tea. You want some?"

He slurps up his drool and shakes his head no. I scoot in next to him with an equestrian magazine, remembering how I was so hoping to ride horses this weekend. To entertain myself, I slip into romance-heroine mode, imagining being mounted on a strong dark-haired mare, my curls and pale breasts bouncing with the horse's gallop (it *is* a fantasy, so I *do* have ample breasts for bouncing). I'm wearing a white bare-shouldered top over jeans that are tucked tight into red cowboy boots. The sun lights my hair, and my lips are painted crimson, and who rides up next to me but—

Chris?

No.

You're in Asia, I tell him. *And I'm with my boyfriend, see? You weren't supposed to follow me here.*

I spur my horse to move along, but Chris throws his leg over his saddle and dismounts, blocking my path. He approaches me and encourages me down from the horse, catching me under my arms and lifting me down carefully, so my torso slides slowly against his. We stand staring at each other. He brushes my hair behind my ear and tells me that my face is as beautiful as my mind. He wants us to share our taste in art and music forever and build a life together touring the world—New York, Milan, Paris, the Pacific, anywhere we've ever dreamed. Does that sound like something I could manage? He wants to come home after a long day and drink a glass of cabernet with me at the kitchen table, he wants to try my Tuscan recipes for dinner, he wants his hand to hover over my heart when he makes love to me. He wants to give our children formal names and do yoga with me on Saturdays, and when we have grandchildren, he wants to sell all our properties and buy a house on Treasure Lake.

His stallion nudges at my mare and leads her into the field. *It's just us two,* he says. *How did God create two people with such perfectly similar interests?* Before I can answer, his hands run up to cradle the back of my head and he kisses me gently, the motion of our heads like a first-time slow dance between a couple with natural rhythm.

"What the heck are you reading?" Tucker says. I jump out of my skin, remembering where I am. He throws the sheets off and says, "I gotta take a leak."

IN THE MORNING we brave the wilderness despite the relentless downpour and Tucker's amplifying cold. "This is our only chance to get outside," he says, and it sounds like a threat. "We're leaving first thing tomorrow morning because I don't want to miss the Steelers on TV." I pin my fishing license proudly on my jacket and kick on my hikers like I was born doing this. When we arrive at the canyon, we start down immediately, and by the time we reach the first layer of trees, we're drenched straight through to our underwear.

My mascara is running down my face and I shout to Tucker over the rush of the waterfall. "We're going the whole way, no matter what!"

I expect he'll turn to me and smile at my determination, but he's trucking down the hill so fast that I wonder if he'd rather be doing this alone. About a quarter of the way down the gorge we come to a railed platform and Tucker stops and points. "See all the trout flying down the falls there?" Ah, I do notice the swarms of fish flopping helplessly against the merciless rush. "If this rain stops tomorrow it'd be the perfect time to grab our poles," he says. "Fish are most plentiful after a good rain."

"Oh good, so you're thinking about staying later tomorrow and skipping the game?"

"No."

It's so late in the month that the trees are now barren and our hike is challenged by impossibly wet leaves. Tucker forges ahead as I navigate the trail with the same caution as when the boys in my neighborhood would go swinging on grapevines in the woods. This is wild, and it's beautiful, but it doesn't come naturally to me. My steps are clumsy and subpar. I don't find myself longing for a camera to capture the scenery the way I used to capture the sailboat pond in Central Park on Sundays. I don't think to take note of the mist rising here from Pine Creek like I paused to memorize the Dolomiti Mountains one afternoon in the Alps. And it's not the exotic factor that's leaving me unwowed—I just don't connect with this rugged sportsman approach.

Tucker, on the other hand, is perfectly at home on these trails, and seeing him here in his natural habitat makes me wonder if I should want to give my feelings for him a last-ditch effort. I could drop to my knees and beg him please, let's try to have more in common with each other; please, let's like the same things . . . but he barely seems to remember I'm here. When we reach the bottom of the gorge, he points out the foot-high stone pyramids that couples sometimes build together on the river's shore as a sign of their commitment to travel together and withstand life's elements. "Huh," I say, and we both stand there with our arms crossed, genuinely intrigued. After a minute he turns slowly to lead back uphill. Something about this hike has cemented for me the understanding that this is the end of the trail for us. *Dead end*, I can almost see in front of us in bold letters. *Steep ascent ahead.*

Suffice it for me to say that the rest of the weekend sees this same aware disconnect between us. For dinner we find an impressively metro-looking Italian restaurant. (They even have a Peroni beer sign in the window! You rarely find that outside

New York.) Tucker bellies up to the sleek marble bar so he can watch college football on the wall. I glance at the bistro tables behind us, watching other couples and groups of friends whispering and laughing and passing bottles of wine. "Tucker," I say, "do you want to try the Sicilian pizza with me?" No, he says, he wants chicken wings, and quite frankly there's not enough surface space under our elbows for us to order both.

The bartender asks us, "Are you sure you don't prefer a table? I'll be happy to transfer your tab over."

I look to Tucker. "Sweetie, a table just opened up right behind us, you'd still see the TV perfectly."

"Nah, I'm good here," he says, his eyes fixed on the flat screen over the bartender's head.

When we compromise for our appetizer, it almost appears as though dinner could turn into an engaging experience after all. Tucker's so impressed at his first bite of calamari that he actually unglues his eyes from the TV to look at me. "Wow!" he says. "You were right, this is good!" For dinner he gets a pizza burger, and I order a white pasta bejeweled with tiny clams and mussels that sounded on the menu like a dish I had in Portofino last year. In one of Chris's e-mails last week he went on about the abundance of seafood he ate in Thailand, and while I too had hoped to savor a fresh catch this weekend, the lack of grilled trout will not keep me from enjoying fish altogether. When the dish arrives it resembles Grandpa's famous white spaghetti with anchovies recipe. I twirl into the first bite, and the white wine butter sauce drips down my chin. "Oh my God, Tucker," I say, "you have to try this."

"No thanks," he says. "I have to be in the mood for seafood. Hey, your bra's sticking out."

"Oh." I pull the scoop neck of my sweater up over the lacy cup of my bra, wondering if it's normal for a guy to be so fixated on football that he doesn't even care to admire the cleavage that's heaving right under his nose. Geez, even *I* think my boobs look good in this bra . . .

I pretend that my boyfriend is keeping his energy in reserve and that when we get back to the cabin Tucker will slam the door behind us, take my face and kiss me hard, rip my sweater over my head, and press me up against the wall for a fervent episode of nobody-knows-us-here vacation sex. But instead he announces that he's freezing, and he draws water for a bath. I watch him climb into the tub and sprawl out lazy-boy style, never actually considering that another human might intend to join him in the space as well. "Oh," he says. "You want in?" When he finally makes room for me, our legs tangle up so that I have to throw myself onto my hands and knees to break free. When at last we're almost comfortable and I nestle in against his chest, he informs me that with the steam in the bathroom and the weight of my body against his, he's finding it difficult to breathe.

That officially makes two of us.

The next morning after he smacks the alarm, scratches himself, and mumbles to me to get packing or else we'll be late to catch the Steelers, I decide it's time to draw the line on Tucker's attitude. He asks me whether ten minutes are enough for me to cross the property to the owners' home to grab breakfast for the road and say thank-you for their hospitality. Meanwhile he says he'll pack us up in a hurry. I meet him at the loaded truck with a blueberry muffin, a banana, and a cup of coffee.

"You took fifteen minutes," he says. "Now I'm gonna have

to floor it to get home in time for the game. Oh, why'd you get me coffee?" he whines. "I don't want to have to hold it while I drive."

I stare at him, dumbfounded that he's treating my concern to make sure he eats as an unbearable chore. "I'll hold it, then," I tell him, trying to scoot the truck door open with my hip. "I was trying to feed your cold." Tucker's listening to a game on the radio, and when one of his players scores a touchdown he pauses from shifting the car into drive to grab my shoulder and shake me. The entire cup of coffee projects across us both and the heap of luggage that he's wedged idiotically between us. I find tissues to wipe coffee off my face and Tucker's shirt, but instantly the truck smells like a Starbucks garbage bin trapped inside six square feet.

Ten minutes later we're in the back parking lot of a gas station, desperately scrubbing down the seats of the truck like two old maids over their lord's broken washboard. We work in silence until Tucker suddenly stops scrubbing to point his finger in my face. "I didn't even want to do this weekend," he yells. "This was a waste of money and time."

Slowly I place my hands on my hips, then throw down my rag and slam the truck door from the inside. "Close your door," I tell him. He looks at me, then goes back to scrubbing. *"I said close your goddamn door!"*

Like a maniac I react, diving across him to reach his inside door handle and slamming it with such force that it smashes against Tucker's thigh. I scream with the windows rolled up, only barely concerned that the shrieks in my voice must be carrying out to the busy front parking lot. I tell Tucker how dare he speak to me that way, that we'd both planned this weekend and that I've done everything I can to make it a time for us to try to reconnect. I tell him what the fuck does he care about the money because I've paid for everything for the last three months, and that unless he starts making school as big of a priority as following the NFL is, he better make sure his next girlfriend is as generous a sugar mama as I am.

He slams his fists on the steering wheel. "I do my best for you!" he hollers. Two guys in fluorescent orange pull in and hop out of their truck to examine a tire, but when they see the theater happening inside our windows, they reverse straight out of the lot. "And you know what? We're done!"

"Oh, we're done all right! In fact," I go to open the door, "I'm not riding home with you." Tucker hurries and hits the child-proof lock. "Tucker, you let me out!"

"It's two hours back home, Krissy, just where will you go?" He's challenging me.

"I'll call my dad to come and get me." Then, just for dramatic measure, I rip off my Steelers jersey, revealing a turtleneck underneath. "*Hines Ward?*" I scream, holding the jersey in his face. Then I clench my teeth and roll it up in a ball. "You take it, I hate football. I only bought this because you kept saying how hot girls look in jerseys." I hold it back to launch it in his face. "Who *says* that to his girlfriend?"

He catches my arm mid-toss, clenching his fingers hard around my wrist. His face gets in mine and he's talking through his teeth: "You throw like a girl."

"*I am a girl!*" I wrangle my wrist from out of his fist and cradle it gently against me with my other arm.

Tucker slams the truck in reverse and whips out of the parking lot too fast for anyone to get down his license plate. Down the road I'm bawling with my head in my hands, ashamed at the monster this relationship has just brought out in me. I've been here before, years ago in an interminable high school first love where I lost all control, along with the rest of myself, to what he wanted. This is the point of no return—we have crossed every boundary of respect for one another. "Look at us, Tucker," I say between hyperventilations. "We're not happy!"

"Yes we are." He takes deep breaths through his nose and lets them out calmly. "Just don't talk."

For the next two hours I concentrate hard out the window, with my hand holding my chin firmly to keep it from quivering. I stare into the gray Sunday fog and the dismal, skeletal trees with their branches reaching up, begging the sky for sun. By the time we arrive back in Treasure Lake two hours later, my face is too red and puffy to go straight home. Tucker tries to lighten the mood by suggesting we order a pizza, but I tell him I'm not hungry. "Why," I mutter. "Are you?"

"Nah."

We drive in silence to the Landing, and when I sit on the couch adjacent to where he's sitting, he asks me to move next to him. Part of me wants to . . . but I hesitate. I feel like we shouldn't be here together at all. I feel like the whole world heard our fight today, our animalistic display of *Springer*-style drama. And the shame is only one of the symptoms that this relationship is dying. My head's booming, my heart aches, and my wrist throbs from Tucker's grip. This is not the kind of love my family raised me to accept. Before he leaves the Landing, he hugs me and sobs into my neck, saying he's sorry. "What can I do to make you forgive me?" he asks.

I shake my head and pull away from him. "I don't know." I find myself holding my wrist, even though it's not hurting now. "Tucker," I say, "I don't want to get melodramatic here so I'll just say it. I planned this weekend for us to enjoy together, and I know you agree that it was awful."

He looks at the ground.

"I feel like we don't have fun anymore. I think I saw you smile three times all weekend. And everything you wanted to do, I wanted the opposite."

"Well, why didn't you say so?"

"Because I wanted to try it, for your sake. I thought maybe I could be interested in the same things you're interested in, and maybe I could, except we're not . . ." I search for the right word. ". . . connected to each other. I just feel like . . . this is really hard to say. But I feel like we're too different."

"You want things that I can't give you," he says.

"No. I want things that you *won't* give me. There's a difference. We don't want the same things in life."

"What do you mean?"

I tell him that I don't want my weekends to revolve around whatever football game is on TV. On Friday nights, just sometimes, I want a break from pizza and wings to relax with a glass of wine and cheese, or sushi.

"Hey, I liked sushi when you made me try it!"

"Tucker, you said it was little and raw." The two characteristics that make sushi an appealing dish to many people are the two characteristics that Tucker spotted as its tragic flaws. I point out how every time we drive past a house sitting high on a country hill, he sighs in longing while the thought of being so far removed from other people makes me start to panic. He likes trucks; I prefer cars. I like passionate, dynamic sex that could go all night; he's turned into a wham-bam four-minute man. I used to live abroad; he thinks a passport is pointless. He's a little bit country; I'm a little more rock and roll. I say tomato, and he says . . . McDonald's. Our lifestyles are completely different, I explain.

"Maybe," he says. "I think I caught a glimpse of your old life in that Italian restaurant last night."

"Really?" I ask him. "When?"

"The waitress told you she always wanted to live in New York, and you said how amazing it was, how you were never bored and how every girl who ever wanted to live there should try it. And then the owner came over and started speaking Italian with you." I'd forgotten about that. "Your eyes went all excited like you were hosting a TV show, and you were talking with your hands. And even though I'd never seen that side of you, you just seemed more . . . yourself."

"Wow." He's more observant than I give him credit for.

"And I know you need somebody with a lot of goals who finds a lot of happiness in what he does . . . but for me, I just don't know what that is yet."

I know that everything he's saying is true, but I want to protest—somehow this has turned into *him* breaking up with *me*. I watch him staring at the ground, that long, far-off face that's recently turned so familiar. Tucker doesn't know what he wants to do with his life yet, and he's blaming himself for it. I can't keep piling my own needs and plans and expectations on him. He and I have to worry about ourselves now.

TONIGHT I MOVE my vitamins and hand lotion and holy water onto the nightstand in the guest room to prepare for my bedtime routine. Ever since high school, I don't like sleeping in my own bed after a breakup. In the morning I need to wake up to new scenery, to light jutting in from a new angle, to the sense that a new day has the chance to start in a fresh space. I feel like my own mattress might swallow me whole in its defeated embrace. Plus the firm pillow I brought in from my bed smells like Tucker from our sleepover the night before we went camping. Stupidly I had insisted we should spend every waking minute of the weekend together.

I know this breakup is the right thing; I understand perfectly well that Tucker and I weren't cut out for the long term—but it doesn't change the fact that I've just lost another man I care about. It will feel lonely at lunchtime not to get his usual call; not to have a happy hour buddy on Friday nights; not to reply to the half-dozen weddings I have coming up with a plus-one. I didn't move back home to be alone, but here I am, hoisting myself high onto the guest bed—a queen-size, which I haven't slept in since I stayed in London with Adam Hunt. On the nightstand there's a photo of Grandma and Grandpa at my cousin's coming-out ball in St. Louis a few years ago. Grandpa's decked out in a sharp tuxedo with a sleek satin vest and bow tie, and Grandma's in a long indigo gown with crystalline drops dangling from her ears and around her neck. Grandpa's arm folds protectively around Grandma's shoulders, and while their torsos are touching securely, they're both very comfortable and relaxed. Into Grandpa's intense eyes I say, "I want someone like you." Warm, dashing, self-assured. He smiles back to promise me that amazing men exist.

I can't believe I feel *so sad* about this, as though I didn't see it coming. There's no confusion, nothing to analyze, nothing to talk about; yet I'm burning to just blurt out to someone: "Tucker and I are done." I don't want to tell Mom because she'd warned me this would happen . . . and e-mailing Chris would just smudge the boundaries of his role in my life even more. Can I call Grandma? No. It's nearing three. I'm sure she's been in bed since right after *60 Minutes*.

At some point sleep must have heard my pleas, because I wake up with the sun blasting through the guest room window. My eyes feel hot and still heavy, my whole body sore from such little rest. I could keep sleeping, I think, but the sun doesn't look like she'll allow it. Downstairs I hear the jarring open and close of cupboards, the stem of a wooden spoon pounding against a pot.

I need coffee.

In the kitchen, Mom is orbiting between her counters, still in her pajamas with the dogs at her feet. "Good morning, sunny day," she says as I waddle in for a hug. "Uh-oh, somebody didn't sleep well."

"No." I duck under her arm for a spoon. "But I better test your sauce."

"We used up all of Grandma's when we were there for Grandpa's birthday. I want to send her a few containers just to have in the freezer."

I tell Mom I'll run it in this afternoon, then call Grandma

to tell her I'll be heading into town shortly. Does she need anything?

Her request is this: "Just you."

I DECIDE AGAINST the mile-a-minute Hollywood entrance that I feel I could bring through Grandma's front door. *Our weekend was terrible and we got in a fight and he hurt me and just look at the bruises* . . . Then I'd wipe my nose with my sleeve, too distraught over my romance gone wrong to hold any regard for manners. *And I didn't even catch a fish!* At this point I'd crumble into a lifeless pile on the ground, wailing at Grandma's feet like an infamous sinner in the Bible. *Please, heal me!*

Instead Grandma ushers me inside, wiping her hands on a dish towel. "You're coming in with a full load and you'll leave with a full load!" she says. "I'm baking bran muffins for your hou—*whoa*," she says, grabbing the edge of her counter as her focus meets my face. "You look like you haven't slept in days."

Under her gaze I feel a massive pimple rising from under the skin on my chin. It's going to be one of those mean kind that Celeste once nicknamed a "rude tenant" because they refuse to vacate for weeks after you demand them to, and they always leave a mess.

"Traveling this weekend sure took it out of you, didn't it?"

"Yeah, Grandma." How do I tell her that I'm dense and as it turns out I don't understand anything she's been trying to show me about men and women. "I need to understand something, and I need you to give it to me straight." Today I've actually carried a notebook with me, reasoning that if I take down Grandma's love lessons in the scholastic manner in which I approach every other goal in my life, maybe I'll finally learn their real-world application. (Yet I call myself out for employing this science-project lingo. When will I learn to stop hiding my emotions behind my intellect?)

Grandma asks do I want something to drink?

No, thank you.

Can she offer me a snack?

Really, Grandma, that's generous, but I have no appetite.

Would I like a pencil with an eraser?

No, I'll take these notes raw. Nothing will be erased, and I'll be writing every word. I need Grandma to point out for me the difference between compromise and losing yourself in another person. I ask her to shed light on the characteristics behind couples that just . . . *go well* together. I just spent the past weekend trying to muster up interests in someone else's passions, and it wound up hurting us both. When will my longing to bond with another person stop being so lethal—most of all, for me?

I swallow Grandma's words like she's just pulled the lever on an M&M machine, consuming every piece of insight till I'm totally spent and my brain is full. I ask her to be as clear and straightforward as possible so as to shed a candid light on what I'm not getting.

As she has explained to me, Grandpa was, in her words, "looking for his career." She says by now it should be clear to me that his work goals were his priority.

Okay. I follow.

And she reemphasizes the fact that she had a choice whether she was going to accept that or not. It was a choice she made every day, over and over, and she always chose to choose it. It was an independent decision, and she lived with it, even when she'd accompany him to a meeting, sitting out in the reception room waiting for him because, as she explained, "I wasn't allowed inside." She wasn't allowed inside the building because she was a woman.

And she has no regrets. All her life she *chose* to be okay with this.

But when she was little, she was born to a single mother and raised by four adults: her mother's sister, her mother's brother, her grandpa, and, least involved, by her own mother. My great-grandma made it very clear through her languid parenting that Grandma's birth was not planned and her existence was to be merely tolerated. She was the result of a relationship that she was always forbidden to talk about—

"Grandma, wait," I say. "Who forbade you to ask?"

"My mother's sister. The message was, 'Just don't ask who your father is, you'll upset your mother.'"

"Ah, okay. Please, go on."

Grandma opens up about something that I'd always gathered just based on hints she'd dropped: she had a very lonely child-hood. She grew up in a big Victorian house full of rather stuffy adults who could hardly be bothered by the existence of this precious little girl in their midst, longing to be adored. Grandma says they always had cats, but the house was so strict that never once did the cats set foot outside. She went to the Catholic school (one that has a minuscule enrollment today, let alone seven de-cades ago when the entire grade school fit in the same classroom) and didn't have many friends her age because she was very shy (thanks to the lack of confidence being fostered at home).

I remember my great-grandmother. Before she died when I was nine, she always wore her fingernails long and polished with fire-engine red. She wore big, bold jewelry and bright glossy lipstick. She never smiled, and she was always reading. When we'd go to visit her in the high-rise, she'd click her fingernails slowly on the wooden arm of her rocker, as if she were a queen waiting for us to either do something to piss her off or to leave. My dad told me a few years ago that she used to sleep for days on end and that when he puts it all together, he thinks she suffered from severe depression. Whoever Grandma's father was, it seemed like Grandma Leona lost herself when she lost him. She lived her entire life like the ghost of a woman after he left her.

"When I was little," Grandma raises her voice to drive this point home, "*I wanted six kids.*"

"You *did?*"

She dips her head with certainty. "I did. That was my goal. I wanted a lot of kids, and a lot of activity. And I did have six pregnancies, but the one after your dad, you know, I lost. I wanted to make sure that when I grew up, my life wouldn't be lonely and boring like my childhood was." Her voice drops with her gaze. "I just don't have happy memories of my childhood."

Got it.

Grandma reminds me that it was just a few weeks ago when she told me that I had to figure out what I wanted for *myself* before I could lock anyone else into my dreams.

Right . . .

So, here's the equation: she knew what she wanted—kids— and Grandpa knew what he wanted—success. And when they united their lives, they were both able to achieve their individual goals. The price that came with it, all those dinners without Grandpa present with the kids, having to wait for him in the reception area of office buildings? "I just accepted all that as a part of my life," Grandma says. "I was always up for it."

Then she continues, asking me to promise never to tell anyone whom she's about to refer to. I agree. So she tells me a story about a couple she and Grandpa knew who had a miserable marriage for many years. "Everything had to be just so with her," Grandma says, referring to the wife. "She always made the decisions for him and he was just so *weak*, but away from her, he could be really talented."

"In his work, you mean?"

"Yes, in his work. In everything, really. Their families came from different backgrounds, and hers was *very* traditional, and he had to give up the way he did everything to be with her."

"Such as . . ."

"Such as the way he celebrated the holidays. It always had to be done her family's way, and he never got to be with his side of the family. And at social gatherings, everybody had to wait for her. She was out to show that," Grandma sticks out her chest, "'Others will have to do what I want.' She was a selfish, self-serving, self-centered woman." Grandma explains that the gentleman she's talking about had to live for a long time with none of his own needs fulfilled. He ignored the promises and the desires that he'd once held for his life. He lost himself.

"He lived his whole life that way?"

"Oh, not his whole life," she says, and suddenly it's as though she's got something up her sleeve. "Eventually he got fed up with her badgering and then it turned the opposite way, where he always tried to keep so much from her. As long as she didn't know anything he was doing, they got along fine. Your grandpa never would have married a person like that."

Then what kind of a woman was Grandpa looking to marry? Or more pointedly, what should we all be looking for in a partner? I also wonder whether the old saying "Timing is everything" is a cliché, or if there's really something to it. In my experience there have been moments when it's seemed as though I'd found *the perfect person*, but we reached a fork in the road and painfully parted ways (or at least *I* was pained, thankyouverymuch, Adam Hunt). Could it simply be that the timing was off? I ask Grandma how she knew that all the circumstances between her and Grandpa were lined up for her to commit to him forever.

"I liked him in school," she says, "but he claims he did not know me . . . which shows you the two different levels we were on. If we'd gotten together in high school, it wouldn't have worked out. The point of a relationship is for two people to grow together. Your grandpa needed a few years to mature and figure out what he wanted to make of himself."

"And all that happened when he was in the service."

"I would say so, yes. When I saw him at the ice cream store on that Saturday night that I've told you about, he and the guys were holding windows up in the front." Which explains where the term *hanging out* comes from—before the days of air-conditioning, when young people wanted to socialize, they'd open up the windows and doors in whichever establishment they chose to congregate and stick their heads outside to chat with friends and passersby.

Grandma says Grandpa sort of captured her that night. He was the same handsome, charismatic boy she knew from school, but he actually picked up on how unique she was. "See, Kris, you want someone on your same intellectual, emotional level." She explains that when the right partner comes along for me, no, we won't have serious conversations *all* the time, but when we do, I have to feel that he bears an impeccable capacity for hearing me—not just the words I speak, but the desires in life that radiate from inside me. He'll see all that, and he'll choose it. My hopes won't be a threat or a turnoff; he won't make me feel too high-maintenance or complex. In turn I'll prioritize his goals as if they were as important as my own—and sometimes even more important than mine. And, this will bring me some of the greatest fulfillment I'll ever experience.

When I think about what Grandma's saying, I realize that this is exactly what was missing with Tucker.

"And this next part is the most important thing I'm gonna tell you."

"Okay."

"I know I cared about what Grandpa was doing when he was away from me—"

"You mean you were suspicious he was spending time with other women?" I've wondered at times how Grandma dealt with all his traveling . . . didn't she have her suspicions?

She squeals, "No, no!"

Okay, guess not.

"I'm saying I cared about what he was doing when he was away from me, which, as I've told you, was often. So when we found a moment, we'd check in with each other. Then as long as everything was okay, we both went back to our work." The bottom line? "You live your life, and he lives his."

Wow, I actually really like that.

She continues, as one by one she places muffins into a plastic container for me to tote home. "Look here, for example: the muffins on the bottom have dates and walnuts—they're for your mother. The plain ones are for your dad, he's hated nuts since he was a baby. When your mom makes my muffin recipe, does she put walnuts in all of them?"

"No. She sticks a plain batch in the oven for Dad, then adds berries or walnuts to whatever's left of the batter for herself."

"Right, so you see? She and your dad don't always have the same opinions of things, but they don't force their likes on one another."

"But they share the same values," I muse, getting her point, "which is why they're both eating bran muffins in the first place—to be healthy." I think of the fresh fish Chris got me craving, versus the chicken wings drowning in grease that Tucker had eaten the other night. It's growing clear why I feel like I connect so much more with someone like Chris, someone who enjoys growing and trying new things; a man who loves reading books and finding work in different countries and brainstorming ways to help others form themselves into the people they were made to be. Football and pickup trucks just don't inspire me that way . . . and that's essentially a microcosm of why Tucker and I broke up last night.

Grandma places the last of the muffins inside the plastic container and seals the lid. "Remember, plain on bottom, dates and walnuts on top."

"Okay." The concentration that's occupying my face isn't about that, though. I'm still trying to process everything we've just discussed.

My hard face makes Grandma giggle, startling me from picking up my purse from her foyer floor. "It's easy, my dear," she says, coming over for a hug and saying into my ear: "Your role is to be an individual," I pull away and look in her eyes, "and to let your partner be one too."

In the car going home I try to repeat Grandma's lesson, but in Italian. *"Il tuo lavoro è essere la persona che vuoi, e lesche il tuo fidanzato essere una persona anche."* It's preschool-level translation, but the trills and rolls off my tongue thrill me. I hadn't realized how much I missed speaking Italian until the dinner the other night when the restaurant owner and I chatted in front of Tucker. With my hands going and my voice rising and falling with the delicious drama of the words, I carry on a one-sided conversation with my great-grandma Angeladea (which translates beautifully to "angel of God"), figuring she's the only person I know who can hear my Italian in heaven. *"Nonna,"* I ask her, *"per favore, com'è hai capito che il mio biznonno era il giusto signore per te?"* How did you know my great-grandpa was the right man for you?

Grandma Angela was Grandma's mother-in-law, and in the early years of Grandma's marriage, Grandma Glo says that Angela didn't take to her. Grandma says she doesn't know why, but I think maybe it's because Angela liked women with a lot of backbone. When I was little my great-grandma once instructed me in her thick Italian accent not to have a baby until I finished college, and whatever I do, to marry a man who's nice to me. It's widely considered that my grandpa got his independent manner of thinking and his degree of likability from his mother, and there are two stories about Grandma Angela that I love to play over in my head.

In one story, when my parents first got married, they went to visit Grandma Angela in the apartment she kept after my great-grandpa Zaccharia died in the late seventies. In front of my parents her parrot kept singing the phrase in English, "Son of a bitch, son of a bitch!" Grandma Angela looked at my parents and said, "I don't know *whosa* teaching that bird to swear," and my dad told her, "It's you, Grandma! He's speaking with your accent!" They say she threw her head back and laughed till she had to wipe the tears from her eyes.

I find the other story to be just as adorable, but much more telling about the strength of Grandma Angela's character. After she and Grandpa Zachary (as we refer to him now) had gotten their near-dozen kids settled on their farm in Pennsylvania, Grandpa Zach got involved in some entrepreneurial endeavors. He did considerably well for an immigrant but was away from home a lot (I suppose Grandpa got this trait from his dad), and Grandma Angela was finding structural issues around their house that needed tending-to. The water pump in the yard was terribly slow and needed to be replaced, and she had been asking Zachary to buy her a new one so she could do her ten kids' laundry and her other work around the house. Story has it that Zachary wasn't intentionally putting her off but his projects kept getting in the way, until one day while he was out, Grandma Angela was juggling babies and dinner and laundry . . . and the water just stopped running. She went out to the pump with a hatchet and beat the living terror out of it. When it finally lay in ruins across the backyard, she brushed her hands, satisfied. Then when Grandpa Zachary got home, she told him calmly, "The water pump broke today. We need a new one." The next day he had a team of friends in the yard installing a state-of-the-art pump.

It's the only story I've ever heard that paints Grandma Angela as anything but lovable and kind, but she was tough when she needed to be. She made it clear that a woman's needs and requests are just as important as a man's . . . but I wonder if Grandma Glo's unwillingness to speak up in her marriage got on her mother-in-law's nerves.

I imagine Grandma Angela looking down now and laughing, both at my poor relationship judgment and my poor Italian. *Sempre fai la cosa furba nel momento importante. La piu bene via al paradiso è vivere come si sta gia li—senza la paura. Sei unica. Esista come la persona sei nata essere, e il giusto signore arriverà.* You always do the smart thing at the important moment. The best way to get to your heaven is to live like you're already there—fearlessly. You're unique. Just exist as the person you are, and the right man will arrive in your life.

"Ah," I tell her, my voice quieting, "*forse hai ragione, Nonna.*" She's right. I realize that thanks to the women who came before me, I'm not alone in this conversation after all.

7

Be Prepared to Forgive

MY PARENTS RARELY FIGHT. Sure, I remember a few unpleasant exchanges between them when I was a kid—Mom would spend too much shopping, or Dad would stay out with his buddies too late. But really, for pretty much my whole life I've seen them demonstrate a mutual regard and a fondness that they both know they'd miss terribly if they didn't have each other.

This is why to this day I find it strange that they've never come up with a solution for their annual holiday fallout, which kicks off every holiday season with a less than joyous sputter. The Christmas conflict tends to start with the tree. Dad goes to a farm to chop his own stock, and upon his return in the company truck, Mom stands in the doorway resting her elbow on her wrist in assessment. Hm. What made you go taller this year, Bill? Was the blue spruce all they had? What the heck, did a bear attack this? We don't have ornaments big enough to disguise all these bald spots.

From there it generally escalates, with holiday decorating malfunctions foiling all the fun. The tinsel seems to have shrunk from last year and won't wrap the whole way up the banister, then it looks like someone's misplaced the dogs' stockings—where will we stuff their Dingo snacks?! To top it off (literally), the motorized Santa Claus that we stick on top of the tree sounds like he's dropped his tranny. He waves out to the living room with his hips wiggling suggestively as if he's on a mechanical bull, but the horse carousel he's riding no longer rises and falls with holiday glee.

I remember outgrowing all the holiday thrill right about when I turned twenty-three. By that time the holidays had come to mean leaving work early after a jam-packed day and rushing to Penn Station for eight hours on the Amtrak. I'd arrive home, throw on my sweats, and somehow manage to gain eight pounds in three days, and then immediately tell the family a tearful but rushed goodbye. Plus, I'd climb back on the train to the city with none of my new presents in tow, because they wouldn't fit in my suitcase . . . or my apartment. That period was when I realized why so many people actually dread the holidays: no matter how much you love your family, getting together with them can present some challenges.

But last year at least Grandpa was still here. I'd been miserable in Milan for Thanksgiving, and my friends and I tried to celebrate by improvising a pumpkin pie recipe. The Italians only use fresh pumpkin, so we had to boil it down and puree it, and when we couldn't find brown sugar, we used maple syrup instead. When the pies were finished, they were in fact beautiful, and all night we sat indulging in individual mini-pumpkin pies with a buttery biscotti crust instead of dough. However, I remember feeling that eating a pumpkin pie after a dinner of pasta and salad didn't exactly scream "patriotic," and no matter how grateful I was for the friends surrounding me . . . they still weren't my family. Mom had called me Thanksgiving morning, her time, as she was pulling the turkey out of the oven and bustling for the family to arrive, just as I was picking up the kids I nannied during the usual school run. On my bike, carting little Alfonso to swim class, I dodged the angry afternoon rush of Vespas (no wonder the word translates to "wasp") and vowed never to spend another Thanksgiving away from America again.

Then for Christmas, I flew home. It took me a while to get ready for my aunt's house because I wanted to look really lovely to see everyone for the first time in the six months since I'd moved to Europe. I wore a curvy black wraparound dress that I'd bought in Venice, with jeweled satin heels on my feet. I did my hair big and curly and then could *not* find the right necklace to go with it . . . until I invaded Mom's jewelry box and found a large rhinestone ornament hanging from five layers of clear, intricate beads. When I arrived at dinner, I made great fanfare of gathering all the cousins for a photo op in front of Aunt Lori's jumbo tree, and between camera flashes I kept glancing across the room at Grandpa, who was smiling at his grown-up grandkids' commotion. But, there was no missing it: he was seated in a wheelchair.

I carried on more festively than ever, engaging in toasts and laughter and Guitar Hero as though it wasn't difficult to see

Grandpa that way. I would catch his eye and wink, pretending for his sake—and for mine—that the holiday gathering was like any one before it, even though we all silently understood that this would be the last one we'd have with him. A month later when Grandpa died and I pulled on the same black dress to give his eulogy, I realized why I'd gone to all the trouble trying to look so lovely at Christmas: I knew it was the last time he'd ever see me dressed up.

This year I'm feeling an aching pulse in my stomach, wondering how in the world the family's expected to celebrate when the person we love the most won't be here. Aunt Anna, the wife of Grandpa's youngest brother (and my great-aunt who taught me to make gnocchi when I was eight), sends me an e-mail the week before Thanksgiving:

Hello Dear,

Hope you and your family will have a great Thanksgiving with your grandma. She said anticipating the holidays makes her blue. That's the time when we miss our loved ones the most.

You take care, God bless you.

Love,

Aunt Anna and Uncle Frank

xxooxx

As part of their bereavement aftercare program, the hospice nurses have advised Grandma that some families choose to acknowledge a deceased loved one's absence by placing an empty seat at the dinner table for them. Grandma says no, *no way* could she stand that. I, on the other hand, wonder if it would be worth a try, but I can't criticize or push her. If I'm having a hard time preparing for the holidays minus Grandpa, I can't even imagine what Grandma's experiencing right now. She's been going out of her way to avoid department stores, with their decorations and Christmas music, saying that the holiday spirit is affecting her in exactly the opposite manner it's supposed to.

Two Sundays before Thanksgiving she and I attend a grief lecture together at the hospital. It's called "Holiday Hope," a talk on coping with the season's festivities in the first year after a family member has passed away. From the information Grandma told me, it sounds as though it should be geared toward widows. But I can tell that she's not feeling totally brave about the thought of going alone, and anyway, I'm interested in the psychological aspect of what they have to say.

When we arrive, the dozen folks around the table are actually all different ages. Grandma's getting herself a miniature bottle of water when I hear the woman who's seated across from us tell her husband she doesn't think she's going to handle this very well. I gather they've lost a child. As people solemnly file in they fill out a ticket to win the door prize, then at a long table against the wall they can collect colorful little pamphlets on the normal stages of grieving and how to brace oneself for the holidays. Grandma takes a few, whispering that most of them are probably too grave for her. I collect one of everything.

The speaker is a tall woman who looks to be in her early

sixties but whose skin somehow appears weathered beyond her years. She has her doctorate in education and usually speaks on how to help children grieve, but when she sits down in the middle of the U-shaped table, she reveals why her eyes appear so benevolently exhausted. When she was twenty-eight with two little kids, she lost her husband suddenly to cancer, and then when her son was twenty-seven, he was killed in a hunting accident. She says she can relate to the grieving process because she's experienced it firsthand, twice. Three decades after her husband's death, she tears up telling us that just before Thanksgiving on his deathbed, he had arranged for the hospital Santa Claus to visit his children at their home after he passed.

The woman tells us that when tragedy struck her, she realized she had to take care of her own needs and shut out the "shoulds" that people were throwing in her face: you *should* celebrate the holidays the same way you always have, you *should* put on a smile in front of your family, you *should* work on getting over this loss by this time next year. But exactly thirty-three years have passed since her husband died, she says, and while the pain lessens, you never "get over" death. She says we're never the same person after we lose a close loved one.

"The holidays mean family," she says, "but this year, for you, someone who's supposed to be there isn't." For a person who's lost someone close to them, the holidays present a period of what she calls "regrieving," or experiencing the sharpness and sadness of the immediate loss all over again. "Those people are still part of the family after they die," she says, and out of the corner of my eye I can see Grandma wiping under her glasses with a tissue.

But, our speaker explains, hope is the one thing that gets us through the tough times in our lives. We can have hope that the holidays will bring joy again one day instead of such desperate sadness. Also, she says, we can keep a special candle on the table or an object on the tree to express that "this is what that person meant to me, and this is what I have left of them." We may not be able to see them physically, but we can remember them with an ornament, a bursting poinsettia, some visible representation that the person who's passed is still present in our heart and in our home. She adds that this keeps the memory of their physicality close, helping to maintain the hope that, if you're a religious person, you'll see your loved one again in heaven or in whatever afterlife you believe in.

At the end of the talk she holds a small ceremony, lighting four candles and leading us through a verse:

We light these candles in honor of you, our lost loved one. We light one for grief, one for courage, one for memories, and one for love.

This first candle represents our grief. The pain of losing you is intense. It reminds us of the depth of our love for you.

This second candle represents our courage: to confront our sorrow, to comfort each other, to change our lives.

This third candle is our memory of you—the times we laughed, the times we cried, the times we were angry with each other, the silly things you did, the caring and joy you gave us.

This final light is the light of love. As we enter this holiday season, day by day we cherish the special place in our hearts that will always be reserved for you. We thank you for the gift that your living brought to each of us.

I quietly rub Grandma's shoulder as she sniffles loudly with the rest of the group. The leader walks around to light the votive candles that are placed in front of each of us. I'm seated at the end of the table, so she lights my candle first. "We light this candle in memory of . . ."

Oh, she wants me to answer. "George Gasbarre."

She proceeds on to Grandma. "We light this candle in memory of . . ."

Grandma takes a deep breath and pauses between the two words for strength: "George . . . Gasbarre."

Then she allows us each to choose a translucent ornament from a box. She explains that we'll open the bulb, write a tiny note to our loved one, and stick it inside. I say to Grandma, "What color bulb would you like?"

"Green or blue."

"Me too! How about you take one and I'll take the other."

Grandma selects the green, I think because it reminds her of Grandpa's logo and because it was his favorite color. I take the blue because it reminds me of Grandpa's eyes.

And, in its sparkly shade of ocean, it reminds me of Chris's eyes too.

I fold my note so my words are hidden and private, but Grandma surprises me when she lets her note face out. I wonder if she's curious to see what I've written; how I've told Grandpa that everything I do is for him, that I know he's taking care of every detail in my life, and that I love him.

When I catch a glimpse of Grandma's note, I can see part of what she's written to Grandpa: *You are the light of my life.*

The following Friday—one week before Thanksgiving—we're not even out of the airport parking lot and Chris is dialing his phone. He has six weeks' worth of patient follow-ups this weekend, he says, and I try to sympathize, but I make the appearance of sympathizing, I'm so nervous to be sitting next to him again that I barely hear his words. He's all splashed out in veteran travel gear: cool nylon cargo pants and a sleek black track jacket, meanwhile sporting his old college baseball cap over smooth hair. He just has this one call to make right now, he whispers over his receiver, and then he wants to tell me all about the trip. I nod and reach out to the cup holder for my iced coffee, trying to act casual.

In the first two minutes of his call he fumbles with my navigation system, searching frantically for the Down volume. *Okay, this is gonna drive me nuts*, he mouths to me, pointing at the electronic box sitting on my dash.

"I need her," I whisper. "I don't know Newark." He crashes defeated into his headrest but then stays calm through the rest of the call, arranging a meeting with a colleague on Monday after a full weekend's sleep to get back on East Coast time. When he hangs up, he's shaken off the attitude and wants to know what's new with me.

"Well, I sold two stories in the last six weeks, which made me pretty happy," I say. "And then, well, this isn't quite as happy . . . Tucker and I split."

"I'm really sorry to hear that." A piece of me is hoping that he's not being sincere. I'm fine with it, I tell him. These things happen, and I actually feel a lot more centered. "If you're more centered, that says a lot," he replies.

"That's what I figure. I've lost six pounds just from cutting out the pizza and beer."

"I was gonna say, you look fantastic."

"Yeah?"

"Yeah, super."

"Although . . . I'm embarrassed pointing this out, but what do you think's going on with my face?"

"You're having a little breakout situation, eh?"

"I'm on the oral antibiotic you gave me, but for some reason it's not helping."

"Are you on birth control?"

Whaaa! Where is he going with this? "Um, well . . . I . . . was."

"When?"

"Until . . . two weeks ago."

"Well, see, we may want to talk about going back on that, because the hormones can help regulate—"

"Chris, I really try to be mindful of taking that kind of thing when it's not necessary. There's nothing about my cycle that isn't right as rain on its own." Oh. My. God. Not only have I answered his question, but I also have just found an ingenious way of informing him that my reproductive system is favorable for childbearing.

Just—you know—in case he'd ever wondered.

We both sit silently a second. "Okay then," he says, apparently satisfied but backing off. "That's excellent news, actually. That's something you don't hear many women say."

"I just hate messing with nature. But," I tap gently on my chin, "I seriously do need to see this clear up."

He says I can come into the office tomorrow morning; it'll be Saturday and he only has one procedure. "And for now," he reaches into his backpack between his legs on the floor, "forget anything you've ever heard about chocolate exacerbating a breakout. It's totally untrue." He pulls out a brown glossy box wrapped in a sleek pink ribbon. "Sorry, but it's so worth it. Indonesian dark chocolate. Kris, it's amazing."

"Oh, whoa." With my eyes on the road I locate a smooth cube, a superdark chocolate that Chris thinks has orange liqueur inside. I bite in. Yep, orange. It bursts onto my tongue and melts in with the chocolate inside my cheeks. Incredible. After we've polished off a minibox, we start in on the snacks I packed in the back—bananas, oranges, and organic graham crackers.

"These graham crackers are good!" he says.

"Right?" I hold out my hand, and he cups a bunch of tiny bear-shaped crackers into it.

During the five-hour ride he catches me up on his trip—how warmly the hospital administrators received him and showed him around, how smoothly his presentation went, and how different the customs are there. He explains how immediate the culture of Southeast Asia is, with an openness and warmth one just doesn't find in America. "Even the administrators, Kris, they'll be in the middle of a business conversation with you and they'll just reach over and do this." He places his hand over mine on the steering wheel and rests it there. Immediately the contact of his skin on mine sets off a tickle of electricity beneath my belly button.

I feel my eyelashes flick sheepishly, and involuntarily, my throat clears. "They must be friendly," I say quietly.

"They are." He removes his hand.

When we arrive back in town we stop at the hospital to see a sixteen-year-old patient who slammed into a tree driving her friend's truck. Chris introduces me simply as Krissy and makes no attempt to justify my role there. He takes the bandage off from around the girl's dread-locked head to examine where her jaw's been fractured. "Was there maybe a little alcohol involved here, hun?" he asks the girl, whose tattooed arm is wrapped protectively around a beat-up acoustic guitar.

Through a wired-shut bite she replies, "I don't know."

"I see."

"Actually, there was maybe a little alcohol involved."

"There was, okay. I just need to know this stuff because if there are still any substances in your system, it can affect how your body reacts to the treatment. I'm not trying to put you on the spot."

"Okay."

Chris asks the girl why doesn't she play something on her guitar for us. "I'm not that good," she answers. She's wearing a

Led Zeppelin T-shirt and baggy jeans with a mangled hem that dangles down way past her feet.

"Please," I coax. "I love the guitar." The girl taps on the guitar's neck, and I can read that she's considering whether she wants to open up to us. She shrugs, then breaks into a few tough measures that face down conflict like an abused dog that's finally full-grown and has learned to fight back. On the last note her ring finger wiggles heavy on the string—a lonely vibrato note that communicates resignation to defeat.

"See?" I say. "That was awesome."

"You came up with that?" Chris asks incredulously.

"Yeah," she chuckles, embarrassed. Chris shakes her hand and tells her he'll check on her over the weekend. "Oh, hey, do you feel like you're in the bathroom a lot?" he asks.

She thinks a second. "Yeah, I guess I have been."

"Okay, I'm gonna have the nurses turn down your IV. You're probably just a little more hydrated than you need to be."

"Hey, Doctor," the girl says, obviously shy about how to address Chris. He turns around. "You gotta get me out of here soon. I don't have any insurance. And my parents . . . they got enough problems."

"We'll take care of it, honey," Chris says. It sooths me when he speaks affectionately to his patients. "The only thing you worry about is healing up, and I need you in here another week."

I stay arm-to-arm with him as we exit the hospital, sweeping straight past the necks behind the nurses' desk that are stretching out one by one like a single file of ducks. It's wild fun to leave them suffering over who that is with Dr. Christopher.

These are the same hospital halls I navigated with Grandma just last week when we came for the holiday grieving lecture, except she and I stood at every crossroads in the corridor scratching our heads and wandering aimlessly. "Your grandpa was always the one who had a knack for directions," she'd said.

"I know," I told her, "and unfortunately it's something I didn't inherit from him." I was impressed, though, when eventually her instincts led us to the correct room, but here with Chris it's completely different. We cruise fast through the halls, and with the scan of his ID badge he gains bold access through even the tightest locked-down doors. Although, as I hustle along with him, it's not his status that wows me as much as his expertise—how does he get a kid who was drinking underage and who clearly can't afford to pay her hospital bill to confess to the fact that her illegal activity and bad judgment is what brought all of us into this sad scenario together? And then who so kindly considers to ask the girl if she's uncomfortable because she's peeing too much? Chris has a way of sauntering into any hospital room and instantly locating the hand sanitizer, the stethoscope, and any obstruction to the patient's well-being. I just feel *safe* with him.

I walk a step behind him out of the exit doors and decide that if anything bad ever happened to me, he's the one person I'd want directing the scene—no matter how personal or frightening. When we reach the parking lot he asks me to toss him his car keys, saying he'll drive us home to the lake. It doesn't faze me for a second that he hasn't slept in more than a day: I totally, unabashedly trust him.

He drops me off at my house, and I wonder why he climbs out of the car as I make my way to my front walk. "Kris?"

I turn back in the lamplight.

"I have something for you." He crosses my driveway with a rectangle of fabric resting across his palms. A thoughtful wrap protects what's inside, the complimentary mesh kind they give you when you buy a designer purse.

I look up at him. "What did you do?" He places it in my hands. "Should I open it now?"

He nods.

I let loose a soft scarf that unrolls all the way down to my feet. It's a deep charcoal color, embroidered with tiny blue and pink flower buds all connected to one another by a delicate green vine. For some reason the first thing I do is hold it up to my nose. It smells faintly like him. "Chris," I whisper. "Thank you." And, like his gesture, what I say next can be taken as either neutral or romantic: "This is the most beautiful thing a man has ever given me." It's true.

"It's pure pashmina," he points out.

"It's exactly something I would have chosen myself."

He says it reminded him of me one night when he was out touring an Asian city capital. I go in for a hug. My God, I actually want to cry! *Stop being stupid. Remember what we are.* But still, I have to force myself to detach from him. As I continue on to my front porch he heads back to his car.

"Chris?"

He turns.

"Your family's not around. Do you have plans for Thursday?"

"Thursday . . . what's Thursday?" he says.

"It's Thanksgiving."

Thanksgiving, that's right! Well, let's see . . . he takes off for another course in New Jersey on Friday, but wow, Thanksgiving. No, come to think of it, he doesn't have plans.

"You're more than welcome to join us. We have dinner at my aunt and uncle's up the road, but not till the evening, so, you know, you have the day to get things done."

That sounds perfect, he says, a really nice invitation, and he'll even bring something.

I'm racing through the house like a woman on fire as his SUV lights pull down the driveway. *"Mom!"* I holler. *"Chris is coming to Thanksgiving!"*

THE NEXT MORNING I get online and order a silk blouse I've been eyeing. It's matte sea-foam green with romantic puffy sleeves, and with black pants it'll be the perfect Thanksgiving ensemble. *Thank you for this lovely and accomplished man who has joined my family on this most American holiday.* And even though the suede ankle boots I've been admiring will cost me ten hours of work for him, I put those in my virtual cart too. Thanksgiving is only five days away—I better lay out my underwear and jewelry now!

By Sunday the phone is ringing off the hook. My aunt calls, asking if there's anything Chris doesn't prefer to eat and do I know whether he has a favorite cocktail. "He's like me, he'll eat anything. Although truly, he's not a big drinker," I answer. Balancing the phone on my shoulder, I dig my pushiest push-up bra out of my top drawer. Just as I'm hanging up with my aunt, Grandma beeps in and talks a mile a minute. "I know, Grandma, I'm really excited too! The poor thing didn't have any plans at all."

Thursday morning I go for a run, then clean my upstairs. Chris and I have planned to go over some paperwork in my office before we head out with my family, and I want my living space to be in perfect presentation shape, as this is the first time he'll get to see it. I get so carried away putting things in order that I begin to organize my personal files and closet, chucking items I've been meaning to get rid of since college. Just as I'm wrapping up my cleaning spree, I shut off the vacuum and notice that I have a missed call. Ah, it's him, he must want to confirm the time.

"Hi, Kris." *Yay!* "Wishing you a happy Thanksgiving morning. I'm spending my day getting ready for this cheekbone course in Philly . . ." His voice trails off for a moment and he sounds tired. "And look, I really hate to do this, but please don't count me all in for tonight. I got called out for a surgery last night and I'm exhausted." *Oh no . . .* "I'm gonna get some sleep and give you a call later to let you know if I'm up for visiting."

My heart sinks into my stomach. Like a zombie I turn and walk downstairs into the kitchen. "He doesn't know if he's coming," I tell my mom blankly, just as she's sprinkling brown sugar over a mountain of sweet potatoes.

"Oh no! Oh, honey . . . what'd he say?"

I shake my head. "I guess he got called out to a surgery last night, and he's tired and he has to get ready for this trip he's going on tomorrow—"

"But it's Thanks*giving*," Mom says, visibly crestfallen. "He has to take a break from work sometime. Is he definitely not coming?"

"Well, he made it sound like there's a chance, but Mom," I lower my chin, saying *Get real*, "I'm not holding my breath."

"Yeah," she says, peeling off her apron. "You're right, we shouldn't have had our hopes up."

All this time I could have been pitching in with stuffing or pie or drying dishes, and instead I was primping the upstairs with the detail-orientedness of a Brazilian wax.

Which is clearly *another* thing I wasted my time doing this week.

I wear the blouse anyway, deciding that my family deserves to see it even more than some silly no-show did. Just as I'm ready to go out the door with Mom and Dad, I get a text that he's still up in the air. *Come and honor God and America with your celebration,* I reply. When we arrive at dinner everyone seems to wonder why we're not eating right away, and my phone goes off again.

Uncle Phil approaches me smiling. "Will Chris be joining us?" he asks.

"No, Uncle Phil. I just got final word."

Before we make our way through the buffet, Uncle Phil gives a toast, then, with most of us still hovering around the bar and the hors d'oeuvres table, we bow our heads for grace. Once I make my way through the buffet line I wonder whom I'll sit next to now that my date's turned out to be such a turkey. At the end of the far table in the dining room, I spot someone sitting silently, all alone: Grandma. Her eyes raise up to me when I place my plate next to hers, and we both force half smiles as I descend into my seat. She has tears in her eyes, and I can tell she's relieved someone's sitting next to her.

The demise of tonight's plans leaves me too weak to cut into my meat. I'm afraid that if I make eye contact with anyone, I'll start bawling, and I wonder if Grandma is fighting a telltale face like I am. The two of us combined are deflecting any potential company at this table with the miserable energy that's radiating from us, two pitiful peas in a pod. I blink back my tears with such concentration that it's difficult to even focus on my plate, and I don't know whether I feel sadder for myself or for Grandma. Finally, she breaks the silence: "He's not coming."

I can't force out more than a whisper. "No."

She dabs at her mouth and places her napkin next to the plate, already throwing in the towel on dinner. Then she links her pinky through mine on my lap and whispers, "I know how you feel, dear." I know she does. "But eventually, you'll forgive him. Forgiveness is peace, when it comes." A tear crashes down my face and seeps through my silk blouse.

Around us my aunt's second floor whirs with activity. Grandma and I are the only still figures among the sounds of ice in cocktail glasses, the crackling fire, and the hum of couples deciding which is the least crowded table at which to sit. This is the price I pay for wanting someone like my grandfather—look: tonight, they're both absent. The crowd laughs and silverware clinks, and through the fog that's clouding my ears I hear my aunt suggest I should be drinking champagne. With her eyes,

Grandma shields me from the scrutiny and "shoulds," panning around the table to make firm eye contact with the family members who are eagerly filling the seats around us. *Don't question how a woman deals with defeat*, her glower says; and with their incessant chatter and nosh, they honor her.

Grandma and I continue to carry on this way, unable to control the actions of some significant other person. We're like the centerpiece candle in front of us, flickering feebly without control of the activity around us; simply wanting to be tucked away, invisible.

Indeed this year's holidays won't be easy, for at the season's kickoff tonight I feel as though we two Gasbarre women have been widowed by hope. I lift a private prayer that, unlike Chris and his dear patient who must be spending Thanksgiving alone, at least Grandma and I both have someone to share the loneliness with.

8

You Are the Prize

Sagittarius: the Zodiac sign which the sun enters on November 22 and exits on December 21, the winter solstice. Sagittarius is a strong, positive sign manifesting characteristics of social competence, physical energy, self-sufficiency, future-orientedness, honesty at any cost, and a longing for adventure and stimulation. A person born under the sign of Sagittarius craves the company of others but will also be proud to survive independently, and will seek a romantic partner who is positive, well-groomed, ambitious, charming, gregarious, risk-taking, self-aware, and unpredictable.

Grandma's birthday falls on December 11, exactly ten days before my birthday, which marks the first day of winter. My mom once told me that when I was born Grandma gently recommended that my parents always separate my birthday celebration from Christmas, as a girl deserves her very own day every year.

There are similarities between Grandma and me that continue to surface as we both wrestle with confusion over our unwanted single status and our respective futures. Until now I've never given much thought to the notion that my birthday falls on the very last day of Grandma's Zodiac, but perhaps now's a good time to pay attention to the sign that binds us. Side by side we're two fiery, independent women . . . who, at the moment, happen to be starving for male companionship. By Sagittarian definition, however, we're often too stubborn to voice what we need, and too impatient to find out what will happen next.

Since I was a kid, our family has celebrated Grandma's birthday by reserving the back room at the little wood-paneled tavern on the edge of town known as the Pine Inn, where Grandpa always held office meetings and company holiday parties. Our whole family has known the owners of the restaurant for decades, so on Grandma's big day we've sat down to a family-style feast surrounded by twinkling white lights and silk poinsettia centerpieces on the tables. It's not an extravagant locale by any means, but it's private, and it's tradition. This year, Grandma informs us, she doesn't want any of it; but after Thanksgiving Uncle Phil insists to her that we should celebrate her eightieth year on the planet with the biggest bash yet.

Two weeks before her birthday the family murmurs collective frustration over whether we're supposed to proceed with the planning. Grandma continues to resist deciding whether she wants a party, and when my dad and uncles nudge her for progress, she grows increasingly obstinate. I call her one afternoon when one of my old college roommates is pressing me to make weekend plans. "Grandma, is this because of Grandpa?" There's silence on the line. I cautiously proceed to tell her that sitting around because Grandpa's not here would be the absolute worst thing for her spirits—she gives off this air that she's blaming him for her predetermination that her birthday's going to be miserable. "God forbid, Grandma, if things were reversed and you weren't here, we know that Grandpa wouldn't pass up a celebration just because *you* weren't around," I tell her. "He loved parties, and he loved when we were all together." I tell her that we want to have this party for her simply because she deserves to be celebrated, but if *she* doesn't want to have this party, then that's a decision she'll have to live with. "But I think you're cutting off your nose to spite your face, Grandma. Grandpa will be there in spirit." I pause. "And if he's not, it's his loss!" Her laugh erupts in my ear.

Two days later Uncle Phil sends out a family e-mail informing everyone that Grandma has agreed to the party and he's booked a block of hotel rooms for us in Pittsburgh that weekend. We travel the two hours in a caravan, and when we arrive I watch all the family's happy couples taper off to their rooms to slide into their dresses and suits. "Let's go, roomie," I tell Grandma, slipping her overnight bag over my wrist and linking my arm through hers. Aunt Marie has already arrived from St. Louis, and Grandma squeals to see her eldest child and only daughter.

The lovely Uncle Phil has seen to it that the setup of our room will suit us three girls just fine: Aunt Marie and Grandma both have their own bedrooms and bathrooms, and I'll take the couch in the suite's living room and share the powder room with Grandma. I have to stay mindful to keep all my toiletries organized and out of her way—her sink at home is always in minimalistic, perfect order.

I slip into a new black dress with white silk ruffles on the bodice, and Grandma puts on the silver dress she wore to my cousin's debutante in St. Louis. When the family arrives for drinks in the suite that we three are sharing, my dad pins a white rose corsage on Grandma's lapel. "See that?" I whisper to her. "You're beautiful."

As we all board the shuttle up to Mount Washington, I count a solid seventeen of us. The maitre d' takes our coats and escorts us to our table overlooking Pittsburgh's nighttime skyscape and Point State Park, where the Ohio, Allegheny, and Monongahela rivers famously meet to create a curving Y-shaped waterway that resembles the midsection of an inviting female. The back of the menu states that *USA Weekend* has voted this the second best view in America. As we crane our necks to point out the glimmering landmarks we recognize below, it's no wonder why.

The dominating pattern around the long dinner table is boy-girl, boy-girl . . . until you reach Grandma, who's seated next to me. Our tuxedoed waiters fuss over her with innocent flirtation, kissing her hand and pouring her champagne with theatrical delight. When I lean in to ask her what she's eyeing for her appetizer, I find that she's immersed in a comical story with my uncle seated on her opposite side. My mom kicks me under the table to point out that Grandma is actually having an awesome time, and my dad snaps a photo of her giving the A-OK sign to the camera. *You all win*, her expression says. She, like every member of our family, is convinced she deserves to be adored tonight by us, if not by Grandpa. A woman is too precious to compromise her good time or her happiness because things haven't gone her way with a man.

When we return to the hotel after midnight, everyone reconvenes in our suite for cake and presents. We sing over the birthday cake and I brace myself to see tears, but Grandma smiles massively before releasing a successful exhale across the sea of candles. I'm betting that right now Grandpa's *really* grateful we did this. When the gang finally gives Grandma loud champagne kisses good-night, she goes into the bathroom. When she exits, she finds me in her bedroom.

I pop her pillow to fluff it up. "Climb in, toots."

"You don't think this is too big for one person?" she says.

"It's a queen," I say. "It's all you."

Early the next morning when I return to the room from the gym, she meets me in the doorway with alarm. "I couldn't find you," she says.

"I was just at the gym."

"The gym? Heavens, what for," she says, pouring me coffee from the minibrewer. "You're gorgeous the way you are."

GRANDMA'S EIGHTIETH BIRTHDAY is a night I want to remember—my twenty-ninth birthday, on the other hand, is not. First of all, who wants a Sunday birthday with the Monday dooms hanging over your head? Dad's not in the mood for Luigi's, and when we go there anyway, my brother points out the way I hold my knife. "No, I disagree," he says. "That's not how the Europeans cut their food."

"Yes it is. I lived there for a year; you studied there for a summer and met like *one* Italian person. And he wanted to be an American rapper. So he doesn't even—"

"You two, enough." Mom breaks up our argument as though we're still in junior high while Dad glares down to our end of the table. Grandma sits at the far end straining to participate in our conversations, and the whole family is so visibly agitated with the unpleasant rhythm of the evening that when the cake arrives, the expressions around the table as people sing "Happy Birthday" look more like mug shots than party faces. *And many moooore!*

THREE DAYS LATER Christmas Eve comes and goes for me with the same apathy, and again Grandma blends quietly into the scene around our living room. When each of us grandkids opens our annual savings bonds, the note inside looks lightweight and lonely:

Love,
Grandma

Her signature looks so lopsided without Grandpa's name next to it. I glance at her, sitting alone at the bar. Then I look up at the ceiling: *This would all be a lot better if you'd stuck around, you know that, George?*

I'm jealous when my cousin's fiancée selects the confetti-cut paper shredder that I've donated to the annual blind gift exchange: what, she gets a hot-rod PowerShredder *and* an engagement ring? I should have gifted booze. I lazily look up from my mulled wine (of which, for yet another year, I am the sole maker and drinker, big fat hooray) to inform her, "You can shred credit cards with that thing, you know." The princess-cut diamond on her left hand sparkles in the light as she crinkles the wrapping paper into a carefree ball and beams ear-to-ear. Someone is having the Best Christmas Ever, and it's definitely not me.

On Christmas morning Mom and Dad are hunting for a gift receipt in Dad's den when my phone echoes through the first floor. "Kris?" Mom hollers, her voice bouncing off the hardwood. "I think your phone is ringing!"

She doesn't know that I'm standing a room away from her in the foyer staring at the incoming call. It's Chris, whom I hadn't heard from since the Thanksgiving flop. "I got it," I say as I hit the Ignore button and disappear upstairs.

Half an hour later when I return, my parents are still in the den, now listening to the Kings of Leon disc I gave Dad in his stocking. Mom wants to know, "Who called?" *Oh, here we go.*

"It was . . . Chris."

"Oh! You see? He's thinking of you, how nice! What'd he have to say?"

"I actually missed the call."

"Well, did he leave a message?"

Ufff. "He did."

"Well?" I don't need them shoving the importance of forgiveness down my throat, but with them both staring up at me over Dad's desk, there's no way around the truth. I give them the seven-second summary of Chris's two-minute message. He told me he's hanging out with his brother in Chicago, that for some cosmic reason I'm in his thoughts right now so he said a prayer for me and he has a lot of confidence that God has great things in store for me. He said he's reading a novel that's changing his life.

In the last month I've begun to see his attributing every mortal event to God and the universe as his way of wiggling out of any active decisions or commitments. He wants no responsibility, no one depending on him for anything, not even to show up on Thanksgiving. If he's not paying me, then he doesn't want to hang out with me. I feel like I've been prostituting my companionship for the last four months.

"Are you calling him back?" Mom asked.

"Probably not."

My dad pipes up. "It's not fair for you to make judgments about him."

"Pardon me?"

"You don't have all the answers."

I can't wait to move out of this place I think, as I stomp upstairs. When I slam the door that closes off the second floor from the first, I wait for my dad to spring upstairs and yell at me like he did during my junior high moody phase: "Just because you're mad at the world, there's no excuse for eye-rolling, stomping, or slamming doors!" In fact I am in my mad-at-the-world mode, but as an adult I've realized that this misery simply translates into feeling frustrated with my own existence. This self-loathing only ever occurs as the result of an unhappy transaction with a boss or a romantic interest, and as I remain unemployed at the moment, it's the not getting my way with Chris that has my emotions more tangled than an old string of Christmas lights. I just can't figure out how to unwind myself and brighten up again.

But I won't call him back. Dad's criticism—"You don't have all the answers"—shamed me, but after the pang of disappointment I experienced at Thanksgiving, there's almost nothing that could persuade me to make myself vulnerable to him again. Even if we were to run into each other at the grocery store next week, I'd stop my cart, stare at him calmly, and then continue on my way. (I would, however, be sporting lipstick and high boots in case of the good fortune of a run-in.) At this point I'd feel gratified if he wanted me, but me not showing desire for him would be empowering.

MY FRIEND KENNETH from high school and his boyfriend throw a New Year's party at their house in Pittsburgh, and on Facebook three of my old classmates and I make arrangements to go. On the ride down my friend Margie reveals to me that the guy she'd been dating since high school has turned out to be a criminal and a polygamist, that she accidentally met three of his other fiancées when she went to visit him in jail in October. Margie is one of the happy-go-luckiest, least controversial people I have ever known (plus she drives a stick shift with better skill than any dude I've ever met—impressive). I can't believe that any man would put someone like her through such hell. "Margie, please tell me you've cut off all contact with him," I say.

"Oh, believe me, I have, are you kidding?"

"Good. And don't go getting frustrated about men—there's going to be a *good* guy who comes to you and tells you that you're the most beautiful woman he's ever met and that he can't live without you."

"Yeah." Her voice quiets. "You really think?"

I look at Margie in the glow of her dashboard. "Absolutely."

When we arrive at Kenneth's house, he takes our coats with grandiose presentation. Except for the fact that I don't recognize most of the faces milling around his marble kitchen, I feel like we're back in high school when he was famous for organizing extravagant dinner parties. In junior high his parents had gone through a brutal divorce and left him to be raised by his grandfather, a local coal mogul. Kenneth always amazed and entertained me as he passed around expensive hors d'oeuvres, finding such wild exuberance in astonishing his guests. "Caviar, for *me*?" I asked him at the first of his high school dinner fetes that I attended.

"Of course, darling, who else." Then he set down his silver tray, and the two of us did cheers with grape juice. Even though I've known since junior high that he was never attracted to girls, he always had a way of making me feel as priceless as a crown jewel. Over a decade after our graduation, I'm reminded of something that's both strange and familiar: every woman needs a man like Kenneth in her life. Here was this person whose family essentially abandoned him thanks to their own unhappiness, and yet Kenneth's sole concern is everybody else's good time—so selfless and noble. To think of my loved ones always so solidly intact with one another—and *I* feel alone and confused?

Kenneth walks around his New Year's party handing out what he claims is Richard Nixon's champagne. He then dings a fork on a glass. "Everyone, I want to welcome you to New Year's Eve two thousand and nine. At this time I invite you to join me in the salon where I've orchestrated an unforgettable round of Dirty Santa." The naughty gift exchange sends us two dozen adults whooping like fifth-graders who just learned how to translate perverted jokes. At midnight we throw confetti and streamers around Kenneth's kitchen, and as the TV airs shots of New Year's celebrations in Sydney, Paris, and Hong Kong, I catch myself feeling a foreign sensation: I'm present *in this moment.* As Ryan Seacrest announces to the world that it's now 2009 in New York City, there's truly no one who I wish were at this party who's not already here. The billboards light up Times Square behind Seacrest's ear-muffed head, and around me there are blasts of laughter and huddles of hugs. There's no reason I shouldn't find total contentedness in the life around me. My friends, my work, my family, my interests are more than enough to keep a girl satisfied: why would I ever be okay with *striving* for someone's attention? I make a silent New Year's resolution to *have fun* this year and to stop fretting that I'm somehow incomplete. I say a prayer for Grandma, who planned dinner with her friends and an early bedtime to ring in 2009. I hope her resolution was similar.

Around me, men and women—and men and men—hug and

sway and blow plastic horns to "Auld Lang Syne," and it's as though someone has bestowed on all of us a momentary state of perfect bliss. It's time I start finding joy again in the *people who are in my life*. I am complete, I tell myself. I am alive. And even though I don't have romance, I have love. I am loved . . . and most rewarding of all, I am in fact capable of loving others.

JANUARY RUSHES PAST in a bright white gust as I make trips to Cleveland to catch up with old college roommates, and to upstate New York to see my best friend since kindergarten, Emma. This may be the last time I see her in an ordinary state: she has designated this year as the one in which she and her husband will make a baby. But even with all the visits with old friends, I have found that during an emotional period in life, there's often a single companion who fills a particular yearning . . . right now, that's Celeste. Her presence makes me feel more understood than anyone else's.

Celeste finished out her nanny contract in Italy and has been back in Ohio living with her parents since October. With our shared states of transition, we agree that we're both desperate for some together time. She makes the three-hour trip to visit me for Valentine's weekend, and on Saturday we pop into Grandma's for a hug. Energy bounces constantly between Celeste and me like a Ping-Pong ball, and our eye-rolling jokes about living as two exasperated Americans among the old-school Italians make Grandma double over. I sense that this visit with my closest friend from college may have answered a silent plea Grandma had for some company. She flips on lights as we walk from the living room into the kitchen, and it dawns on me that she'd been sitting in the dark before we arrived.

"Dig into those peanut butter melt-aways," she says, gesturing at the box of candy that Celeste and I have brought from the local chocolatier. We lean over Grandma's island counter as she sits down at the kitchen table to slice open the oversized gold envelope that we've handed her. She spreads the card open and reads about St. Valentine, who, according to legend, was a healer who was thrown in jail and tortured for his faith in God. Valentine also disagreed with the Roman law that kept citizens from marrying, as it stated that married men made poor soldiers, so secretly Valentine performed wedding ceremonies for couples who wanted to spend their lives together. The jailer who was guarding Valentine's cell was desperate for him to restore his blind daughter's sight. According to legend, Valentine agreed to try.

He and the daughter, Asterius, became close friends throughout her therapy (*very* close friends, it sounds like, although the religious section of Hallmark isn't exactly known for its juicy romances), and because she was bright but not educated, Valentine began teaching her about nature and history and God. One day Asterius asked him if God really hears the prayers of little old her, and Valentine explained that if we simply believe in God, He will always do what is best for us—there's nothing we have to do to earn his love. Then right before Valentine's execution, he gave Asterius a love letter with a flower tucked inside and a message to continue seeking God. Immediately after Valentine died, Asterius gained her sight. When she looked in the mirror, she saw how beautiful she was, and she read Valentine's letter saying that she'd been the beautiful red rose of his gray, wretched life. In that moment Asterius learned that her insecurities about being loved and taken care of had always been unwarranted.

In the card I've given Grandma is the prayer to St. Valentine:

Teach me to love generously and to find infinite joy in sharing,
Enable me to bring out the best in others
And to project my love into the world.

Maybe the secret to fulfillment is to stop wondering what we're lacking; to stop seeking love and instead to start accepting ourselves and loving the people we encounter. Two weeks ago in late January the one-year anniversary of Grandpa's death passed, and this humanistic prayer to St. Valentine today with Grandma reminds me of the kindness that overflowed from my heart and my actions in the weeks immediately following Grandpa's passing. Suddenly I understood everyone I encountered as a person who had suffered significantly at some point; who knew struggle and chose to smile anyway. When I returned to Italy after Grandpa's funeral, I couldn't help but hold open doors for the old ladies in the village, to kiss up the kids I was nannying, and to pick up Celeste's tab at bars when her boss forgot to pay her. Losing my grandpa made me want to be more caring, and I noticed that when I was giving love, I wasn't so starved to receive it.

Celeste heads back to Ohio the Sunday after Valentine's Day, and Mom packs up a heart-shaped meat loaf for me to take to

Grandma. I know how she hates eating alone, so while I'm working on quieting the emotional hunger inside of me, I do bring my appetite to Grandma's. Across the kitchen table she sets down her fork and says to me, "You know, you seem different."

"Yeah?"

"You've lost weight, haven't you?"

I nod and swallow my mashed potatoes. "A little, five pounds maybe. After the holidays, it sort of just came off."

"That's not all, though." She's squinting, studying me carefully. "You seem happier."

I scrunch up my nose. *"Really?"*

"Mm-hm."

"Well, so do you, you know. Maybe it's because you've survived your first year without Grandpa."

"I imagine that has something to do with it. But you," she muses. "Something's definitely different."

Could it be that contentment makes us more attractive? I remember the first time I ever saw a Bon Jovi video, in 1986. Jon Bon Jovi had this tough-guy look on his face through the first verse of the song, and watching, you're going, "Oh sure, y'know, he's a cute enough guy." But then at the chorus he flashes a huge movie-marquee smile at the camera and every girl in the room—well, my babysitter, her friend, and me—swooned to our knees going, *"Oh . . . my . . . God!"* Everyone's better looking when they're expressing happiness and radiating warmth and self-assuredness from inside. It's why we use the word "attractive": a person's positive affect magnetizes us to them.

But I wonder if that actually works from the other side of the world. I explain to Grandma that Chris has been back in Asia since late January, and, after a little of my own internal resolution, we've returned to cordial terms. She sets her plate aside to hear that he first made contact with me when he needed help locating a document I'd worked on. While I kept my end of the initial exchange short but sweet, he told me how indebted to me he was for my willingness to always lend a hand . . . though I can never tell, does he say such kind things because he's genuine, or because he loves to hear himself say perfect words?

I brushed my hands of the question until a few days later when he called me at seven in the morning. I answered the phone groggy and confused, and he apologized with a hush. "No, no, what is it?" I said.

"Don't worry," he whispered. "Check your e-mail later."

After I woke up and poured my coffee, I sat down at the computer to read his note that—oh, wow—he'd passed his board exams, which was one of the projects that kept him so secluded from other people for the past few months. He said he knew I would appreciate what it meant and that I was the first person he'd called to tell.

There is a bottle of Cakebread behind my bar with your name on it, I wrote back. I'd remembered him once mentioning his favorite wine, and months ago I bought the bottle, hoping we might share it some evening. *I shall gladly find a way to get it to you when you're back in PA.*

"His loss," Grandma shrugs.

I tilt my head and push my plate aside to meet hers in the middle. *His loss.* She's turning the tables on me, feeding back the advice I gave to her. "His loss that he never got to share wine with me?"

She nods.

"You really think so?"

"I'm proud of you," she says. "You've done everything right."

"With him, you mean?"

"With him."

Isn't she being a little generous with the flying colors she's just pinned on me? I wouldn't say I've done everything right—far from it. First of all, my parents had me thinking I was cold-hearted for not wanting to speak with him on Christmas. And now, almost three months after the Thanksgiving disaster, I can't help but maintain the impression that Chris's ducking out of dinner was based on a series of rotten excuses. *I need to study. I'm traveling tomorrow. I had surgery.* I never did come upon proof that in fact he'd performed a trauma surgery the night before Thanksgiving. I still feel embarrassed that I'd put so much energy into preparing for the whole thing, that my entire family looked at me with both hunger and excitement in their eyes as they waited for him to arrive at the top of my aunt's stairs with a dessert in his grip. On top of it all, why can't I just let the whole thing go? Yes, I've forgiven him . . . but every time I think of him, I catch a disappointed jab to my stomach—that confirmation: *he's not coming.* He's not here.

Celeste's mother once gave me one of the most useful pieces of advice I've ever received. One summer weekend in college when I was visiting Celeste in Ohio, her mom said, "Remember, on your way home, if you don't know which lane you're supposed to be in on the Interstate, always stick to the middle lane." That rule has come in handy dozens of times since then, even in desperate moments on the Italian highway when I could barely read road signs or operate a stick shift with the crazy drivers around me sucking all my attention. *Stick to the middle lane,* I'd remind myself, and instantly I would feel my blood pressure slow down to a normal rate. This weekend I brought Celeste up to speed on the Chris situation from summer to winter, and this afternoon before I left for Grandma's, Celeste e-mailed me to tell me she'd gotten back home okay. (Our friendship, the quintessential two-way street.) She writes:

> I briefly told my mom about your boy situation, and she said that with the Thanksgiving invitation, you pretty much put it all out there. Now you need to "pedal softly." If a guy cares about you, it's his move to make. My mom also said, "You tell Krissy to remember that she is the woman, which means she is the prize. He is not the prize, Krissy is the prize!"
>
> I hope that helps!

I think it helps—but I want to run it past my coach. "What do you make of that advice, Grandma?"

Grandma says she agrees completely, that even in the age of e-mails and "those little messages you kids send each other on your phones," a woman has to operate with grace in any relationship. She explains that when she was young, women "didn't ever want to be chasing a man. *Back off.* That was the custom, and if you ask me, it's still that way. Men don't want to be approached just any time."

"Hm. What if the guy's thinking the girl's going to call him?"

"Listen, you're asking my opinion. I'm telling you that Cecilia's mother is right—"

"Celeste."

"Celeste. Her mother is right. You're the prize. It's up to him to *get you*. If he wants to call, he'll call. If he wants to see you, he'll see you. Men still think they're the ones in charge. It's their biological nature." *Biological nature?* When did Grandma go all pop psychology?

I like it.

But what if, just what if you can't help but reach out to a guy? Grandma says the savvy way a girl would see if a guy liked her when she was young was to somehow drop a hint about where she was going to be later. "We'd make it known where we were going without being bold," she says. Ah, like a Facebook status update. "And when I first started dating your grandpa, I really thought he was seeing other girls. So I'd make plans to go out with my girlfriends. I wasn't going to sit at home doing nothing." Years later she found out that Grandpa really had just been cruising around with his buddies. "That was another thing I learned—when I wanted an answer out of your grandpa, I never pounded it out of him. Give him some time to explain himself," she says. "You'll find out a whole lot that way."

Give him some time to explain himself. Her words keep playing in my head, reminding me how months after a breakup, even after the worst of your wounds have healed and there's really no part of you that aches missing the other person anymore . . . there's still that one tiny, unjaded, optimistic little ounce of your heart that would welcome hearing from him. It's the solitary—however improbable—hope that just maybe you could forget all the conflict and find excitement in each other again. Good friends have massaged it into my brain that I'm a treasure rich as gold, and though I genuinely get that now, my chest still feels hollow sometimes.

Blast him, I know there's still a part of me that would make room for him. If he were to call again, I'd still have to formulate how I'd answer the phone: act bubbly or aloof? Fill him in on everything that's new, or hold a quiet grudge? I'm not ready to count on him again, but I still care about him . . . and I'm afraid that if this prize can't learn to compromise, then I may be sitting alone on the shelf for a very long time.

Although as long as this prize loves herself, then maybe being alone is better than being with the wrong person.

9

Recognize an Open Door

In late March it's as though a magic bellman has opened the door into a secret world so sunny that it blasts away the last smudge of winter's grayness—both barometric and emotional. My new year, new leaf approach successfully holds Zen like a scene out of *Wayne's World*—"Live in the *now,* man!"—and a new energy cracks bravely out of its shell inside me. In fact, I think I'm ready to make my next move. I begin pricing apartments in Brooklyn, and out of the blue Isabella, the mom from the family I nannied for in Italy, e-mails to ask me to return because little Francesca misses me. I miss them too and the kindness is difficult to decline, as is the salary both Western Union and I loved . . . but no, I decide. I still need to be close to home.

One afternoon in early April, I'm sitting at the beach across the road from my house when Emma calls. "I have some news," she says. "Are you ready?" I tell her to wait while I sit down on a rock: she must be pregnant. She tells me calmly that she's expecting a daughter in the fall, and the image of her caressing the cheek of a baby on her breast triggers me into a giddy laugh-cry on the phone. Emma tells me she's heard the baby's heartbeat and seen her fingers and toes in an ultrasound.

"She's you and Sean, together," I tell her. "I would have cried if I would have heard her heart."

"I didn't cry, but seriously Krissy . . . it was so cool."

For two and a half decades Emma and I have shared everything—we're talking celebrity crushes, family secrets, and vital science fair projects that consisted of mixing two perfumes—Exclamation and Malibu Musk, Benetton Colors and Debbie Gibson's Electric Youth—to see if they'd cause an allergic reaction (rest assured, they did not). When she got married four years ago, my mom and I hosted the bridal shower and made favors for the reception. Then I held her bouquet on the altar as she pledged her life to the guy she'd been mad for since high school (he's now a sought-after chef whom I credit with teaching me the recipe for authentic salsa).

Selfishly, I'd hoped she'd wait at least until I got married before she got pregnant. This baby is the first development in her life that she'll experience ahead of me—*without* me, really—and the six-hour car ride that stands between us could make her little girl and me mere acquaintances at best. When we hang up after her announcement, I remember that on vacation the summer before eighth grade we'd pinky-sworn that our kids would call each other Aunt Krissy and Aunt Emma. When I leave the beach and arrive home, I send out my résumé for an editorial job at a marketing firm outside Albany, close to where Emma and Sean live. A week later the firm gives the job to somebody else, noting my geographical transfer as a financial and moral risk. "If it doesn't work out, then both you and we are stuck with the mistake."

I assure them that I understand their decision, but inside, anxiety strikes. Not only am I growing ready to leave my family and get back to real life, there's also no viable source of income anywhere in my crystal ball. So when Chris calls on the first Friday in May to ask whether I can man the Saturday reception desk at his office, I quickly accept.

When he blasts through the office front door, he shocks me: his hair is short and slicked back. In fitted charcoal slacks and shiny shoes, he approaches the reception desk and takes my hand in both of his. It's been a while, he says. I count five months and eight days, to be exact, to the last moment I saw him when he was smiling in my driveway, committing to bringing a dessert to Thanksgiving. But standing here facing him, I lose the will to hold onto my anger, surrendering to the fact that under any circumstance, I could never hold the substantial gap in meetings against him. He's my dear friend. Regardless of whether he's ever let me down, the sincerity in his eyes proves that he's worth remaining present for. "Your hair's short," I observe gently.

"I'm representing my country now." He takes one of the whole wheat chocolate chip cookies I've baked for his staff, and the whole gang follows him into the exam room to preview the day's cases. "Your hair's short too," he calls from down the hall, turning the corner into full doctor mode.

I touch the hair at the nape of my neck. The morning I was leaving Italy for good last June, Celeste hugged me goodbye and asked me to swear I'd never cut my hair until I'm a mom. "It's your best feature," she'd said. I broke the promise after my "you're the prize" discussion with Grandma. A woman's beauty, I'd concluded, is often not about her best physical features. Toward the opening of spring I felt the lightest and most independent that I had since returning home almost a year ago, and I'd read once that when a person cuts his or her hair very short, it can be an act of emotional liberation, like the shedding of an old skin. I wanted a change, and I wanted a fresh look that showed how I felt.

At noon Chris emerges with a credit card and asks me to run out and get lunch for the six of us who are working. I take charge of the task and order very liberally, emerging from Ruby's curbside pickup with a backseat full of turkey burgers, broccoli soup, and salad. When I return to the office, I set up the spread in the lunchroom and go back to him with his card and receipt. "Let's allow the others to eat first," he says. "Then you and I will go together." When the last of his four assistants returns from the break room, Chris asks her to watch the front desk and gives me a quick wiggle of his hand, inviting me to follow him.

The lunch menu I've selected is perfect, he says, using two plastic forks to transfer salad from the to-go container onto his plate. He pulls out a chair from underneath the table and sits in the one opposite. "It's good to see you, Kris," he says.

I nod assuredly. "I'm happy to see you too."

He looks down at the floor. "You know this is my last Saturday in this office."

"You mean forever?"

He nods, and looks out the window over the gardened court-yard. "Forever." I'm relieved when he then searches the table for a soup spoon, because I can't pick up the expression on my face. I must look like a lone lover on an old train platform. I reach for my hair again, wondering whether I'd feel less vulnerable right now if I hadn't cut it. When he looks at me, I regain focus. "I have the grand opening of the practice in Asia in a month," he says. "For the next few weeks I'll be seeing patients an hour away in the office of a friend of mine."

We both sit quietly, then I look at him. "I'm sad that you're leaving."

This appears to energize him. He jumps up to grab another turkey burger off the counter. "How's your family doing?"

I tell him Grandma was having a couple good months but she's fallen back into a slump. "She's finally started going to a widows' support group every week. But my mom's mom is pretty under the weather too. She's been having terrible trouble with her eyes and she can't cook or work in the garden anymore. My parents are away on business this weekend, so I'm taking her to church tonight."

Chris's eyes light up. "*Hey,*" he says, "you know what . . . I think I know something that could cheer them up." He says his grandparents are in town for the next month for a surgery his grandma's having on her hip. "They came in from near India-napolis, and I've set her up with some good doctors here."

"How nice of you." *Where is he going with this?*

"What do you say we organize a grandparents' brunch?"

Is he serious? "Yeah, ha, a grandparents' brunch." I try to chuckle the idea away, thinking how strange it can be to have both my punctilious grandma and my *I Love Lucy*-esque nana together in the same room—let alone in front of someone like Chris, whose impression I like to manage as meticulously as possible.

"Yes, that's it, a grandparents' brunch! When you see your grandmother tonight, invite her to get together tomorrow. Then call the other one. I'll call you in the morning and we'll make reservations somewhere nice."

The awareness is creeping over me that this is a disaster waiting to happen. I imagine Chris's grandmother as being even more proper than Grandma, staring down her nose at how we small-town folk behave and picking at her food with a fork, saying she prefers her Hollandaise on the thicker side. Plus, I know that because Chris is both male and swamped, the arrangements will fall on me. If the whole meal turns out to be a bust, the blame will be mine.

I cannot let this grandparents' brunch take place.

But when I mention it to Nana, she *loves* the idea. She hasn't been to brunch in a decade, she says, and while I know that she's notorious for her exaggerations, I figure that statistic isn't too far off the mark. I hold her hand up the stairs of her ancient duplex house to her bedroom, where she opens the closet for me. "Pick out my outfit, baby," she says. "I'll even wear high heels to meet your friend."

Grandma takes a little longer to climb on board, saying she doesn't know if she's up to meeting new people. "Call me in the morning," she says. "I'll let you know my decision before you make your reservation." But ten minutes later she calls me back, saying what the hey, she's sorry for being a stick in the mud and she'll join us.

So help me if you back out of these plans, Christopher. I will take my grandmothers to this brunch whether you show up or not.

I'm still in bed when my cell phone rings. "It's a go, Kris," he says in my ear. "Want to plan on one o'clock?"

One works, I tell him, and I'll make the reservation at the country club in town. I dig through my closet to find something to wear, tucking a white camisole into a fitted skirt from Tuscany that's embroidered with flowers that are each a color in the spectrum. I start to panic looking for a jacket of some kind—I can't be late picking up Nana or I'll throw the plan off schedule. Just as I'm about to change skirts for something easier to match, a plum-colored cardigan jumps out at me. I step into tan heels that are the same color as my skirt. *Whew!*

Grandma is waiting in her car when Nana and I pull into the country club parking lot. The three of us walk in together, and when we enter the grand ballroom, not a soul is present at any of the tables. Near the buffet, there's a table with a card on it that reads GASBARRE. A hostess in a bow tie peeks around from the bar area. "You're expecting three more, correct?"

"Yes," the three of us answer in unison.

"You're not closed, are you?" I ask her. "I called."

"No, we're open. But brunch ends at two o'clock, and if the rest of your party runs much later, I'm afraid we'll have to tear down on you."

"I understand, but see, my friend is a surgeon and his grandparents are in from out of town, and . . ." I explain how he's always late and can never seem to help it, you know doctors, and the hostess folds her arms.

I knew this was going to be a nightmare.

"What can I get you three to drink?" Grandma and Nana light up.

"Nana, what will you have?"

"It's been five years since I've had a glass of Chianti," she says. "Grandma?"

"Just a cranberry juice, if you please."

"And I'll have a mimosa, please."

Grandma pipes back in. "Actually, change mine to a mimosa too."

Through the window opposite the golf course outside I see the door to a large pickup truck slam. From the carpeted front lobby three shadows slowly approach the dining room, and after a few seconds Chris is the first of them to turn the corner. When I see him, I have to catch my breath. He's dressed in a sharp light gray suit and wearing edgy black-framed glasses, and I'm so flustered that I have to paste on an easy smile, which must certainly appear forced. He beams as wide as the doorway when he sees me, and I recover my senses and rise from my chair. Behind him his grandma is a head taller than both of my grandmothers, and her skin radiates without a touch of makeup. She's wearing a sweater with bluebirds embroidered that reminds me of something Grandma owns. His grandpa, meanwhile, follows close behind with a cane and pulls out his wife's chair.

Chris comes to me and kisses me on both cheeks. When we

separate, there's satisfaction in his smile. "Ah," he catches himself. "I brought this for you." He hands me a check for yesterday's work, and I'm impressed that he made a priority out of paying me right away, right here at breakfast. I float around the table to introduce myself to his grandparents while he introduces himself to mine. The chef winks at me from behind the omelet bar. After everyone has their drinks, the six of us mill around the buffet. Chris and his grandparents go for salad and soup, while Nana, Grandma, and I flock to the buffet's opposite end, using tongs to select breakfast sweets like French toast and pancakes and doughnuts. "Honey girl, come here," Nana says, and from across the room I can feel Chris's eyes on my bare calves as I help Nana pour syrup.

When we return to the table, Chris suggests we say grace, and he's looking at me. My grandmas and I make the sign of the cross, and I pray the Catholic mealtime prayer:

Bless us, O Lord, and these thy gifts
Which we are about to receive from thy bounty
Through Christ our Lord, Amen.

Then I add: "And thank you for the family and the new friends that join us around this table." Over my folded hands I watch Chris open his eyes and give me a slow blink: *Well done.*

His grandparents talk about their most recent fishing trip, and Chris says he has a jar of his grandpa's freshwater salmon to let me try. Nana acts as though she may dominate the conversation, telling the crowd around the table what an amazing singer I am. "She had a chance to go to Broadway!" she insists.

My mouth drops and I look at Chris. "No, I definitely didn't," I explain. "I did some theater through college, but that was it."

"You got paid for two shows out of high school!" Nana adds. "She's always so modest."

Chris sets down his fork and presses his palms together on the table. "Now, Kris, wait, are you wasting some of your God-given talent?"

My cheeks go hot and I feel a sweat break out across my upper lip. "No, no, there's really not all that much talent to waste. And besides, I sing in the car."

"And in the shower, I'll bet!" Chris's grandma says.

"Exactly, in the shower as well."

"What was your favorite play you ever had a part in?" Chris asks.

Nana pipes in. "That one about that French artist . . . you know, George something? He worked all the time till his lover left him because she'd had it up to here?" Nana whacks her hand against her forehead like a sloppy soldier.

"*Sunday in the Park with George*," I say.

"Georges Seurat!" Chris says. "I love his work!"

Chris asks Nana about her religion, and I bury my face in my hands when she breaks into a straight three-minute monologue about the importance of rejecting the devil. "And do *you know* that *in the Bible*, it says . . ." and when she's in the middle of reciting a verse from the book of Genesis, Grandma, who's been quiet till now, rescues my sanity to ask Chris about his work. I'm impressed when he keeps the explanation to a minimum—he really wants this gathering to be about the elders.

I tell his grandmother how proud she must be of her grandson and his unparalleled success, and she says indeed he amazes the whole family but she only wishes he would stay closer to home. Chris's grandpa engages Grandma in a conversation about World War II, and they determine that he was in Germany at the same time my grandpa was. Suddenly Grandma is locked in to him, erupting at moments like a teenage girl at his stories about getting into trouble with the soldiers in his squad. "What rank was your husband when he left the army?" he asks. Even beyond eighty years old his nose comes down to a perfect bulbous point, as though it was crafted by an artist; exactly like Chris's.

"He was a corporal," Grandma says.

"Impressive," Chris's grandmother pipes in. Grandma goes quiet.

"He was very impressive," I chime in. "Wasn't he, Grandma."

She nods. "He was."

The waitress comes around with two separate tabs. "Can I get you all anything else?"

"No, thank you," I say, accepting the bill.

"How about a driver, *dah*ling," Nana says. She thinks she's Marilyn Monroe. "I haven't been this drunk since my third husband died!" Chris pauses from tucking cash inside his billfold to smile discreetly.

Somehow I've recovered my pulse by the time we all exit the restaurant together. Chris kisses both my grandmothers gently on the cheek as I hug his grandma and wish her well with her operation. Over my shoulder I hear him tell Grandma that the aquamarine in her vest matches her eyes perfectly, and when I turn to see her blush, Chris comes to me. "This was beautiful," he says as he leans down and places his lips on my right cheek— so tender, his touch—then on my left. His hands run down the length of my arms, and—I know I'm not imagining this—our fingertips linger against one another for a second. Desire strikes me like lightning as he and his grandparents make their way to the pickup, which I now understand is his grandpa's.

I hold Grandma's and Nana's arms down the steps. "What'd you think, girls?"

Nana says, "His lapel was wrinkled." I was referring to the lunch, not just to Chris, whose lapel was definitely not wrinkled . . . and isn't she legally blind? "You know how picky I am when it comes to my granddaughters' suitors." Okay, hold on: first of all, how much better does it get than a handsome, caring, international surgeon? And second, who says Chris is my *suitor*?

"I thought it was perfect," Grandma says before she gets into her car. I'd been fidgeting to hear her opinion of Chris.

I take Nana to the grocery store for milk, bread, and a carton of Parliaments before I drive her home. When I put her groceries away, kiss her goodbye, and get back on the road, my phone rings. It's Grandma. "Dear?" she says.

"Grandma! I'm so glad you called because I forgot to tell you something at brunch. You'll never believe it: Emma's having a baby!"

"She is? Emma, why, how wonderful! Were they trying?"

"Yeah, they've been married five years, they were ready."

"Oh my land." (This is a phrase I have yet to pick up.) "I'll be sure to light a candle at Mass. Dear, the reason I called is that I just wanted to tell you . . . today was the most marvelous afternoon I've had in a very long time."

"Oh, Grandma, I'm so happy to hear that."

"I could tell there was someone else who enjoyed it as well."

"Who, me?" Oh no, did I make my crush obvious?

"Well, yes, I suppose you. But I was referring to your friend." Suddenly she's addressing the issue of him with heightened mystery, leaving his name for me to surmise on my own. *You're a real minx, Grandma.*

Although the possibility occurs to me: what if I am completely confused and we're talking about two different people? "You mean Chris?" The question jumps out of me uncontrolled, and the subtext to it is a *Grease*-esque *Gee whiz, Grandma, you think he really likes me?* I should really make a priority of reeling in these junior high emotions . . .

"Yes, I'm talking about Chris."

"*Really?*" I pull into the post office parking lot so I can concentrate on our conversation.

"Yes. And you want to know something, I thought he was definitely more relaxed this afternoon than he was the first time I met him."

"Well, that's an interesting observation."

"And I think he's most relaxed when he's interacting with you. I sure noticed him smiling at you a lot."

"Really." I say it with confident curiosity, but my heart is pounding, begging Grandma the love expert to be right.

"I have a hunch you bring out a side to him that most other people don't. Well, heavens, it's not my place to make the judgment based on one family brunch . . . but," she indulges us both again, "indeed that was my sense. Plus," I hear mischief rise in her voice, "he sure looks handsome in a suit, doesn't he?"

"Did you *see* him, Grandma?"

She giggles.

"I guess we have the same taste, don't we?"

"Yes," she says. "I'd say we're known for loving the same men."

"Grandma, wow, thank you for calling and . . . telling me all this."

"But really, dear, what I called to tell you was—" Suddenly she turns solemn. "—that was such a lovely afternoon that . . . when I walked in the house just now, I cried tears of joy."

I INVITE CHRIS and his grandparents to a Mother's Day luncheon with our family the following week. However, by now, after last week's brunch, he's disappeared completely—responding only to the e-mail I'd written to tell him that Grandma Glo was glowing after our get-together.

"Glad Grandma Flo liked it," he replied. "If only I could remember which one she was!"

Flo?

I'm disappointed, but certainly by now I'm not gullible enough to imagine that he'd have stayed very close for long.

But in Nana's kitchen on Mother's Day it's definitely better that Chris is not present. After we three generations went to

Mass together, my mom's navy seersucker suit and long strand of crystal beads strike a stark contrast to the old-fashioned wood panel atmosphere inside Nana's house. Mom gestures at the body lotion on Nana's kitchen table. "She liked the scent you picked out," she whispers to me. Then, stretching her neck toward Nana's bedroom, she yells, "Hey, Ma, who delivered the pie on your counter?"

"Punk," Nana says, referring to her brother, an ex-con who lives in a trailer on the edge of town. "He wanted to stay but I told him you were coming." Nana's siblings and their kids all avoid my mother and her professional ties to the town's law enforcement.

"Keep your purse close," Mom mutters to me. "Uncle Punk could come back."

Right then Nana busts out of her bedroom. She's a vision in her peach golf shirt from church, teamed with crushed-velvet green elf shorts boasting bells that hang off the jagged hem. Mom and I turn to each other, and Mom's horror and confusion must mirror my own. Her voice comes out a squeak. "Just what the hell are you wearing, lady?"

"It's very chic," Nana says, adjusting her red elastic waistband. "I gotta show you this dance I did in Punk's hospital room a couple weeks ago before Jesus brought him back from death's door—I swear, it's just like Lazarus."

"Hospital room? A dance for who?" Mom says.

"Why, all the nurses."

Mom's head collapses into her hands. "Please don't tell me Ruth McGee was there."

"Ruth McGee was so! I'd swear every nurse in DuBois was in the room to see this. Now, look up or you're gonna miss the show," Nana says, already bouncing in place so the bells on her hem set a rhythm for her song. "Friendship," she sings, "friendship. When you need me I'll be there . . ."

"Well, what the . . ." Mom wonders aloud. With wide eyes and mouths she and I take in the TV-tray cabaret in front of us. Mom's hand blindly walks around her chair to her purse in search of her camera.

Nana gives the jingle a grand finale with her arms shaking in the air. Then she looks down. "Hey, do these shorts give me kangaroo paw?"

Mom looks at me, dazed and confused. I wince and cover my eyes. "I think she means camel toe."

Nana starts to laugh so hard at us—like *we're* the freaks—that she has to grab her freckled knees to catch her breath. Her legs are white and hearty, skin flapping where muscle tone once was. Amid the laughter and Mom's bewildered critique, I quietly observe that I inherited Nana's thick legs. Did I get *none* of Grandma's delicate traits?

Mom takes a minute to recover from bewilderment. "You mean to tell me you did that in front of *people we know?*"

"Well, sure," Nana says. "They performed a regular miracle on Punk, he was swollen like a whale from his diabetes. I wanted to show them my moneymaker."

"Dear God," Mom says. "Just so you didn't show them your baby-maker."

At that Nana and I begin howling, and Mom looks at me shaking her head.

"See why I married your father?" she says, and turns back to Nana. "Heck with the flowers and body lotion. We should have gotten you a gift certificate for a spray tan."

DAD'S CAR CLOCK READS 6:22 and Grandma's watching golf in front of Grandpa's big screen when I shut my car door and ring the bell to her house. I give her a hug and kiss, handing her the body lotion wrapped in the same girly cellophane sack as I'd presented to Nana. I gesture to the TV. "Where they playing today?"

She shrugs. "Oh, I don't know." She has it on because golf was Grandpa's favorite thing to watch on Sundays after church. "Have a seat, you want a glass of wine?"

"Sure—if you're drinking it too."

She gives me a sly smile and lowers her voice. "Your uncle Paul and aunt Martha were here today. We killed a bottle of white zinfandel. But sure, I'll have a glass with you."

I follow her into the kitchen, where I have the urge to take over the task of pouring the wine myself. Dad's barbecuing for Mom, and we're planning on dinner at eight. I look at the clock: already 6:32. I step aside, out of Grandma's way.

"You want some leftover spaghetti?"

"No, no thanks, Grandma. Dad's doing hot dogs for Mom in an hour."

"Oh." She's disappointed because it means I'm not staying long. "Hot dogs?" She makes light of it, handing me my glass and leading me back to the living room. We take seats in her side-by-side recliners and toast each other.

"Happy Mother's Day, Grandma."

"Oh, thanks, Kris. Hey, before I forget, did Carisa get ahold of you?"

"Yes," I take a sip, "she e-mailed me. I was so excited, she said she wants to ask me how she'd go about getting into writing. Grandma, you know something? That girl's a writer. Her blog when she was studying abroad, did you read it?"

"Yes, but I didn't always understand her lingo and things."

"Oh my gosh, I was obsessed. She's hilarious." Carisa, my second-to-youngest cousin, embodies our family's work-hard/play-hard philosophy, giving it her own twist: she works hard at one thing, and that is playing hard. Before she transferred to a state university in Missouri to be closer to her parents, Carisa went to a college close to Grandma and Grandpa's Florida house. The week I was there, before Grandpa's chest pains started, he and I got such a kick out of listening to her stories about her classes and antics. He looked at me with the devil in his smile and said, "She's a troublemaker."

"I know," I told him, as though we were initiating her into our exclusive club of family adventurers. "I approve."

I realized then how much I adore my cousins—especially the girls. I've wished at times that I could take them all away on some retreat vacation or move them into a *Real World*–style house, full of just us, and give them advice on guys and work and living alone and all the things I had to learn the hard way. If I love my cousins as much as I do, I can't imagine how much love Grandma must feel for her granddaughters.

"I just think about all you girls," Grandma says, looking into her wineglass. "Carisa and her free spirit, you with your projects and traveling, Maggie's not coming home from school this summer—neither is Gabby for that matter, they both got internships. Trish is moving to San Francisco at the beginning of June . . . and have you heard? Kenneth Cole promoted Nicoletta to senior merchandiser and switched her to a nine-to-five schedule during the week."

"That's good, she'll be able to get home more often instead of dressing windows during crazy weekend and holiday hours."

"That's true." Grandma sits quiet a second, then says, "I'm really happy for you girls and your careers. It makes me sad sometimes that you're all going your own ways in the world. You're leaving."

"Grandma, that's what grandkids do. If we don't leave, then we'll just keep hanging around, driving our parents crazy. They need a break. And you've had more time with your adult grandchildren than most grandparents ever see."

"I know, I wasn't finished with my thought. Because when I think about it, it's much better today than when I was young."

"*Better* than when you were young?" This is the first time she's ever acted wishfully about what it's like to be a girl my age.

She looks at me. "Yes. It is."

That's all she'll say. To fill the silence I tap on the base of my wineglass, then nibble on a few almonds, sitting back into the noisy leather of Grandpa's old recliner to fully appreciate what she has just said.

Then all of a sudden she announces, "I think I'm going to go away for a trip."

"*Yeah?*" I put down my glass. For months we've all been telling her that a change of scenery might snuff out the last of her grief. We've even offered as a family to pay the cost of her flight if she wants to go visit Aunt Marie in St. Louis. "Grandma, I think that would be wonderful for you. You'll be amazed at how a vacation changes your perspective."

She slaps her knee in epiphany, suddenly upbeat. "That's what I've been thinking."

"Remember my first vacation to Italy, how refreshed I was when I came home? I felt like a new person. Grandpa said I had 'the Roman glow.' " Then it dawns on me, and I ask, "Grandma, have you ever traveled alone before?"

"No, but . . ." She begins talking quickly, as though the idea's coming together right before her mind's eye. "Tricia said if I want to go in June when she moves to California, we can fly together and she'll make the stop in St. Louis so that I have a travel companion."

"That's perfect! Then you'll come back and we'll all be at the Landing for the Fourth of July, then first weekend in August we have bocce, then two weekends after that is, geez, that's Zach's wedding already."

"I'm looking forward to seeing Uncle Bill at Zach's wedding." Uncle Bill is Grandpa's favorite brother. He never had any children and he lost his wife—my dad's favorite aunt—to cancer fifteen years ago. Uncle Bill loves being with our family, and even though he's always lived hours away, I think he considers my cousins and me to be like grandkids. I raise my eyebrows. "You think you and Uncle Bill will dance?"

"Kristine!"

"What, Grandma, it's an innocent question!"

She shrugs irreverently. "I told you once that I found all your grandpa's brothers to be handsome, didn't I?"

I gasp in mock shock. "Gloria Delores!"

"I need to look forward," she says. "My puzzle club tried to talk me into going to Florida, but all our friends down there live in our old neighborhood, and I don't want to face that place without Grandpa."

"Your puzzle club?"

"Yes, it's new. We meet down at the community center once a week."

"Are there any single men? Think you'll find your missing piece?"

"That's enough, young lady. This wine is getting to us both."

"Oh Glo, lighten up. So in St. Louis you and Aunt Marie can shop and go to museums, and Uncle David will probably take you out to eat and to a Cardinals game."

"Right. I don't want just a few days. I'm thinking two weeks." I think of the burden this will take off my dad, who calls Grandma most nights before dinner, after working a full workday and then his marathon training. This will also be a relief for my uncles, who chip in and take a lot of responsibility for Grandma's loneliness and well-being too. She looks at me. "I'm done with the antidepressants."

I sit quietly a second, then smile gently. "I think that's really positive, Grandma." The pills have helped her get through the worst of her grief, but it's true: we're not women who are content to depend on outside sources to make us feel happy.

When I go to hug Grandma goodbye, she's still perky and lit up. Never before had she hinted to me that she wasn't perfectly accepting of the life she lived; that there are parts of her granddaughters' lives that women her age may actually envy. Also, never before had she taken ownership of her own independence or even dreamed of traveling without my grandpa. The conversation makes me all the more okay with the fact that Chris wasn't part of today: I discovered my grandmothers all over again.

A WEEK LATER Chris rings me to ask if I can come in and work at his satellite office for the next week or so. "Chris, I'm sorry," I tell him. "I'm on four deadlines, and they're intense." I tell him I know a college student who's looking for summer work, and he hesitantly agrees to take down her number.

Two nights later he calls me again. "Hey, the girl you sent me is decent, but I really need you," he says. "Nobody sees a project through like you do."

"Chris," I say, firmly, "I wish I could." I pause. "Look, I have a light at the end of the tunnel next week. If you get in a jam with Kylie, let me know and I'll see what I can do."

"Awesome. Kris, I really need you."

"Well," I say, "we'll have to see." Geez, Grandma's don't-chase theory works!

"Well, then when are we going to have another one of our grandparent brunches?"

I laugh. "I don't know, you're leaving in two weeks, aren't you? How long is it this time?"

"Four months."

Yikes.

One night Mom and I are heading out to meet Dad for dinner when my phone rings. "Is he calling every night now?" Mom asks.

"Just about."

"Honey, he needs your help," she says.

"Oh, *fine*." I answer the phone. "Hello, Dr. Christopher. Are you calling to inquire about my assistance?"

The next morning I put on a blue dress and pastel heels. Chris picks me up in my driveway and opens my car door. "You want me to drive so you can make calls?" I ask him.

"Good idea." We do a Chinese fire drill around his SUV. "You know," he says, climbing into the passenger side, "you're more than welcome to keep my car for the summer while I'm gone. I realize it can't be fun sharing wheels with your parents."

"Oh, Chris, thank you," I tell him. "That's so kind of you, but really it's not necessary." It would be an honor, he insists. I tell him, "Listen, how about this: if you bring it up again, then we'll discuss it."

That morning I sit at his desk, plowing through everything he'd had on our to-do list—paying invoices, booking flights, picking up his suits from the tailor. "So you're all set!" I say. "You could leave the country tonight and everything would be taken care of."

His eyes go wide and panicked, and he asks me can I please return in the morning. "There's more," he says.

But the next morning our agenda takes me only an hour— I fill most of the day catching up on my e-mail and making changes to an article.

At lunch he pops his head in. "Kris," he says. "Can you join me for dinner tonight?" The question catches me off guard, until he explains that he's meeting with his accountant this evening and would like me to be there as an extra set of ears.

Ah. "Yeah, I can join you. Besides, you're my ride."

Speaking of that, he says, he meant what he said about my using his car this summer. "You should take my laptop too," he says. "Yours looks like it's on its last legs." I glance over at my Mac with its perpetually dim screen and the external keyboard I've been using since last summer when I spilled a bottle of water, frying my keys.

"Okay," I tell him. "It's a deal."

Before we leave the office he changes out of his scrubs into a button-down shirt and slacks. He dresses just around the corner from me so we can keep talking, and I can hear the rustle of clothes, the zip of his zipper. He peeks around at me. "Do I need a tie?"

"No," I smile. "He's an accountant, not an investor."

He carries both of our briefcases out to the car. "Ooh, Kris, you carry this thing around?"

"Heavy, right?"

"Yes, a little."

"I have a strong back."

When he climbs into the driver's seat, I feel like we're headed out for a date instead of a business meeting. "Where should we tell him to meet us?"

"Luigi's," I say. "If you're up for Italian."

He calls his accountant. "Well, it's DuBois, so it's Luigi's or Luigi's." He whispers over the receiver to me, "I have to stop at the hospital first."

I nod.

In the hospital parking lot Chris walks around my side of the truck to help me down. "I love those shoes," he says, pointing to my satin heels.

"Oh, thank you," I tell him. "We have the same taste, don't we?"

"In shoes?"

"In general."

The nurses point us back to his patients' room. The man is in his early fifties and just had his gums grafted. "Dr. Christopher?" he lisps as Chris removes the tongue depressor from his mouth. "I'm really feeling some stress about something. I don't like the dentures my dentist designed for me."

"Okay," Chris says, slipping out of his rubber gloves and crossing his arms to listen. "Let's talk about that." The poor fellow says that the dentures just look too big, and he's afraid to spend a couple thousand dollars on something he doesn't like.

"If I may interrupt?" I say, sitting on the chair in the hospital room.

"Sure, Kris," Chris says.

"Is it that you don't know what your options are?"

"Exactly!" the patient says.

Chris tells him that as a doctor, there's only so much he can do for a patient's health and satisfaction. "When a patient's not happy," he says, "I want them to tell me. And I know your dentist, and he's the same way."

The guy is in much better spirits when we leave, and he winks at Chris as he shakes my hand. "She's a looker," he says.

Chris smiles and shuffles me out the door.

When we get back out to the car, I buckle into my seat belt. "Chris, you are . . . an *amazing* doctor." That patient was so distraught about his appearance and the money he was about to spend on something that didn't suit him. "I mean look at you:

you've been with patients all day and you're headed to a business dinner, and your concern is to make sure your patient feels heard."

"That means the world to hear you say that, Kris. I was glad you spoke up the way you did." He pulls the vehicle onto Interstate 80. The evening sun is shining down on the cornfield ahead of us, and, my God, this is the same road we traveled home from our first date.

I feel that we're even more connected right now than we were that night, when we shared Swiss gum and music and an intimate dinner and the wind blowing through our hair; the night I fell into bed trying to memorize his face. Over the last year there have been moments when I felt I knew him better that first evening than at any other point in our friendship— this complicated character who requires so much support and understanding in his quest to share his talents with the world. If I weren't so happy to be riding in his co-pilot's seat right now, I'd be devastated. After he leaves for Asia next week, it's possible I'll never see him again.

That reminds me. "Hey, do you need a ride to the airport on Tuesday?"

"Yes!" he says, and grabs my hand in my lap, gripping it excitedly in his. "Thank you for asking!" He gives me a solid squeeze, then lets go. I pretend to nonchalantly look out the window, even though the feel of his hand has left a sensory impression in mine.

He calls a patient from the restaurant parking lot, so I go inside to meet his accountant at the bar. "His name's Dick," he says. *Great.*

Dick and I introduce ourselves and make small talk, but by the time Chris joins us, my head is already spinning. "He seems to think I'm managing your books, Chris," I seethe as the bartender takes Dick's drink order. "I'd do it if push came to shove, but I'm afraid it would be over my head." He tells me not to worry. We muddle through the conversation, which covers international tax law and other totally foreign topics.

"Exactly when are you planning to turn in your payroll report?" Dick asks.

I lean in to Chris. "Dick, it will get done when it needs to. Chris never leaves things unattended." Somehow my hand has found its way to the warm spot between Chris's shoulder blades. It lingers there, and I can feel the toned muscles under his shirt. Chris doesn't move a millimeter . . . but *maybe* two chardonnays are enough for me. I do some quick math, figuring it's been eight hours since I've eaten anything. "I'm starving," I whisper.

He nods. "We'll eat after he leaves." But Dick doesn't leave, and Chris and I wind up scarfing down dinner as a waitress runs the vacuum under our bar stools.

On the way out I show him the picture of me with my arm around Giada De Laurentiis that hangs on Luigi's front wall. "Our families are from the same region in Italy," I tell him.

"That's unbelievable. You know, you two could be sisters."

As I turn out the exit door, I laugh and tell him that he's just paid me the highest compliment anyone can pay me because I think Giada De Laurentiis is the most beautiful woman in the universe.

"Well, like I say," he says sheepishly, "you two could be sisters."

This is the first time he has ever made any reference to my looks or whether he finds me attractive. For a year his approval of my appearance has been an obvious detail missing from the prospect of romance with this man. I share a longing with every woman in the universe to be wanted by the man I want; to be desired for my beauty and my spirit. It's the female's core need, and it's taken what feels like a long time for Chris to fulfill it . . . but he just has. He opens my car door and holds my hand as I get inside, same as he did on our first date. "Thank you, Chris."

In my driveway he walks to the back of his SUV to pull out my bag. Together we walk to the porch, and when I open the front door and step into the house, he sets my bag just inside the door. For a moment he remains standing there on the stoop with his hands resting politely in his pockets. "Good night, Kris."

"Good night." I click the front door closed and watch him make his way across the driveway to his car. I'll help him in his office for the last time tomorrow . . . and then I don't know when I might ever see him again.

I make sure he's around the corner before I turn off the outside lights—realizing we've turned many corners recently, haven't we? For the second time today I feel the way I did the night we first met. He opened my car door that night, same as he did multiple times today. It was a gesture that demonstrated his care for me, his kindness toward me, the compromise of his own position to see to it first that I was comfortable in mine. The first time we ever encountered each other he'd torn himself away from studying the peculiar tree in my yard in order to join me in a shared space, to share an evening with me. I suppose that was when my hopes started to build. I suspected perhaps this man might make a rule of setting aside his own curiosities and fascinations to just . . . *be* with me. I've seen that he's capable of it; it's just that his work trumps everything else in his life.

This is the one dilemma that Grandma's insights can't seem to solve. I ignore the dogs' barking as I slump up the stairs. Mom's grandfather clock chimes midnight. Chris and I have an early morning tomorrow. I'll spend the day running around to pick up farewell gifts that he wants to give to his staff, and I know that when I hand over his credit card at the chocolatier, at the greeting card store, at the café for the staff lunch, the women behind the counter will eye me, wondering who I am to Dr. Christopher. I remember the time I told Grandma he needed a wife. *I'm cut out to play the role of the person who takes care of you*, I want to tell him. *We've been opening doors in each other's lives since we met . . . so why won't we let each other in?*

10

Love by Existing

THERE WAS AN AFTERNOON in early March when Grandma called me in a breathless panic. She'd had a dizzy spell and blacked out in the hallway; somehow, she said, she'd managed not to fall. "I just called the doctor's office and they think I may have had a ministroke," she told me. "Can you come and take me there?"

There was no car at our house, so I dialed my brother and asked him to rush home from work and drive me into town. I stayed quiet in the car so he could zip around the slick roads with high concentration—winter had pounded us for what would be one final time this year, casting the sky in the same bleak tone as the slush that lined the highway. My temple rested against the cold passenger-side window with the same hurried dread I felt flying home when Grandpa was dying.

When the receptionist called Grandma and me from the waiting room, the nurses hardly acted concerned. One stuck a tongue thermometer with a spiral cord under Grandma's tongue and gazed up at the ceiling while another slapped a blood pressure sleeve around Grandma's arm. "That's cold!" she said, as alarmed as a child poking his little foot into a scalding bathtub. I stared astounded at the nurses in their autopilot rush, shocked that they weren't a little more careful of my grandmother's comfort. I didn't care if this was her third visit to their office in a month: she was scared, and I could see the staff's impatience flustering her even more. My hand crept inside my purse—I wanted to text Chris: A *little concerned by what I'm witnessing at my g-ma's doc visit*, I'd write. *We need you*. I didn't dial the message because I never disturb him while he's working, but I could imagine the nurses snapping into their best behavior if he whisked in the door. In reality I'd have to act as Grandma's only advocate: part of this staff's job was to be sensitive to her.

The one nurse removed the stethoscope from her ears and the Velcro sleeve from around Grandma's elbow. She said the problem appeared to be that Grandma's blood pressure was high—it wasn't major, she told us, but she wasn't sure why it was happening. She said the doctor had decided before we arrived that he wanted to do a full-on exam.

The nurse handed me a blue cloth gown with ties in the back; just like the one Grandpa wore in Florida when he was admitted for his heart blockage. "It gets a little drafty in the back, Mrs. Gasbarre," the nurse told Grandma. "Maybe your granddaughter can help tie you in."

"What do you need her to remove?" I asked as she turned to go out the door.

"Everything. She's getting the whole shebang today," the nurse said. "I noticed on her chart that it's been five years since her last pap, so we're going to run that too."

"Oh heavens," Grandma whispered.

The heavy wood door slammed hard on the nurse's exit, making both Grandma and me jump.

"It's chilly in here, isn't it?" she said.

The fluorescent lights highlighted the lines around her eyes unforgivingly, and the doctor's kids stared down at us stoically from a black-and-white photo on the wall. Good God, are they Amish or just unhappy? "Yes, it's pretty cold." From the mood to the antiseptic soap on the sink, the entire room felt completely sterile and just about the last place on earth a woman would want to get naked.

Grandma sighed loudly and unbuttoned her petite pink cardigan. Carefully, I unfolded the chilly blue gown that I was about to help her into. "I guess as Grandpa would say, whaddya gonna do?" she said. "Anything for my health."

I held out my hand and pretended to be casual as my eyes wandered any angle of the room except at my disrobing grand-mother. I heard the rustle of fabric as one by one, very slowly, she removed each article of clothing and placed it over my wrist. After I counted her sweater, her blouse, her pants, and two knee-high stockings, I extended the hospital gown to her. "Here, Grandma, I won't look, but let's get this on fast so you stay warm, okay?"

"Wait," she ordered me, and I felt a piece of satin fall care-lessly into my hand. I turned, shocked, to find a flimsy silk camisole trimmed in lace. Painting on composure, I folded it carefully, trying not to react. What else does this little stinker have up her sleeve?

When I heard her stand, I looked the other way and spread open the blue gown. Her arms tugged into the sleeves, and I pulled the strings together tight so that no one could see her body. She smoothed over the bottom of the gown the way one smooths their church dress over their behind to sit in the pew at church. When she was seated, she slowly angled her back to me. "Dear," she said, "could you please unfasten my brassiere?"

Brassiere. Such a womanly word that no one uses anymore. (Later I looked up its etymology and found that it comes from an old French word referring to a child's jacket, and no wonder—a brassiere, or a bra as we know it now, was created to protect innocent and delicate subjects.)

The brassiere. I rubbed my hands together to warm them up before locating the hook and eye between the gown's breezy gap. Grandma slid the straps down her arms and swiftly removed her bra through the sleeve of the hospital gown, reminding me of the fourth-grade sleepover where I learned to take off my training bra while still wearing a shirt. *Ta-daaaa!*, I'd yelled, swinging it around my head. By accident, on Grandma I see that it's the same type of thing that I might wear. *My God, my grandma wears underwire and lace!* She nimbly folded the tiny cups into one another so they were spooning like newlyweds. She tucked the bra under the folded pile that I'd draped over her chair, then slipped her white loafers back on. I noted that in fact I have inherited some aspect of femininity from my grandmother: when I'm at the doctor's I always carefully fold my clothes and protect my unmentionables by stashing them respectably, hoping that if the doc sees I take good care of my belongings, then he'll take good care of me.

When I knew it was safe to look, I held her hand so she could climb up on the examination table. Her back rested on its incline, and her tiny legs dangled over the side. I thought of lightening the mood with some cheeky *I hate having my girl parts examined, don't you, Grandma?* comment, but I figured she was almost certainly attempting to think about something else.

When the doctor walked in, he gave me a curt nod, then asked me in a whisper, "How's her memory?" I wiggled my hand back and forth, as if to tell him, *So-so.* He and I hadn't been seeing eye-to-eye about Grandma's health. On our previous visit he lectured her about how her mood swings should be stabilizing with the antidepressants. She hated the side effects, she'd told him, and was afraid of dependency, so I innocently asked him what he thought of her seeing a psychologist to talk through her grief of losing Grandpa. "Maybe it would help with her memory too," I'd said. "That's not getting . . . any better." *Please, help us,* I wanted to beg him, but he'd lowered his gaze and narrowed his eyes and told me very firmly—too firmly, with contempt— "I have more physical symptoms to address before we resort to *that.*" I remembered from studying psychology in college that within the medical community, psychotherapy's not always regarded highly . . . and I sat seething in the examination room while he seemed to condescend to my grandma with his notion that she was imagining her symptoms. Again, though, these medical issues are out of my hands. Doing my best means being present and relaying the results to my dad and uncles.

The day of Grandma's alleged stroke, somehow, the doctor

seemed in a bit lighter mood than last time. He yanked the stirrups out of the side of the exam table and curtained off a private curve of space around her. *Thank God!* I love Grandma, and I'm not shy, but on the other hand, knowing her discomfort in exposing her body would've made me squirm too. From the other side of the curtain I could hear the doctor telling the nurse to heat the speculum, and I heard a lamp click on. "Ooh, that's bright," Grandma said. The doctor told her to relax. I held myself in my seat and then heard cues of Grandma's increasing cooperation.

As he quietly checked the parts of her body that she kept all her life for herself and her husband, the understanding slowly occurred to me: Grandma is a *woman*. Until these last few months I've always thought of her in relation to the people in her life: as a wife and a mom, a grandmother, a player in a bridge group, a member of her parish, a pesky customer in a restaurant, a patient at the doctor's office. I've insisted on picturing her as a part of her surroundings, a character in a scenario, a subject always reacting to some outside stimulus . . . but never as a person with thoughts and feelings inside, independent of the situation that happens to surround her. I hear the doctor ask whether it hurts when he presses here, does she feel pressure there, can she take a deep breath so he can hear her heart. Meanwhile my own heart is pulsing noticeably in the subtle discovery of this moment, and inside, I realize, Grandma and I are composed completely the same. We have hearts that beat (and break), minds that think thoughts both spoken and private, parts of our bodies meant to serve both beautiful form and life-creating function. We've both loved, made love, at moments felt sexy and experienced high passion. We've both laid alone at night crying and tortured to understand why our loves are—our love is—gone. Grandma lay there behind the curtain quiet and obedient as the doctor went through his cold procedure to determine the general condition of her very existence. Is she healthy? It depends: does a broken heart count?

In the waiting room I'd assured her that the doctor would take care of everything, but deep down I was as worried as she was. A *stroke*? Could something serious be happening? And if it came down to it, could I consider putting my life on hold to care for her?

There was something Grandma told me late in the summer that pops into my mind often, for no reason: you have to decide on the things you want in life, and address them, before you can commit to sharing a life with someone else. No matter what stage of life a woman is in—in a relationship or out of a relationship—she holds visions for herself in her heart. Grandma's visions have included walking down the aisle to join a hero on his adventure, acting as head of a wild household, and enjoying a retirement where she and Grandpa could kick back and enjoy their grandkids. My visions have been quite different from hers: I wanted to work in New York and spend some time traveling while I was young . . . and now that I can tick those goals off the list, I can start to think seriously about my future: it may involve partnering up with somebody else so we can combine our individual narratives into a love story that's better than fiction . . . or it may not, and I'll live my story on my own.

But Grandma and Grandpa did it together, and I do believe that relationships like that still happen. Love just documents itself a little differently today than it did when they met and got married. When two people committed their lives to one another in Grandma's day, the motive was often a practical one—just take her and Grandpa: she craved a family, he wanted support to be successful in his career. It seems that back then, young people weren't encouraged to be picky about their partners or to consider a young adulthood of self-discovery. Why, if someone fancied you, you simply accepted his kind invitation to spend time together. Picking apart the way he dressed or smelled or acted may have created a social ripple in the community, and in the interest of communal peace and long-term personal contentment, you just said yes because if he was asking you out, he'd probably decided that his feelings for you had the potential to be serious.

Grandma has explained to me that from there, when a boy and girl began to like each other, and after he came around to her house to meet her family a few times, the pair would begin hanging out with packs of their friends. After they'd been spotted out together consistently—"steady"—it was well understood to their peers that they were officially "going out." The transition between courtship and a relationship was generally an easy process to detect for both the couple and the community, and the relationship grew more serious as the couple grew more intimate and attracted to one another. When—usually not if, but when—they reached the point when they were prepared to marry, their plans for the wedding and their life together were modest. Remember, many women didn't work back then, so in most cases there was only one income coming in, which didn't leave a lot of room to splash out on extravagant dates and exotic vacations together. For my grandparents' honeymoon in 1948, they traveled through the Smoky Mountains of Tennessee. They stopped to picnic and snap photos of each other along the road, and recently Grandma flipped through these pictures with all of us granddaughters studying over her shoulder.

In the snapshots, she's classically feminine in a long coat with a dress under it (I couldn't determine the dress's color from the black-and-white image, but she remembered it was navy blue). I imagine what's even deeper beneath this outfit; soft silk and flowered lace, a satin slip that probably both frustrated and thrilled her new husband to keep unwrapping delicious layers before he finally discovered her milk-white skin. She stares into the camera with a look that could be either sultry or shy. Her arms float down to her sides, as though she knows just where to place her hands. Her sexiness is subtle, but knowing. I froze her in my mind, wondering if the day I gaze that way into someone's camera will be sooner, later, or ever. Finally I'm prepared for any of these realities.

In these photos, Grandpa is in sharp slacks and a white button-down shirt with the sleeves casually rolled just past his wrists, and a tie—a tie!—for the honeymoon drive. The Tennessee highway spirals above and behind him, far into the forested mountains, and his rear rests against the wooden guardrail with one leg propped up against it like a model's pose. With his right hand leaning on the rail he stands regal with the landscape . . . only Grandpa could make Tennessee look so irresistible. His pose is the epitome of what I imagine American malehood was like back then: strong, effortless, adoring, *handsome* . . . with a capacity to strike amour in the simplest of settings.

It seems to me that back then, romance was found in the everyday. I imagine couples swaying slowly in the dark to the phonograph after the kids had been tucked into bed; the rattle of ice in a man's scotch glass as his wife took down her hair after a tiring day. I like to think that the men proved their maleness with their character instead of, say, their unmatchable lifestyles or their salaries, and the women didn't compromise themselves to get men's attention the way I've caught myself doing in the past. Although I haven't done it lately . . . and certainly never with Chris.

As a matter of fact, his attention is fixed, not begged for or earned. It's the old-fashioned kind: the slow-building familiarity between us that's transformed patiently into fondness; his nature, which is both kind and strong . . . like my grandpa's. There's an intrigue that sparks just from his looks, definitely, but the more you come to know him, the more magnetic he is. I've found myself so scared of him because he's been a challenging read: he's not the rousingly sauntering bad boy whose mouth tastes faintly like smoke and lime when he kisses me in the bar; he's not the guy who would put up with a woman who gets wrecked on the first date. He stays out of moral trouble and has high standards of behavior and character for the people with whom he surrounds himself, and he finds beauty in a late-night swim in the lake as well as in an old woman's eyes. He's complex, but understanding him is so basic: Chris is the most American man I know.

Maybe if I started looking for what's important in romance—not on the high degree of reckless abandon that a man triggers in me or how much fairy-tale effort is spent to facilitate our physiochemical interaction, but on the integrity and authenticity that a man brings to the table . . . then maybe I'd land lasting love the way my grandmother did.

I'm finally ready to be a *woman* in a relationship. Up to now, for a long time, there were graces that I was sadly convinced I lacked. I remember the night I told Grandma the story about getting so drunk on my date with the twenty-nine-year-old CEO that my own friend had to lecture me about my behavior in front of men. Grandma said to me, "You ruined his image of you," and I agreed yes, I had. She told me that when she and my grandpa dated, she might have drunk *a* glass of wine with him—but back then women who got drunk in front of men were considered "loose." I, meanwhile, can't even count the number of times I've been drunk in front of men; in fact, I can't think of the last time I've shared a sober first kiss with a guy. Junior high, maybe? What does that say about me? I've been scared to share myself with someone without a chemical encouraging me: *Go ahead, it's safe to open up to him. I'll make it so meaningless that you'll probably forget about it in the morning.* What if I'd only ever kissed guys based on their respect for me, not based on the compulsion of our attraction to each other? I guarantee I wouldn't have entered into some of the heart-breaking messes I've gotten into in my twenties. In some cases it's probably best that I can't remember half of what happened.

Getting to know my grandmother better has shown me that the female graces I didn't think existed anymore are actually in my capacity—and in my blood. It's a true skill for a woman to allow another person to care for her . . . and the good news is, it still happens. *I deserve love.* That's all I've had to learn. It's like the Descartes supposition, "I think, therefore I am." I'm a woman, therefore I am wonderful. All we have to do is exist, and for that simple state, we hold the title as World's Most Radiant Creatures.

But that sets the bar for my behavior sky-high. I've learned from Grandma that if I want to be regarded as someone who's intelligent, respectable, and top-shelf, then that's exactly the person I need to *be*. I teach the world how to treat me by the way I treat myself, and the way I present myself.

AFTER THAT DAY when I learned that my Grandma dresses in a camisole under her everyday clothes, I started wearing slips again. It was something I hadn't bothered with since probably my First Holy Communion, but it feels right. There's a layer between the world and me now. Grandma has taught me that whether I'm involved with a man or not, there are parts of my female experience that are only for me. She confided in me one night that no way would she have considered having sex with my grandpa before they got married. "You have to live with yourself afterward," she told me.

Meanwhile a neon sign with the number twelve was blaring in my head, as I'd defensively told my gynecologist at a recent visit, "That's only an average of one a year since I lost my virginity." What have I been *doing*? If I've given a man—multiple men—my most beautiful, sacred form with nothing required from them, then no wonder that's left me feeling worthless at times. Why weren't they calling, why weren't they trying to see me again? It's because my feelings didn't matter to them, because for a minute, probably after too much wine or a few Jagerbombs with my friends, my feelings didn't matter to me. I had wanted to be desired without expecting that these men should want to know my heart first—and they should!—but now I see the value of reserving my most precious self. Besides, as Grandma told me during our sex talk: "Do you think *you'd* like leftovers?" Unless it's Thanksgiving or Mom's spaghetti, not so much. Grandma said that if a woman treats herself as something special, then men are more likely to view her that same way rather than if she carried on like one of Tiger Woods's mistresses. "You'll get more from him, and from the relationship," she explained. These days shots and crop tops are rare in my world.

There were so many presumptions that I'd allowed to be built in my own mind about what a wife should be. I thought she should be a show-stopping cook and a brilliant entertainer, a nonstop quick wit, a wild thing in bed, an effortless nurturer, the bearer of an upbringing that appeared perfectly bred and super achievement-oriented . . . but, if I can be honest, my grandmother was none of those things and she still enjoyed one of the most legendary lives and marriages that I've ever seen. I thought I had to be good at *everything* in order for somebody to love me. I've been trying so hard to get where I'm going before I'll let anybody in, but when my grandpa first noticed my grandma, she was *walking down the street*. She wasn't doing anything superlatively sexy or admirable; she wasn't in a huddle at a party responding cleverly to questions about living abroad; she wasn't wearing the dress that her designer friend in New York made that's been hanging in her closet for four years waiting for the right opportunity to be worn. She was going to meet her mom after work . . . she was just *being*. Grandma has taught me that a man doesn't love a woman because she strives; *he loves her simply because she exists*.

However, I maintain that it's good for a woman to feel inspired by a man. Knowing Grandma, she'd agree. In my college psychology days, I studied a theory stating that every human is born with a drive to self-actualize; to grow and develop to be the best person he or she can be. From what I've witnessed between Grandma and Grandpa (and the relationships that haven't worked out for me yet), a partner should make us want to improve ourselves constantly, and urge us to maximize what we contribute to the world.

When we left the hospital that day, Grandma's doctor sent her home with no worries and simply told her to drop one of her meds that's known for causing dizziness. "No stroke?" she said.

"We'll schedule a CAT scan, but no, I'm quite certain this wasn't a stroke." He paused for a second, and placed his hand over the edge of his clipboard. "And Mrs. Gasbarre, I want to promise you something: your memory is not something that concerns me right now."

She looked up at him.

"You're taking your medication and we're keeping a close eye on you, but the tests always come back normal, and your symptoms aren't severe enough for me to pursue anything more. I'll ask your granddaughter." He looked at me. "Has she always been a little bit of a scatterbrain?"

Grandma snapped her head to look at me. I shrugged and scrunched my nose. "Well, maybe . . ." I looked at her to confess. "Grandma, you have. Especially without Grandpa around to direct you."

She surrendered. "Fair enough."

"Doctor, I do have a question, though: when will she get her pap results?" He said a nurse would call in the next couple days but that with her history, there were no concerns. I ushered

Grandma into the hallway to check out. "Let's go," I said. "I think this calls for ice cream."

"But it's still winter!"

I stopped and turned to her. "You would skip a root beer float in the middle of the afternoon because there's a little snow on the ground?" I shook my head in mock judgment. "What would your husband say . . ."

Of course at that she agreed, asking if I would drive her car since the roads were a little slick. "Now wait a second," she said, stopping again in her tracks. "The better question is, do you need a ride home? Didn't Jeff drop you off at the hospital to meet me?"

"He said he'd come back and pick me up wherever I need him to." I drove Grandma's car, and after we took our ice cream from the walk-up window, I took a bite of my Oreo sundae and opened her car door. "You know, Grandma?" I said. "There's only one thing that could make this afternoon even better."

"Better!" she laughed. "You think a doctor's visit was exciting?"

"It turned out okay, didn't it?" I climb into the driver's seat and move it back a few inches.

"Well, then, what would make this afternoon better?"

"A visit with Grandpa."

She sat quietly.

"Would you like to go see him?"

"I don't know." She rested her small root beer float in her lap and tapped her toes together. "I was in a hurry to see the doctor so I grabbed these slip-ons instead of boots."

"Okay, well, listen. My feet are a little bigger than yours, but if you don't mind my getting your shoes a little damp, then you can take my boots."

She stared at me, dumbfounded. "You're going to . . . wear my shoes."

"Yep."

We decided to switch shoes at the cemetery to give my feet less time to stretch hers. "These are nice," she said, lacing up my hikers, which I've been wearing all winter thanks to their water resistance and warmth. My heels hung off the back of Grandma's spring loafers, but I was careful not to crush them down as I walked around to help her out of the car.

She braced my arm. This is a habit that strikes me constantly these days, when I think about how intimidated I was to take her hand the day I arrived home from Italy to tell Grandpa goodbye. How we've grown individually, and together.

Her every step across the snow was conscious and precise as she looked up occasionally to measure how far we were from Grandpa's headstone. "Grandma, don't worry," I said. "Just tromp through it, get them wet." I kept her pace, allowing her to hang tight to me, while balancing her kept my mind off the cold seeping through the heels of my socks and spreading around my feet entirely. In my rush I'd grabbed my long black ankle-length coat from the closet, the dressy one from New York that I'd worn in this very spot for Grandpa's burial just over a year ago. The wind at St. Catherine's Cemetery seemed to love the coat, billowing its bottom without a break. With my bare hand I slid the snow off the ledge of Grandpa's stone. Grandma stood silently.

I welcomed wandering thoughts, as they helped keep my

mind off the chill. *What's she thinking?* I wonder if it's more than a myth that older married couples enjoy very active sex lives. And I know this may be odd, but I wonder if Grandma misses being intimate with Grandpa. When she cries, is it ever for his hold around her body, his warmth, his breath against her mouth? I remember reading something by an author—I wish I could remember who—who said that while she was living in New York, she used to go get manicures just to be touched by another human. When we women live alone, not being hugged or kissed enough is one of the most throbbing realities to live with. I linked my arm tighter through Grandma's.

Around the cemetery the flags had been taken down to protect them from winter, and it was undeniable: for four gray months a year, these grounds truly mark this life's end. Uncle Phil bought the fanciest flag-holder on the market for Grandpa, but it sat empty, bouncing against the wind. Grandpa's here resting the way Grandma wished him on, I thought. *In peace.* I squinted at the snow's brightness, wondering which one of us, Grandma or I, needed the other's support worse. *I'm walking in Grandma's shoes.* I wondered if she felt more secure wearing mine than she did when she left the house. We stood quiet until she said, "I never come here alone, you know."

"I know. That's why I came with you."

"Do you?"

"What, come here alone? Yes, all the time. Sometimes I think about bringing a picnic here and eating it, or bringing a lounge chair and tanning here next to him."

"That's strange!"

"Well, I've never actually done it, but I've thought about it. It's just peaceful to be here with him. I could always tell him anything." I looked at Grandma. "You too?"

"I could've, I suppose . . . but I didn't. He had enough to worry about without me bending his ear."

"Oh, Grandma, that's silly. You two were close." Again, our relationships with Grandpa highlight Grandma's trademark cautiousness versus my typical audacity. "I took him literally when he told me, 'You can do anything you want to do.'"

"I know you did!" Her laugh is hushed by the cushion of the snow.

"But I have yet to pack a picnic."

When we get back to her house, Grandma puts both pairs of our shoes by the heater and goes to get me warm socks. When my brother arrives and stands in the entryway, Grandma holds me long and tightly in a hug, until she pulls away and stares into my eyes. "You saved me today."

"I wouldn't have had it any other way." With Grandma's phone call to the doctor—and her lifelong philosophy on her body—she saved herself. *Anything for my health*, she'd shrugged. Her simple approach is a good lesson. In her relations with a man or when she's completely on her own, a woman has a duty to herself to keep a sound body and mind.

Grandma may have saved herself, but maybe today she saved me too.

11

No Angry Goodbyes

THROUGH THE OPENING in my curtains it's clear this is one of those Saturdays most people wait for all year. A bird bounces from a high branch to one lower and sturdier, its tiny voice narrating its wings.

My clock says the day is creeping on noon, and when the neighbor's lawn mower stops, there's the hum and happy splash of boats on the lake. It's been ten years since I've witnessed Memorial Day at home; this perfect few days that epitomizes the concept of *weekend* and marks the start of the Treasure Lake summer.

The weather outside would make the last two hours that I've spent crying in bed totally uncalled for . . . except this feels *so good.* Tears trail consistently from the corners of my eyes and drop fast like pinewood derby cars over the slope of my temples, landing in the ditches of my ears, or when I look up at the ceiling, in the pool that's collecting in the back of my hair and soaking through my pillow. These sobs are both torturous and fantastic.

I know this feeling: I'm in love.

I didn't know what to say yesterday at Chris's satellite office when his partner Joe invited me to the farewell dinner he was holding at his house for Chris. "You're welcome to join us," he said. "You've been important around the office these last couple weeks."

"Oh, thanks, Joe." I played it off casually, but my eyes shifted to Chris, whose jeans and Italian vest didn't exactly lend themselves to the hunt for files he appeared to be conducting on all fours. "That's very generous."

"So are you coming?" Joe coaxed. "Come on, I'm barbecuing!"

I wanted to discuss it with Chris first because I really didn't know whether I belonged at a Friday evening dinner with his full office staff. Logistics-wise, however, it was the only plan that made sense. Chris was my ride home. "I'd love to," I said.

A month ago when Chris arrived home from his last trip abroad, he'd mentioned treating me to a glycolic facial peel. I was surprised, given that I've seen his patients spend anywhere from three to five hundred dollars for a peel or two. When he first offered, I was cautious in assuming he planned to do it for free. "It'd be right up my alley," I told him, "and it's generous of you to offer. I just don't know that I can afford it right now."

He paused from studying an X-ray he was examining to look up at me. "Kris, I'd be insulted if you thought I would ever take your money."

It was gentlemanly! When I told Grandma about it, she shrugged and said, "Why not take him up on it, you know how many women would line up for that?" Of course I'd do it, I figured, while Grandma excused herself to the bathroom. Wait a second, it occurred to me. Just why does he want to give me a chemical peel? Is my face screaming for help so loudly that it's going to keep him up at night when he's on the other side of the world? That's it, isn't it? When he's looking at me, he's picking apart my flaws. The bump across the top of my nose, the lines that are starting to indent my forehead after I've been sitting at the computer too long; and now this, my chin, eternally inflamed with breakouts.

I felt my face flush in anger until I caught the photograph plaque of Grandpa, smiling in his suit and tie, inside Grandma's curio cabinet. *Krissy, Krissy, Krissy,* he sighed. *How many more meals will you have to share with your grandmother before you realize that there are men walking this earth who simply want to do kind things for you.* I imagined his signature Italian shrug-and-frown: *It's a facial! An hour at the spa! You and Emma applied sillier solutions to your skin with things you pulled out of the back of the refrigerator when you were eight!*

'Twas true. So after we wrapped up Chris's very last day in the office before his weekend of packing and then his flight to Asia, I cheerfully obliged him by sitting in the reclining exam chair as he stirs a large blush brush in a porcelain bowl. "You're gonna love what this does for you," he said. "It's going to peel away all the dead skin cells on your face to reveal your healthiest layer."

"My youngest layer, right? That's why women pursue this as an antiaging tactic?"

"Exactly. And when I'm back in the fall we can proceed with the next step. I'll put you under the UV lamp to sterilize your skin down to its deepest layer." It sounded so delightfully Dr. Oz. In relaxation, I settled into the chair till I realized: there's an unspoken understanding that I'm not to tell anyone else he's doing this for me. "You took off all your makeup, right?"

"Yes." I'd done so reluctantly, the thought occurring to me that I've never really let a guy see me without makeup, until, well, I wake up next to him in his bed. *You're moving kinda fast, Chris!* I joked in my head. I wish.

Then he touched lightly on my jaw to tilt my head backward. *Oh, if every man understood the appeal of hand cream the way he does!* He stroked his fingers slowly over my forehead to clear my hair out of the way; then carefully, so carefully, swabbed the area above my eyebrows with a cotton ball, sweeping down my nose and in the crevices around it. He doused another cotton ball to wipe my chin. "Is that witch hazel?" I asked.

"Yes. You like it?"

"Mm," I told him as he swabbed around my mouth. I've always loved witch hazel's fragrance; a combination of floral and therapeutic. I kept my eyes on my feet so our gazes wouldn't lock, then while he stood upside down over me, he took the sides of my face in his hands. "Are you ready?" he said.

I smiled up at him. "You act like this is a serious procedure!"

"Well," he said calmly, "I want to make sure you're comfortable."

"Yes," I told him, settling farther into the chair. "Ready spaghetti."

He began stroking the solution onto my face with his brush. I tried to pretend I was someplace else to ignore the awkwardness of his closeness. *Relax*, I inhaled and told myself. *There is nothing dangerous about being so taken care of . . .* So, I imagined my face was a canvas, and almost immediately his brushstroke turned so calming that I wanted to fall asleep. I remembered being little and not wanting to miss out on the adults' late-night, wine-and-laughter-filled dining room conversations until Grandpa would wave to me to sit on his lap so I could rest my head on his chest. Then he'd trace his pointer finger around my face until I fell asleep.

"Ann, do me a favor," Chris whispered. "Turn out that fluorescent light." His nurses had been hovering in the doorway, having packed up the last of their materials.

"Dr. Chris," I heard Ann say over my head, "you still have some papers to sign downstairs. Do you want me to do this peel so you can finish up?"

"Thanks, Ann, I appreciate that," he said. "But I know Krissy's face well. I need to get this just right."

I know Krissy's face well. I know Van Gogh's *In Arles* well because it hangs over my bed and I get lost in its beauty every day. The way he said that stays with me. I wonder . . . could it be that he pays more attention than I *allow* myself to see?

I tapped my fingers lightly on the chair's armrests, relinquishing my always-has-it-togetherness for one vulnerable moment to feel like a child in this man's care.

"Look at that," Ann said. "She doesn't even have any wrinkles."

"Her grandfather was Italian," Chris explained. "I think that's why."

He remembers, I thought, and suddenly it was clear: he understands where I come from.

Chris, I love you.

What? Where had that thought come from? His wheely stool creaked as he stood to rinse the bowl and place it inside the autoclave oven. I peered around the back of the exam chair, studying his every authoritative move, then sat back when he took the stool again. "Does it burn at all?"

"No."

"Good. No itchiness?

"Nope."

"Excellent. I want you to relax, okay?"

"Yes."

"Ann, we're good here." I heard her remove her weight from the door frame and walk down the hall. Chris wheeled his stool closer. I could feel heat from his face on my ear. "You want to try a relaxation technique that I use with my sleep apnea patients?"

"Sure." His proximity was nerve-wrackingly intimate.

His presence was warm. Again I tried to distract myself with my thoughts: *There's no way he does this with his patients, he'd get sued!* But, oh, why was he getting so close when he was about to move away? I breathed steadily, consciously loosening my hands and shoulders. I imagined his breath on my mouth, his lips on mine. Secretly I wanted that. I inched my head a degree closer to him.

"I want you to imagine that you're wrapped up in a hundred blankets," he said. "They're warm and light and loose enough that you're free to move. Can you feel them?"

Somehow I feel completely normal answering yes.

"Good, Kris. And there's a soft light shining above you, but second by second it's disappearing, and soon the room will go completely dark."

The nurses told us to tell Grandpa to walk into the light when he was dying, I thought, remembering how he'd stop writhing in his bed in pain and discontentedness when we told him that it was okay to approach heaven.

Chris continued. "When the vision of that light is gone, it's replaced by a steady, placid sound that transports you. Don't speak, but think of what that sound is." I heard waves at night on the Landing's shore with the echoed rumble of trucks over the mountain on the interstate. When I was little I swore that was the sound of the world turning. "Now imagine that sound blanketed by snow in the winter, and you're sleeping all season, with nowhere you have to be. Very well done, Kris," he said. "As you've been relaxing, your body temperature's been rising. Your breaths are profound now. They're delivering fresh oxygen to your blood and muscles." I felt almost hypnotized, unable to make a sound. I could only continue breathing. "I'm going to leave you alone a few minutes," he said. "But I'll be back."

Everything was black, until a clear thought surfaced: there are definitely moments when it's actually beneficial to a woman to let a man take care of her.

I'm not sure how long I lay there resting—five minutes? Twenty?—But when he returned he waited to turn on the light until after he placed a warm, damp cloth on my face and wiped away the solution. "I want you to stand up and rinse off your face," he said. "Do you feel renewed?" I turned on the water of the stainless-steel basin and rinsed until I felt him hold a towel against my arm. After I dried off, he handed me a mirror and finished wiping the space between my ear and my jaw. In the mirror I saw that his nurses had returned. "It's beautiful, isn't it?"

I made a face like Mona Lisa, not wanting to draw more attention to myself in front of this audience. My face shone in the lucid way it used to in grade school, when I first learned to use Noxzema. The sensation was so clean, so deep down and thorough, that the tiny lines around my eyes had disappeared and the tone and freckles from the sun had evened out. I considered telling him, *You do good work,* but I understood that this wasn't for his ego—it was for me. And so I agreed: "It's really beautiful."

When his assistants exited the room, he braced his hands around my shoulders and stopped me, standing belly-to-belly, so close that I couldn't tell if he was examining my forehead or staring straight into my soul. "Perfect."

Perfect . . . did he mean me, or his work? As we walked down the hollow hallway together, I slipped into a fantasy, pretending that he'd just created me; this modern Pygmalion sculpting my flawless femininity from his own vision. In an exam room where most patients go to have their teeth pulled, he'd just crafted art; he'd just restored beauty. This fluorescent-lit atmosphere left most people feeling clinical and cynical . . . but I felt gratitude and massive affection.

This is what it's like to be loved by a man. Before a woman falls in love, her beauty is the cause of a man's admiration, the carefree pull that captivates him. But then after she falls in love, even more radiance is the effect. I remembered that the Monday I went into work after I met Adam Hunt, my boss stopped at my cubicle with her coffee and said, "Dear God. You've met someone, haven't you?" When I spun away from her in my chair, she said, "There's no sense in denying it. Look at you, he woke you from the dead." And in a sense, yes, he had woken me up from that lonely, self-conscious bad dream that I experienced as dating in New York, in which I could encounter men on the surface but felt embarrassed for wanting to give them my love. Adam Hunt had cleared away the cobwebs from the warm, loving space inside me that I'd kept locked up for all of my young adulthood. And so it goes: when a female becomes the object of a male's desire—no matter how primitive the concept may seem—it's as though he's kissed a sad, sleeping princess and breathed life into her from his own breath. And she begins, then, to see herself through his eyes, her every movement and glance and emotion turning passionately cognizant, as though she's watching the most womanly version of herself from some priviledged audience. Never before has she been more beautiful; and never before has she been more herself.

When you think of it that way, it's no wonder Grandma misses Grandpa so much. In these last few weeks, though, I have experienced that again. Allow me to backpedal just a moment: I certainly believe that I'm self-assured enough to live without a man's validation; I feel sufficiently lovable on my own. But having the attention of a man again—as subtly displayed as Chris's attention usually is—has made me excited to get out of bed every morning. On days when I dress a little glamorously for the office, I know that he notices; and on days when I dress more demurely, I know he appreciates it. For most of the year that I've known him, I've wondered whether he was even seeing me, even when I was standing right in front of him. So the offer for the facial . . . it showed me that he cared.

I suppose the lack of this kind of attention is what Grandma's trying to cope with right now. It's made her spirit more sluggish. For two decades after Grandma Angela's husband passed away, she used to tell us all with her Roman accent, "I just want to die. Without him I have no reason to live." We witnessed her living a busy life of capability, and Grandma Angela did live a full life without her husband, but for her it wasn't full enough. I know that every morning my Grandma Glo is fighting that same sad surrender . . . but I think she gains energy when she sees how my femaleness is blossoming. She noted the dynamic between Chris and me at brunch a few weeks ago, and looking back I remember how nurturing my actions toward my grandmothers were and how delicately I'd presented myself that day. I sense that Grandma is proud of the woman I'm growing to be, especially when her own femininity may feel like it's fading.

After the facial, Chris carted the last of his boxes to his SUV and then walked with me down the one-block stretch from the office to Joe's house for dinner. It was during this stroll that I felt an emotion transact between us as undeniable as a static shock. I wore a white denim skirt and a little pink Mandarin blouse with white buttons lining the collarbone. We strolled slowly on the sidewalk as the evening sun led us along, and once again the moment felt more like a date where we should reach for each other's hand than a business dinner or a chat between friends. Chris said suddenly, "You know what I really want to see?"

"What?"

"The Princess and the Frog."

"Really?" I started laughing.

"Yeah. It's out, you know." He paused, and his voice lowered. "What are you doing tomorrow night?"

Oh, the sheer misfortune! He was about to ask me out but I already had plans. "My friend Celeste from college is coming in. She's the one who lived with me in Italy."

"Ah," he said. "Maybe another time then." He looked down at my pastel plaid heels and said, "Will those be okay in the grass?"

"Oh yeah, thanks, they'll be fine," I said, glancing at my feet as if to convince him I hadn't tried on half a dozen pairs of shoes with this outfit. Then I made a hasty decision to push my luck: "You speak like someone who's dated a lady or two."

I heard nerves rattle when he chuckled. "Not for a while," he said.

The final confirmation: he wants me to know he's single.

Joe's wife Claire seated Chris and me across from each other at the dining room table because the office staff had occupied the umbrella table outside. As Claire and Joe settled into the dining room with us and opened a bottle of wine, Claire explained that they'd renovated last fall. With the flowing floor plan and sophisticated appliances—right down to the electric wine opener—it was clear they loved to entertain. As Claire poured pinot grigio into my glass, instantly I relaxed into the ambience of their home. The kitchen was dressed in stainless steel and a merlot-colored French toile scene of a couple picnicking peacefully by a lake.

Joe and Claire have been together since high school and she helped put him through med school. Now she manages his office. She told me that ever since their fourth son graduated from college a few years ago, they make an annual trip to Europe or the Caribbean, hoping it will be soon when one of their boys announces a baby's on the way. "Oh, you should meet my mom," I replied. "She's dying for grandkids too." As soon as the words were out of my mouth I realized what I'd said. Involuntarily my eyes shot across to Chris, who stared at me poker-faced.

Over dinner the staff buzzed with different stories from around the office, but Joe and Claire talked with Chris and me about their vacation last summer in the French countryside. "Oh, I *love* France," I gushed.

"Chris, you're thinking about buying a flat in Paris, aren't you?" Joe said, and instantly I darted my eyes to avert them from Chris's. Unknowingly, a few weeks ago I'd told him that Paris was my favorite city in the whole world.

He busies himself with his fork, flipping over a piece of lettuce that's on his plate. "I've been looking into it."

After we cleaned up from dinner, Claire directed all of us to the backyard for dessert. On the way out I asked Chris quietly, "How much longer were you thinking of staying?"

"Actually," he said, "I'm going to spend the night here. Joe and I are going for a bike ride tomorrow morning."

"Oh." *How am I supposed to get home?*

"You can take my car if you want."

I shook my head. "No, remember, my friend Celeste is coming to town tomorrow and I wouldn't have time to come back and get you."

His assistant voiced up. "Krissy, I live out at the lake and I'm leaving now, why don't I just take you?" she offered.

Chris stood, giving me the cue that I should probably jump on that option.

"Okay," I said quietly. "Thank you." But I felt like I'd just been dumped in public, with all the staff staring at me for my next move while their ice cream sundaes melted.

I hugged Claire and Joe, who told me they hope to see me even after Chris leaves next week. "I have your card," Joe said. "You do good work, I'd like to get you involved in some projects this summer."

"I'd love that."

Chris approached me from across the patio. "Sorry, Kris," he said. "We just planned the ride today."

"Don't be sorry," I said, barely attempting to mask my irritation. "This solution works fine."

But a low drum kept billowing in my stomach, even after Chris's assistant dropped me off at the Ski Lodge to meet my brother and cousins for happy hour on the deck overlooking the old slopes. We pounded shots of tequila, and my cousin Jake spun me out on the dance floor, but everytime the thought of Chris sparked in my consciousness—hazed as it was growing—it took me out of the moment. Was my attraction growing that obvious? Did he think I'd be disappointed by his staying at Joe's because it meant we wouldn't be riding home together? Well, I'll admit: I sort of had conjured this image of the two of us arriving back in town and stopping for a glass of wine on Luigi's garden patio or the balcony at the country club that overlooks the lake. No volume of alcohol or music could drown out how poorly it was sitting with me; the way that dinner ended.

I FAINTLY REMEMBER my brother driving me the half mile home from the Ski Lodge . . . and then my mom meeting us at the front door and helping me into bed, which must be why I'm waking up in pajamas instead of with yesterday's skirt up over my head. On hungover mornings like this when I lived in New York, I'd meet my friend Lynne for brunch and she'd shake her head miserably (and hilariously) over the menu, saying, "We need to make some changes." Today I will: I have to address these feelings for Chris.

I'm going to tell him. I'm scared, but I can't keep shoving this down and pretending it doesn't exist. People make themselves sick from that, don't they? Here in bed the words come to my mind effortlessly, like bubbles from the bottom of a champagne glass, and the more I cry, the more the headache and the stress are released from my brain. *This is real*, I want to tell him. *There is an emotional—no, a spiritual exchange—taking place here, and I can feel that there are moments when it's definitely two-way. And I know that I may never see you again, but I need to say all of this.*

Then, these next words surface in my mind:

I think I'm in love with you.

I roll my head into my pillow to wail. *In love with you!* Why does it happen like this! The pain, the delicious misery! I feel crazed. Grandma would be horrified if she saw me like this, her hands covering her mouth in mild terror, backing away toward the door. This is not how a sane woman behaves! This is not the effect that love has on a healthy person! But then I remember how she's told me that at night, and sometimes even in the day, she has to go to her bedroom and scream and wail for Grandpa. Even Grandma does it!

I think—I *think*—my grandpa had a hard time showing his emotions until his later years. One summer evening, oh, I must've been about six, I was sipping at a Shirley Temple at the Landing bar and he was busy drying glasses on the other side. I bit my little red straw, then pointed it at him so he could see me in the mirror. "Hey, Grandpa," I said, "here's a question for you: how come every time I tell you goodbye, you never kiss me and say 'I love you' like my mom's mom does?" Who did I think I was, his therapist? He had no response except to busy himself even more, but that night when I was leaving, I went over to him and hugged him around the waist. "Love you, Grandpa," I said.

And for the first time, he told me out loud: "I love you too."

He was generally very kind with my grandma, but he wasn't always known for being affectionate. She's explained to me over and over that he was always distracted, infatuated by his work. She could never hold his complete attention or get his full disclosure; even when they fought, his method of apologizing was to say, "Well, are you done being mad?"

Chris is perhaps a good deal more progressive than that . . . but when it comes to relating, man, does he have a lot of catching up to do. "How come you never kiss me and say 'I love you'?"

Do I want to spend my whole life asking a man that question? Or, is it possible that Chris has the capacity to open up and take my lead, the way Grandpa did?

Maybe that six-year-old Krissy's question was so untamed and innocent that it was wise: if I'm willing to open up first, it's *within the realm of possibility* that Chris could begin to share his feelings too. I don't know if this makes me strong or weak, but I don't think it's right to let him walk out of my life without him knowing what's developed in my heart. In these last couple weeks he's revealed more than ever . . . not everything, not even a *lot*, really; but enough.

I don't need the world from him, not today and maybe not ever. I don't even need his forecast about where he thinks things between us could go, if he sees them going anywhere. I can tell him how much I care about him and then let him go. I watched Grandma do it. The advantage I have over her is that I already know I'll be okay on my own.

If I tell him how I feel and he doesn't feel the same, at least I've told him. I love him as he is, not on the condition that he loves me too. If Grandma could sum up her message in an airplane banner outside my bedroom window right now, it would probably read like some version of this: "Krissy, you can't control how a man expresses himself. Love him anyway."

I might never get what I want from him. I know this. But still, I care. It's a kind of love I've never managed before: I don't really feel the need to demand anything in return; and I want to prove my care for him with my life instead of with my body. Of course, I wouldn't marry him tomorrow—come on, he still has so much to prove. Could he ever commit? Would he give our relationship the time that partners need to share together? Would *our* future be as important as *his* future? I'm not sure, but it may not matter: in two days he's leaving, and when he returns, it'll only be for a short break before he has to go back to Asia . . . and by then I could be gone. If I don't tell him, then he'll never know; and either way I'll continue without him.

I take a deep breath and smear the last of my tears, itchy on my skin and trickling to my hairline, off my face. *Ah, Krissy, nobody's ever accused you of doing things the easy way.* Why must I always love men who leave . . .

The downstairs phone rings. The machine picks up the call, and it rings again. It takes all of my mental focus to roll my body out of my bed: I'm never drinking again. The phone rings a third time, and when I make it to the kitchen, it's Mom's cell calling. I rub my head. "Hello?"

"Are you just waking up?"

"No." My mouth tastes like Patrón. "I just don't feel well."

"Oh. Dad and I are in town with Grandma."

"Oh, you're planting flowers for Grandpa today!" I need to sit down.

"Yep, we did it." I missed it. "But while we were there, Grandma told us something. We want you to hear it from her."

I sprawl out in the wooden kitchen nook. "Okay." Oh no, something's wrong . . .

"Dear?"

"Grandma?"

She giggles. "It's silly really, but we were talking while we were planting Grandpa's flowers—oh, speaking of Grandpa's flowers, you should see the beautiful red, white, and blue geraniums your mother found this morning, and your aunt put down fresh bark and the flag—and you really won't believe this: when we tipped over the plastic container of blue geraniums, guess what came out?"

"What?"

"A frog!"

I laugh, but it sends my head blaring. "Grandpa was there to play a prank on you, wasn't he?"

She's giggling. "He was." I hear my dad in the background. "Oh right, I'm getting off track. Dear, that day that we had brunch with Chris and his grandparents . . ."

"Yes?"

"Well, I just had a feeling that day . . ."

A feeling? Oh no, I wasn't enough of a lady at brunch!

"Dr. Christopher . . . he's the man for you."

I whisper into the phone. Certainly I've heard her wrong. "What did you say, Grandma?"

"I have a very distinct feeling about this. Chris is the man who's going to be your husband."

"Oh my God!"

She laughs. "I know, dear, it's very strange. But I felt it that day at brunch."

"You mean a premonition?"

"I can't say," she says quizzically. "It was just . . . a feeling."

I speak with caution: "Grandma, it's so strange you're saying this right now. I'm embarrassed to admit it, it's a shame, actually, because it's such a beautiful day out, but I've just spent the whole morning sobbing in bed because I've realized: I feel something really strong for him."

She continues giggling through the phone. It's probably been a very long time since my grandma has felt part of any occasion really important and joyous.

My head isn't pounding, and suddenly I'm dying for something to eat—just like that, I feel better. "But Grandma, I have my hesitations."

"I'm sure you do, dear."

"Right? Because I don't feel that he's been particularly . . . *forthcoming* about how he sees me."

"Dear," she says, "you've been through a lot with this whole situation, how can I explain what I'm thinking. . . . Let's put it this way: I think it's good that you'll have some time away from him."

"'Absence makes the heart grow fonder'?"

"*Not* that as much as that it sounds like you have a lot of feelings to sort out. He's shown you that he's not someone who's going to move quickly, and I've said it before, that's positive. But with him being gone, you won't be able to throw yourself into the romance—"

"Which you've seen me struggle with way too many times before."

"Well," she says politely, "yes. Maybe this will give you a chance to—what would you say—process all this at a healthy pace." She pauses a minute. "Although I will tell you this: something tells me that by your birthday, you'll have a better sense of where all this is headed."

"Really, Grandma!"

"Your birthday, the holidays, right around then. Just take it easy. A day at a time. But I do see something between you two—and I'll tell you, so does he."

If anybody knows what love looks like, if anyone knows the sensation of a male and female pairing well together, it's my grandma. She and I have both been sensing that there's something promising going on between Chris and me. I rest my tearstained, blazing cheek against the cool brick of the kitchen nook. *Grandma sees it too.* Mom gets back on the phone to apologize that there aren't any groceries for Celeste's arrival, but I tell her that we were planning to go to the market as soon as she gets in.

And around five o'clock, Celeste's Jeep rolls up my driveway. When I walk out to greet her, there's a note written on a piece of spiral-ripped notebook paper sitting on Mom's porch bench. The presentation's perplexing, but the message inside says it all: *In case your trusty computer dies this summer,* it says in careful print, *wanted to make sure you had this . . . minus the explicit lyrics.* There's a smiley face scrawled on the paper, under which is resting a CD case with the title scrolled in Sharpie, "Songs to Transport You." It's the jazz CD that I burned for Chris last summer that he's just . . . burned for me? Lower down on the page he wrote, *It's been my sound track for more than one surgery. Thx and Love.*

My confusion turns to shock, then to weak knees. As Celeste tries to maneuver her way into a spot in our driveway, I remember: for a second this morning I thought I'd heard a vehicle out here, and it startled me out of my romantic breakdown. My goodness, it was him! I'd been falling to pieces about him and *he'd been right outside.*

Celeste slams her door shut and hugs me, backing up to put her hands on her hips. "The hair looks good," she says.

"Thanks. It's growing in." I'm still dumbstruck. "You know what, come here. You gotta see this."

She takes the CD, turning it over until she realizes what it is. "And you thought he hated it. I need a copy of that, but call mine 'Portofino Nights.'"

On the way into town we blast the CD in my dad's car and ride with the windows down the way good girlfriends do. As we browse the aisles in the store, I fill Celeste in on the other latest in the Chris saga. I speak hushed as we hover in the tomato aisle. "So two nights ago he tells me that Giada and I could be sisters—"

"Oh boy, does he know the right thing to say."

"I know! Okay wait, tonight: do we want to make dinner, or go out?"

We're at the register sliding grocery bags full of barbecue items up our arms when my phone rings. Celeste shuffles some of my bags out of my hands so I can dig through my purse. I stare wide-eyed at Celeste. "It's Chris."

"Get it!"

"Hi, Chris." I say it quietly in case anyone I know is close by the register.

"Hi. Did you get what I left you this morning?"

"Yes, I did! Thank you so much, how thoughtful."

"You're welcome, I thought of it last night. I found the CD while I was packing. Listen, Kris, I'm wondering if you have a sec."

I point toward my dad's car in the parking lot and Celeste

pushes our cart through the sliding doors. "Well, I'm just fin-
ishing up at the grocery store and my friend Celeste is here,
but, um, sure, I have a quick minute." Celeste and I unload our
bags into the backseat. Then I put my hand on her arm. She
understands the gesture and stops what she's doing. "Okay, well
exactly what is it that you need to say to me?"

He hum-haws around and I anticipate that he's going to say
he wants to sit down with me before he flies out. Maybe there'd
be time to have lunch together on the beach on Monday, after
Celeste leaves, and we could share the bottle of wine I've been
saving for him and something nice to eat, like sandwiches on
baguette (from Paris in March, he wrote and said he was crazy
for the baguettes and brie there) and strawberries for dessert (he
said he'll think of me every time he slices a strawberry, after I
showed him how the Italians do it: two cross sections into four
sweet quarters). His next words over the phone catch my day-
dream from carrying me away: "I told you that I needed your
help with my practice because you're my friend."

"That's right, I am your friend."

"And I told you that I wanted to leave my car with you all
summer because you're my friend."

"Okay . . ." I watch Celeste, who's watching my face fall.
Carefully she drops her bags in the backseat and moves close
to me.

"But, Kris, this one's really hard for me to say. I just left a meeting with Joe, and I've decided: I don't want you in my business."

It's as though someone has pummeled into my stomach and
taken me down, right there by the shopping cart shelter. I can't

breathe. I stumble onto some words that must sound something like, "I'm not sure I understand what you mean," but his response floats through one ear and out the other like nitrous oxide that's already knocked me out. The late-afternoon sun pounds down on Celeste's blond hair as she rounds the car and climbs in—it's really too beautiful a day for drama; why have I chosen today to let this man in—and because I can't independently think of anything else to do, I begin to follow her cues.

He knows I have a friend in town. Why did he have to get this off his chest right now? In my peripheral vision Celeste digs through my purse and places the car keys into my hand. I don't want to drive while I'm talking on the phone. I don't want to sit here either. I don't want to be having this conversation about staying out of the business of a friend who all but begged me to help him through a busy spell. My brain kicks in and I start my dad's car, carefully navigating the parking lot and into the road. He doesn't want me to take this the wrong way, he says, but I can't think of any other way he could mean it. He's not even giving me any reason; just those seven words. *I don't want you in my business.*

I round the industrial park's sharp curve, and at the four-way stop with his old office on my left and my family's factory on my right, I allow the other cars to cross the intersection before I do. Kindness, I think. In my ear, he is still listening to himself talk. Kindness is what I rediscovered in my hometown. There's consideration among this community. The you-go-first, no-you-go-first kind; the old-fashioned kind of relationship between friends and families and husbands and wives where if you're suffering,

I am too; but if you're celebrating, please come around to our house for a champagne toast before you head to dinner. That kind of kindness. It's what's missing from this conversation: I feel like he's slapped me in the face, and he's not explaining why.

When we say goodbye and I finally unglue my phone from the side of my face, I take three seconds to recover. Then I raise my finger presidentially in the air and say, "Well, if he doesn't want me in his business, then he doesn't want me in his life, because the only time I'm in his life is when I'm helping him with his business." Celeste operates in the loving and skillful manner that got us through my high-strung panics in college and Italy: she listens.

"He says he'll come by Monday with my paycheck, and then his assistant is going to leave his car with me after she takes him to the airport on Tuesday. And that's another thing!" From the passenger seat Celeste pumps her imaginary brake into the floor as we come upon a line of Saturday night traffic that's headed toward the lake. "He had asked *me* to drive him to the airport! And just now he says he needs the time to go over a few things in the car with his assistant. What the hell is that all about?"

"Maybe he . . . just needs time to go over a few things in the car with his assistant?"

I look at Celeste, whose intention is always this pure. When I returned to Italy after my grandpa's funeral, she let me sit in a parking lot in Parma and tell her the story of how he died. It was a Saturday night in early February and we were late meeting friends for dinner and shivering in the Fiat the family I worked for let me drive. Meanwhile Celeste had never met my grandpa before . . . but she cried with me. Her tears were silent and self-sacrificing. I could see her feeling my own pain. It was one of the most profound moments I'd ever shared with a friend—and I wasn't going to put her through more misery over another man I love during her visit to see me this weekend.

Oh Krissy, you have such an active mind: I'd imagined everything, hadn't I? Or he had toyed with me, leading me on so I'd keep coming to work to help him. Is this what he does with women? Instantly I'm angry at my parents for encouraging me to be a friend to him, at my grandma for her ridiculous read on our friendship. He'd manipulated her too. Now that he doesn't need me anymore, he's cutting me out. Does he care about the impression he'll have left on my family when he leaves? Does he have no shame for what an asshole he's made himself out to be, to me?

I slam a case of Coronas on my brother's kitchen counter and furiously unload ingredients to grill pizza Margherita on his deck, which is just on the other side of the golf course from our house. Jeff is the only male I care to see tonight, and from the kitchen I can hear him and Celeste laughing on the deck. They are both so *easy* to be around! Those are the personalities I keep around; Emma, whose parents live next door to my brother, is the same way. I chop tomatoes and basil for the pizza sauce, deciding: I'm going to meet new guys this summer. We have Zach's wedding in August, and my friend Joy has been wanting to introduce me to an oncology resident in her med program. Months ago when she first proposed it, I laughed and rolled my eyes at her—"Darling, I seriously doubt there's a future for doctors and me"—but now I like the sound of someone whose job is to help patients cope with their cancer.

I'll call Joy when Celeste leaves. This summer I'm going to get better at bouncing back from amorous letdowns.

On Sunday evening Celeste and I line up wicker love seats with my parents on Dad's screened-in porch to watch *Father of the Bride*—and I laugh to look around and see all four of us cry when George Banks gives Annie away. Every time I've ever seen my dad cry, it's encouraged me about the sensitivity of the male spirit. In the back row of our makeshift drive-in theater, Dad makes us all laugh through our tears when he laughs at himself wiping his cheeks with his hands. I never saw Grandpa cry till he was dying. I wonder if Chris has ever cried at all.

MONDAY MORNING WE wake up early for a two-hour walk around the lake with my mom, and all seven miles consist of a full-on Chris analysis. "Terry, what do you make of the way he acts?" Celeste asks.

"He's so intriguing, and yet so unsure of what he wants. Such a beautiful man. It's a shame, really. He'd make an amazing father." Ah, indeed I've pictured our children, their cheeks like apples, wide American teeth, light eyes, and dark, wavy hair that I get lost just daydreaming about. They'd be so curious and considerate, so incredibly self-assured. I've considered, however, that they'd probably have a father who would never be present for their games and recitals. I *could* do that on my own, but why in the world would I want to? If I have kids, they'll deserve a dad who was as present as mine always was.

When we get home, I have a text from Chris saying that he plans to stop by my house in the mid-afternoon. "Nice." I toss my phone. "He's always so on-time and specific." While Mom cooks spaghetti for lunch and Celeste showers, I don't know why, but I pull the pinkest, paisliest, spaghetti-strappiest sundress I own out of my closet . . . and iron it.

After my shower I slather on the beach-fragranced body lotion I bought in Italy (nobody does silky skin like the Italians do, for what it's worth) and put in tiny iridescent pearl-drop earrings that move with my hair. On my feet, little white flip-flops with baby rhinestones on the straps. Grandma once told me that the first instruction her mother-in-law gave her after she married my grandpa (I guess it was normal for mothers-in-law to dole out these instructions back then?) is that the days when you feel the least beautiful inside, like when you're fed up with your husband and the kids are being terrors—or in my case, when you're rabid-mad at the boss whom you've developed intense feelings for—these are the very days when it's most important to look beautiful on the outside. "How you feel inside is what you wear outside," my great-grandma said, and I could hear it in her Roman accent. "But if you don't feel good, at least look good. Then you'll feel better." And it's true, because when I fold my dress under my legs and slide my chair in to join Celeste and my parents on the back patio for lunch, I imagine I blend in with the breezy pink flower pots Mom has placed on the center of the table and around the patio furniture. In the middle of lunch Chris texts to say he's en route, and it's a French term that would typically warm me up . . . but not today.

"How are you going to deal with him?" Celeste asks. My parents pause from spinning the lazy Susan around the table to stare at me.

"I don't know. I'm just going to see how it goes." For once my strategy at handling Chris doesn't garner any criticism.

I finish my spaghetti and push my plate aside, my stomach tying itself in knots.

We're all carrying dirty plates away from the table when I hear a vehicle pull into the driveway. I hike upstairs to brush my teeth and put on lipstick, and when I reemerge, Chris is climbing out of his SUV and walking through my garage in jeans and a crisp white button-down. Mom and Celeste stand behind the kitchen counter, rubbernecking with their mouths hanging open. "Hi there," I tell him, sliding open the screen door. "Come on in."

In our entryway I flick on the light as he pulls out his check-book. We lean over my homemade time sheet together as I go over the hours I've put in and the expense receipts for which I need reimbursing. "It comes to five hundred eighty-eight dollars." I think I hear my own voice shake.

He writes out a check for six hundred and asks, "Is that fair?"

I look up at him. "Yes, thank you." I could swear he feels what's coming.

He asks me to accompany him out to his car, he needs to discuss something with me. "Look," I tell him. "No more bomb-shells, okay? I get the idea."

Bombshells, he says. No, no. What he wants to tell me is how he woke up this morning and there was a hummingbird outside his window and it reminded him that he wants to get back to painting and sculpting. What am I talking about, bombshells?

I try to look him in the eye, finding it much easier to stare over his shoulder at the trees in my backyard. "What you said about me staying out of your business," I say, shifting my gaze to my hands. "I get it."

"I'm trying to compartmentalize."

"I can appreciate that," I tell him. "Do whatever you need."

"Did you hear what I said as being heavier than the way I meant it?"

That lights me. "I don't know, Chris, because I heard it pretty heavy. And I have to tell you, it's not sitting well with me. You tell me that you don't want me in your business, and honestly, I can level with that. But my concern is that I'm only in your life when I'm working for your business, and if I'm not in your business, then I won't be in your life anymore." I'm controlling my emotions so hard that one wrong word from him could break me into quiet tears, but for now my face remains stoic. Suddenly he feels too unfamiliar for me to freely address him by his name. "Because the only time I ever see you is under fluorescent lights, surrounded by desk chairs and nurses. And, truly, I don't mean to sound threatening. I just have to voice up here—for once, because I never want to bother you with this stuff—but I have to tell you, today, that if we hope to maintain our friendship, then we need to start seeing each other as friends."

That's exactly what he's saying.

Oh bullshit, I want to tell him. I filter my tone: *Calm. Calm.* "Is it? Because, Chris, my . . . *fear* is that . . . we rarely have time together, and now you're leaving the country. And I haven't asked for more because I've wanted to respect your space, and I know you give how you can, really, I see the value in that . . . but sometimes it's not what you say. It's how you say it. And so for you to tell me that you don't want me in your business—"

He looks around my driveway and winces, grappling for words. Finally he blurts out, "Can we take a walk?"

12

Be True

A WALK.

I hope Celeste doesn't leave before I get back.

A breeze rustles through the thick green trees, lifting the cotton of my dress to float behind me. *Please Lord, let the sound of outside dim the racing of my heart, and don't let his medically trained eye wander to my neck, where I can feel my pulse is visible and ready to burst.* Then, my heart stops, and I realize that he really can see straight through me right now: I forgot a slip. But the dress is printed, I remind myself, and it's not going to kill either of us if he sees through to my silhouette. *I'm not perfect.* I'd feel more secure with a layer under this dress, but it can't affect how I feel about myself. I won't let it.

"I'm trying to get better at not letting my work take over my life," Chris starts. When I go to answer this, my responses have gone mechanical. My nerves are vibrating so mercilessly right now that all my earthly concentration goes into absorbing his words. The completion of his sentences seems to push a button in me, causing me to say something automatic, something that I haven't pondered or engineered. Somehow, thank heaven, it's all coming out intelligently. Grandma would be impressed at my composure.

"Well, to that I would have to say that indeed you do draw people to you in your work. This is a good thing, Chris." Now our words seem to take on the lilt of an old-time novel, and a tunnel of trees lines our descent into the rocky beach parking lot.

"But you, Kris," he says, "you're different. You're a special person and . . . I want to hear more from you."

"More from you." It's a phrase I've never heard before. It's so pleasant and plain and, finally, it's one that requires no analysis. "Thank you."

We settle our backs against the wooden fence adjacent to the sand. "But having you at dinner at Joe's the other night . . . something about it just didn't feel quite right."

"You know what, Chris? I felt the same way." I'm conscious not to fold my arms across my chest or I'll look closed off . . . I don't want to set my hands on my hips or I'll appear confrontational. I have no clue where to put my hands. Then, thankfully, he suggests we cross the parking lot to sit on the large rocks that line the shore, away from the noisy Memorial Day crowd that's gathered on the beach.

He leaves the giant rock for me and takes one smaller and lower to the ground. I hoist myself carefully onto the shoreside boulder. Just then one of my flip-flops falls into the grass. Again I'm aware of myself. I gently rap its mate against the rock and knock it off my toes. Finally now that we're seated, my motions feel more fluid, and I know I'm officially comfortable on the rock when my ankles cross. I'm ready to own my half of this conversation. "Was it something I did at dinner, Chris, that made you feel like I didn't belong?"

"No, Krissy, no, no. I can't say it was anything you did, and I don't think it's that you didn't belong . . ." He's searching the sky for better articulation.

"Well, in any case, you see what's happening here?" I make a gesture between us with my hand. "We're agreeing."

"Yes, we are."

"But if we'd had the conversation about your staying at Joe's proactively, then I'd have known to decline his dinner invitation, and that would have alleviated the misunderstanding we're having right now."

"Right," he says. "Sometimes I just think there's a little confusion about what we are because we know each other so well."

How is that a bad thing? I want to ask him, but my point comes out sounding more diplomatic when I tell him, "Listen.. I love knowing you in so many different capacities. I told you what a caring doctor I think you are. I can't imagine that any person could know you completely without seeing you at your work."

He looks at me intently, and after a pause says, "And we're both single, so there's that."

I kick my heels against the rock and look down at my pink toes. "There is that."

"And I just think so much of you that I wanted to throw you a little cash because I know you've been out of work for a while—no, that's not even it, Krissy, it's more than that," he says, tossing his hands in the air and then resting his head in them with his elbows on his knees. "Kris, I don't . . . *think* of you in the same way as I think of all the people who work with me."

"I would hope not."

He looks at me, startled.

"We know each other really personally. I'd certainly hope that my relationship with you is a bit more unique than most other people in your office."

"It is!"

"How so exactly?"

"We knew each other socially first—"

"We dated."

My assertion catches him off guard. I show him some mercy, not insisting to explain: *Look, we made arrangements, you picked me up—unless you needed a lift, then I picked you up; we shared meals, we talked, we laughed, you did thoughtful things for me and we usually exchanged some token of affection when we said goodbye. All, dates.*

"And throughout those interactions I came to find you . . . intriguing, Kris. But I had to keep my mind on my work, and above everything else I knew I was leaving."

I nod gently. "I know that now."

"But I saw, in so many ways, that you have so many amazing qualities, and I saw a way for us to help each other. I needed you."

He stares down at his hands in a moment of self-examination

that strikes me as uncharacteristic and . . . refreshing. "Everything in my life comes together when you're in it."

My stomach leaps. *Calm. Patience. Teach him how to treat you.* "Chris, honestly, I've so appreciated the work you've sent my way, but I have to tell you something." My voice softens and our eyes meet again. He drops his hand from its position shielding the sun from his eyes. "I look to you for more than a paycheck . . . or skin advice . . . or a glycolic peel—"

He dips his head. "Such as?"

I go to laugh casually but no sound comes out. I clear my throat. "Uh . . . wow."

He lift his eyebrows as if to say, *Well?*

"Okay." I exhale. *He isn't going to make this easy, is he? But I have to do this, for me and for him. I know what I feel.* "I guess what I'm trying to tell you is that . . . uh . . . Chris, women like me—young, single women—don't get the chance to meet enterprising, inspired, goodhearted—and *handsome* men very often. And, uh"—*oh God, please make this easier!*—"there are times when I've thought that I'm maybe a little too selective in the characteristics I seek in a man. However . . . having known you for the past year, now I see that . . . there are men who are worth waiting for. Because there are moments when I really believe that you possess . . ." My words are coming out slowly and carefully thought out. I shift my eyes from the water behind him to look straight at him. "You possess all of the qualities that I have ever looked for in a man."

He releases the squint from his face and regards me kindly.

"All of them," I say. "Ever." He stays still for a moment, and then leans in on his elbows. His body language wants to hear more. "But then, on the other hand, there are times when you completely . . . Chris, you *baffle* me. And I feel ridiculous for even considering you would ever care to be someone even remotely significant to my life."

He appears about to start a thought, but I have to finish my own.

"And tomorrow you'll leave the country for, what, five months . . . and when you get back," I lock eyes with him, "I may be gone. I mean, I may still be here, but there's just as likely a chance that I won't be." He rises from his stone and approaches me. "And even if I am, you'll leave again."

He sits and places his hand on my bare back, in the space between my shoulder blades and sundress straps. He touches me so familiarly that all I can think is how foreign it feels. I search across the grass lawn toward the beach for the grace to turn calmly toward him. Instead I look up at the sky. "Please say something."

"Let's go sit in the grass." He picks up the thongs of my shoes between his fingers and leads me to a spot under the shade of pine trees. The lake laps softly beside us, and he sits with his elbow resting on his knee. I face him closely, sitting on my feet with my hands folded delicately until I pick a dandelion and fidget with it to keep my hands and eyes occupied. When I look up, his eyes are fixed on my face.

So, so blue, those eyes . . . so very crystal blue that they deserve their own paragraph.

"Kris," he says. I realize that his knocking off the second syllable of my nickname inches him closer to knowing me more. "I'm hearing that there's something more you need to tell me." I've seen him do this with patients too when he knows that they're not revealing their most serious symptom. Maybe they're scared to learn how severe the diagnosis will be or they're dreading what the treatment will demand of them . . . but every time I've seen him use this approach, they're always relieved to see how good his instincts are. He wants me to feel like I'm driving this conversation, which, as hard as it is, is exactly what I need from him.

Go on, I tell myself, *he can't help you address it if he doesn't know it exists.*

"Whatever it is, Kris," I feel his hand grasp the outside of mine, "I want to know."

"Okay, but Chris, it's difficult." I pause, and for a second I notice distress in his face that I might chicken out. "I guess I just need to tell you that . . . in the last couple weeks, seeing you work and helping you prepare to leave," I tug at the dandelion's tiny petals, "similar to what I hear you saying about me, I've related to you in a very different—a closer way—than anyone I've ever worked for."

He dips his head as if to say, *Go on . . .*

"Chris, some feelings have surfaced for me. And," *be strong* "it's clear to me now that I have feelings of very deep caring for you."

Still he's saying nothing new.

"And . . . my sense is . . . that . . . these feelings of deep caring, could potentially—hypothetically—under the right circumstances . . . turn into feelings of love." When I meet his eyes, there's a half grin on his face. "And I want to know—I mean, I suppose I'd like to know, or I'd appreciate knowing—but, you don't *have* to tell me, of course, although I guess I really would want you to tell me if . . ." *Just say it!* "If you ever felt the same." *There.* "Even an inkling."

"When I feel these things, Kris, it's more than an inkling."

This is what sets him apart from other men, I remind myself, staring up into the pine trees to sort out my next move. *He's complex.* I rest my hand on his knee in a last resort cue to tell him, *Look, I just want to level with you.* But I can sense, same as he relates to his patients, that he has faith I'm brave enough to finish presenting my concerns to him.

"Chris," I tell him. "*If* you've ever had feelings for me, and if you've ever thought about sharing them, then now's the time. Tomorrow you move to the other side of the world and I *don't know* where I'll be when you return. You understand that. And"—this may come out harsh, but maybe it's wisest—"if you ever want me to know of those feelings, if they exist, then now's your chance to tell me. After today, I don't want to know." I twist the dandelion stem around my finger and silently beg him to break the excruciating silence. "After today it'll be too late. And, Chris, if you don't feel anything, then trust me, *that* is okay because the last thing—"

But suddenly I can't continue this sticky self-preservation because there's something shushing my lips, my God, it's his mouth, and when I realize this I let out a grateful sigh that finally he speaks. The touch of his mouth is like a baby rose on my lips, and lovingly his tongue parts them. So sincere. So worth the wait. For so long I've wondered if his medical understanding of what's exchanged in a kiss had forged an aversion in him to this most biological (and pleasurable) of activities . . . but no. This is the most natural first kiss I've ever felt with someone. There is no shame; only beauty; only fingertips on cheekbones and nose hovering next to nose. There's nothing medical, only emotional; and my only reminder that he's a doctor happens when he skillfully, masculinely, cradles my face in his hands. *His touch changes people's lives*, I think. *And today it's changing mine.* He moves his chin close to mine, and instead of submitting to his invitation for another kiss, I rest my cheek against his. Now it's me who needs to take this all in. I don't know how many minutes we sit here, silent, not kissing; just cheek against cheek; eyelashes blessing each other's questions.

I raise my eyes, "Chris, what do—"

Shhh, he corrects me, his finger to my mouth. "Kris, please."

"Okay." I rest my cheek gently back against his.

What do you feel? I need to ask him. *And have you been keeping it from me?* I think of Grandma, how she was so careful not to push Grandpa for his emotions. I'm trying to learn that love doesn't need to know every thought, every feeling, every detail so hysterically. These last few months when I've started to doubt my capacity with Chris, I remember what Grandma told me at Valentine's Day when I told her I was giving our friendship space: "I'm proud of you," she said. "You've done everything right."

We sit quietly another minute with only the sound of water licking land and the pine trees over our heads accepting the wind like the hush of bristled drumsticks in a smooth jazz band. Then Chris breaks our silence with this: "It's such an honor to be sharing this space with you." My eyelash brushes against his cheek as I close my eyes to absorb these words.

More minutes pass, and I decide I either want to talk or kiss again. "Chris," I ask quietly, "do you wonder what's next?"

"Kris." He smiles, his eyes fixed on my lips. "Don't talk."

"Okay."

He can't appease my questions about the future because neither of us knows what's ahead. No man can determine my future . . . that was one of the first lessons Grandma wanted me to understand about being a woman my age. Chris touches his lips to my cheek and rests them there without kissing me. Oh my God, my heart. I try earnestly to remain silent . . . but there are things I want to know. "When did you feel this for me—"

"Kris." He starts laughing, then his voice hushes again. "Always you want to use words. What would you do if there weren't any words?" I look up at him. He runs his finger along my smile line. "Hm?"

"Is that rhetorical?"

"Shhhh . . ." I rest my temple against his face. "Do you trust me?"

I pull away and look at him. Do I trust him? My gosh, I don't know. Does that mean I don't? I look at the grass, and then up at him again.

"Why did you pull away from that kiss?"

"I didn't." The idea stuns me. "Did I?"

He nods, his hand resting on my collarbone.

Did I?

He searches again for my gaze. "There's a melancholy about you today."

I separate my head from his. "A melancholy . . ."

"I knew you had something on your mind."

"Yeah, I'll say! And you know you really—" But his lips are on mine again, making a loving woman of this chatty girl. He reaches the back of my neck with his hand and gathers my hair in his clutch. It's as if he needs me.

When we finally pull apart, my head is woozy from the happy dopamine that must be coursing through my veins, and I need to brace my arms with extra strength—I'm so elated they feel like they're floating. But I take his hand in mine and set it in the grass. "I've learned so much in the year I've known you," I tell him. While he hasn't been *responsible* for the ways I've grown, having him in my life has been behind it. "And you want to know something?"

He tilts his head.

"I'm a better person now."

He takes my chin between his thumb and forefinger. "For the first time in a very long time," he says, "I didn't feel any competition with my work . . . and I didn't want to be unavailable . . . and I wanted to show you how much I cared."

So all along I was giving him things he was longing for? I had no idea. "You showed you care how you could."

"I want to know you completely . . . and I want to share me with you."

Oh my God, finally, this is it! Grandma was right! I keep my eyes down and move into his cheek again. "That's what I want too."

"You realize it just cost me six hundred dollars to kiss you?"

I shrug. "Well, hopefully I've just given you something much more priceless than that."

"Yeah," he says, running his finger down the inside crease in my elbow. "I know where I'd put your IV in an emergency situation." I smile at him as he examines the blue vein making itself prominent from my right arm, and it turns me even weaker, until tears spring up. In different ways we both have ideas of how we could save each other's lives. I tuck my fingertips in the curve behind his ear and down his neck.

"Kris," he says, "do you truly believe that God will make sure we meet again? Is your faith that strong?"

I look out over the lake, and the wind takes my hair. I peel a wisp of it away from my lips. "Yes. It has to be."

"Do you *really* have that kind of faith?"

I look him square in the eye. "Yes. It's all I have."

We don't know how the timing of this will work, the distance or the dynamic. But the uncertainty in my heart is met with an assurance in his gaze, and when we rise to brush the imprint of the grass off my legs and return up the beach's stone lane to my house, I wrap my arm around his waist.

I'm sure that I could never hide
The thrill I get when you're by my side!

"You're going to the hospital today to tell your grandparents goodbye?" I ask.

"Yes."

"Are you late?"

"Yes."

"Will they be angry?"

"No."

It crosses my mind to visit Grandpa's stone later, to sit quietly with him in celebration of what's just happened. I know he's part of this. I look up at Chris. "They want this for you, don't they?"

"Who?"

"Your grandparents."

"They want what?"

I shrug. "Love."

"Is this love?" he asks. He's pleasant, amused. "This is a precursor to love."

"Yes." I unwrap his arm from my waist and link my fingers through his. Carefully he lifts my hand to kiss the tendons that run from my knuckles to my wrist.

"Nah, they won't be mad. I'll just tell Grandpa I was rolling around in the grass with some girl—"

"You were not!"

"Come on, it's a fishing story. It's nonfiction."

"It's narrative nonfiction, and it didn't happen."

His eyebrows raise mischievously. "But it could."

"*If* this is love."

He stops at the foot of my driveway and drops my hand from his grip to raise his fingers in a steeple to his lips. Then he closes his eyes and bows reverently, the way he'd rehearsed before his first trip overseas. "Yes," he says. "*If* this is love."

AFTERWORD

"So, Grandma, you know that in the past few months, I've gotten a little better at being discreet."

She raises one eyebrow. "Have you?"

"Yes! Come on, Grandma. You've noticed." She situates herself in the chair across the room as I log onto Grandpa's computer. "But, I do have to tell you: yesterday he called from the airport and told me that he's really happy about the talk we had. The talk." I do bunny ears, indicating that there was a lot more than talking happening.

"Mm-hm . . ."

What's with that that mock-apprehensive, half-delighted look in her eye? How is she not satisfied yet? Everything she predicted is happening, for heaven's sake. "And there's a part of this e-mail I got this morning that I have to read you. Now *mind* you, I won't read the whole thing. But this part—" I put my hand over my heart; I already have the line memorized "—is so beautiful."

She laughs, finally abandoning her pretend hesitation to get excited with me. "Go on then," she says, urging me with a shake of her hand "Read."

"So, he says he had a good flight and already had a big meeting . . . but here's the good part."

There was this lovably earnest woman who took me down to her lake and kissed me gently. Could you give her a big, warm hug for me, and tell her that she hasn't left my mind.

I turn around slowly, not to disrupt the moment. "How gorgeous is that, Grandma?"

"It's lovely, dear." She looks up at the ceiling. "But I'm confused, *you* kissed *him*?"

"No, Lord, no, Grandma. He definitely made the first move. And the second, and the third, and he kissed me by his car before he climbed in. It was all him. He knows that. With him it's always just semantics."

"Ah."

I wheel Grandpa's desk chair closer to her. "So, Glo? Come on, this is big! This is what you said would happen. You said, '*By the holidays*—'"

"My dear, I remember what I said. And I would *like* you to find the kind of man who deserves someone as beautiful as you one day." She holds up her finger in caution. "But it's possible that I'm wrong. And if he's not in your life by Christmas, or next year, or next century . . . please don't get stuck on it."

"Because there's someone else."

"Maybe, but Kristine"—my family only uses my full name in the most serious of conversations—"all your life, the only one you can *always* count on, *one hundred* percent of the time . . . is you."

I gaze at her, comforted.

"Whether you're with someone, whether you're single. All this time we've spent together, all these days and nights and doctors' visits: it's not my job to tell you how you have to be if you want a man in your life. Right?"

My head tilts in an attempt to understand.

"You're a woman who's had goals, who always knows herself and what she wants. That's the most important thing for a woman to be in this life. And that, my girl, is what you have taught me." She starts to tear up. "I can't tell you how much this has meant to be part of this with you." She shrugs, pulling a tissue out of the cuff of her sleeve (another Grandma trick I've picked up). "So, you'll live your life. We'll all find out soon enough how it goes."

"If this is love," I tell her.

"If this is love."

ACKNOWLEDGMENTS

THANK YOU FIRST to my two blessed grandmothers who have taught me what they know about our family and our faith.

To Janet Rosen and Sheree Bykofsky for your brilliant structural guidance and for being the first to spot the beauty and potential in this story . . . and certainly for finding me a home with the powerful team at HarperCollins, whom I have been so energized to work with.

To that HarperCollins team, including but certainly not limited to Amy Bendell, Lisa Sharkey, Cal Morgan, Jennifer Hart, Carrie Kania, Alberto Rojas, Mary Sasso, Maggie Oberrender and super-publicist Kateri Benjamin, the brains in design, the sales and marketing forces, managing editorial and production, and all the people who worked hard for every piece of this book to happen: I give massive thanks for your support every day.

And Amy, a special note to you—no editor could have been more inspiring or pleasurable to work with. Thank you for guiding me to take this story where I knew it could go, even when I wasn't sure exactly where that was. You have been my dream partner for my first book.

To Joelle Watt for your limitless vision, your time, your talent, and the incomparable bond our work has brought us to share.

To Bethany and David Johnson for being part of the cover concept's genesis—you are superstars.

To Bob Hanak and Matt Taladay, infinite thanks for helping me wade those early critical waters.

To the wonderful people who are connected to our family's business for your investment, belief, and interest in my work over the years.

To every teacher I have ever had in my life, with a special thanks to those who intensively nurtured my writing and my fascination with humanity: Mrs. Barbara Stephens, Sr. Kathryn Preston, Mr. Bill Wright, Mrs. Maureen Kane, Mrs. Star Young, Mrs. Mary Mike Sayers, Mrs. Lisa Blasdell, Mrs. Kathleen Kunkle, Mrs. Carol Korthaus, Fr. Ed Walk, Dr. Jacqueline Schmidt, Dr. Peggy Finucane, Dr. John Yost, Sr. Mary Ann Flannery, Dr. Nick Santilli, Dr. Denise Ben-Porath, Dr. Paul Thomson, Dr. Scott Bea, Dr. John Vitkus, Dr. Paul Levinson; to Mrs. Roz Pete for teaching me how to type (how very important that turned out to be!); to Mrs. Donna Chollock for taking me on my first trip to Europe, which is now my second home.

To my friends at YourTango.com, BustedHalo.com, and LimeLife.com, and to all the gracious editors who have given my work a home.

To the industry elites who first taught me about publishing:

Suzanne Murphy, Bill Gaden, Carisa Hays, Martha Levin, Dominick Anfuso, and especially my dear Suzanne Donahue. Thank you for giving me such a prime foundation and fostering my love of this business.

To Aunt Eva, who so generously linked me with our relatives in our native Rome and Castelnuovo, Abruzzo. It was an event that changed my life and really catalyzed this story.

Alla famiglia Massimi . . . vi adoro!

To the Spaggiaris—truly my family, *grazie di tutto*.

To Eddie and Heather Tate at Luigi's and George and Kimberly Moore at the Treasure Lake Ski Lodge—you've been my hometown favorites for years, and I hope you don't mind that I've just told the world where to find you!

To Joel Weinstein for your direction in taking this story beyond the book.

To Katie Bressack for your eternal enthusiasm, for keeping me connected to friends in the biz like the beautiful Megan McKeever, and for your inspirational friendship.

To E. Benjamin Skinner, my friend and author of *A Crime So Monstrous*, for sharing materials that helped me prepare the book and for the incredible work you've done for women around the world.

To Marty Beiser who promised me that leaving New York on a year of adventure would not ruin my chances of getting published. (Marty, you were right!)

To Leslie Meredith, who first told me this book idea was worthwhile.

To Andrew Paulson for the hookup . . . you got things moving.

Acknowledgments

To Lynn and Alphie McCourt for sharing the article that set this book idea in motion (and to Ashley Davis for sharing Lynn, Alphie, and Allison with me!).

To my precious friends who have been such encouraging supporters of me.

To the men on whom the most enigmatic characters in this book may have been based—you've brought so much to my life, and I really have loved you.

To Sr. Kathryn King, who is magical.

To my brother for always keeping me real.

To my parents, definitely the two most loving people I know. You make the world a better place with your kind and endlessly giving nature. I know how much you've sacrificed for what I do. I love you.

And to God and Grandpa: without you, none of this would be possible. Both, kings in my heart.